THE BAKER ILLUSTRATED GUIDE TO EVERYDAY LIFE IN BIBLE TIMES

JOHN A. BECK

BakerBooks

a division of Baker Publishing Group
Grand Rapids, Michigan

5.41
9/24/18
ED CHRISTNER

Published by Baker Books
a division of Baker Publishing Group
P.O. Box 6287, Grand Rapids, MI 49516-6287
www.bakerbooks.com

Paperback edition published 2017
ISBN 978-0-8010-1966-1

Printed in the United States of America

The Library of Congress has cataloged the hardcover edition as follows:
Beck, John A., 1956–
    The Baker illustrated guide to everyday life in Bible times / John A. Beck.
       pages cm
    Includes bibliographical references and index.
    ISBN 978-0-8010-1413-0 (cloth)
      1. Bible—Dictionaries. 2. Palestine—Social life and customs—Dictionaries.
    I. Baker Books (Firm) II. Title.
    BS440.B27 2013
    220.95—dc23   2012045919

17 18 19 20 21 22 23   7 6 5 4 3 2 1

Interior design by Brian Brunsting

For my soul mate, Marmy. "She is worth far more than rubies. Her husband has full confidence in her and lacks nothing of value. . . . She sees that her trading is profitable, and her lamp does not go out at night. . . . She is clothed with strength and dignity. . . . Many women do noble things, but you surpass them all" (Prov. 31:10–11, 18, 25, 29).

And for Judah, our first grandchild, who joined the kingdom of God during the writing of this book, in partial fulfillment of God's clear encouragement: "These commandments that I give you today are to be on your hearts. Impress them on your children. Talk about them when you sit at home and when you walk along the road, when you lie down and when you get up" (Deut. 6:6–7).

CONTENTS

PREFACE

Our days pulse with ordinary activities and experiences. We wash our clothes, download music, and stop at the store to purchase a loaf of bread. We execute our roles in life as firefighters, software technicians, and grandparents. Similar activities filled the lives of those living in Bible times. What was ordinary for them, however, may appear quite extraordinary to us. The notions of winnowing grain, removing one's footwear during a land purchase, or milking a goat were well known to those living in Bible times. But the very nature of these activities and the connotations linked to them may puzzle contemporary Bible readers. What did an armor-bearer do? What did it mean to be a Pharisee? What social disadvantages were faced by the childless widow? What was the difference between a wife and a concubine? How did people hunt? How were names given? How was someone executed by stoning? How were ancient cities fortified? What was a *lot* and how was it cast?

I trust that Abraham, Ruth, and Paul were not harmed by their ignorance of twenty-first-century culture, but modern Bible readers can be harmed by their ignorance of the biblical world. That is because the Holy Spirit often guided the inspired authors of the Bible to include mention of practices and customs from their time in this important book. God intends for these cultural images from the past to change us. But the rhetorical impact of the imagery is often muted because of the distance in time and experience between the modern readers of the Bible and its ancient human authors.

The goal of this visual guide is to restore clarity and vitality to those portions of God's Word that speak of the activities and social stations of the past. Each article discusses the literal realities that attended the activity or role under consideration. This includes the necessary treatment of the cultural connotations linked to it. The article will then illustrate the ways in which the biblical authors used either literal or figurative reference to the idea under discussion as they sought to change and shape us as their readers. You will find these cultural practices from the past to be fascinating on their own. But more importantly, your experiences with these images from daily life will give you fresh interpretive insights that will deepen your understanding of the most important book you will ever read.

ANOINT

Olive oil was a signature product of the Promised Land (Deut. 8:8), and it was used in many different dimensions of daily living.[1] Among them was application to the skin after being mixed with aromatics. This was designed to mitigate the harmful effects of a sunny, dry climate and also served to mask one's personal body odor in a place where bathing occurred infrequently due to the lack of fresh water (Ruth 3:3; 2 Sam. 12:20; Dan. 10:3). The biblical authors also knew of a unique application of oil to the body that was given a special designation: *anointing*. This was not done with ordinary oil but with oil specifically produced for this ritual. The recipe is given in Exodus 30:22–25, and it is also called "the oil of joy" (Ps. 45:7) or "holy oil" (Ps. 89:20 NASB). A stern set of guidelines accompanied with penalties to match ensured that this special oil was used only for ritual anointing (Exod. 30:37–38). At God's direction, the special oil was poured on the head of a person to mark him or her for special service whether as a member of Israel's clergy, as a political leader, or as a prophet.

Those anointed in this way had their lives change in three important ways. First, the one "anointed by the Lord" stood out from the general population as a leader. The process of

pouring oil on someone's head had no power on its own and could even be misused to designate a leader God had not intended to lead (2 Sam. 19:10). However, when it was done appropriately, anointing consecrated the life of an individual for special service in the kingdom of God (Lev. 8:30). Once marked with this act, special responsibilities and restrictions ensured that this leader would fulfill the intended role in executing God's plan on earth (Lev. 10:7; 21:11–15). Second, the anointed one was not autonomous but was always subject to the will and desires of a superior.[2] The "Lord's anointed" was a middle manager answering

An olive crushing press broke the tough olive skins so that the precious oil could be extracted.

to a divine CEO. Third, anointing meant special protection was extended to these special leaders—protection that was unmitigated by circumstances. For example, David considered it unthinkable to harm Saul, the Lord's anointed, even though Saul's failings had compromised his leadership and even though Saul was the one who stood between David and the throne of Israel (1 Sam. 24:6; 26:9; 2 Sam. 1:14). This protection was enshrined in the poetry of God's people: "Do not touch my anointed ones; do my prophets no harm" (Ps. 105:15).

As the biblical authors share divine truth with us, we find the idea

of anointing mentioned frequently in two locations. Fully one-third of the total number of instances in which anointing is mentioned are found in Exodus, Leviticus, and Numbers. As the Lord was establishing a new worship system for his Old Testament people, he put his stamp of ownership on the physical objects associated with worship and on the clergy who would lead that worship via the process of anointing (Exod. 30:26–28, 30). The repeated references to this kind of anointing join to create a refrain that reminds the reader that there was only one form of worship that God sanctioned in that period of history, and he marked the people and tools of that worship with special anointing oil.

Samuel, Kings, and Chronicles account for the next one-third of the instances where anointing is formally mentioned in the Bible, but in these cases it was not clergy but kings who were anointed. The idea of anointing a political leader was not unique to the Israelites; it appears to have been practiced by both Hittites and Egyptians as a way of protecting those leaders from harm imposed by hostile deities.[3] Special and repeated mention of the anointing of Saul, David, and Solomon helped to confirm the new institution of the monarchy among God's people and prevent contested successions. It is striking that after repeated mention of anointing in connection with these three, there is a relative absence of mention in the pages that follow (limited to 2 Kings 9:3; 11:12;

Although David had the opportunity to take Saul's life in a cave at En Gedi (left), he honored the divine protection that the Lord's anointed enjoyed.

The Baker Illustrated Guide to Everyday Life in Bible Times

23:30). We cannot know for sure whether subsequent kings were anointed, but as formal mention of anointing disappeared from the later pages of the Bible, the absence of this divine sanction highlights the absence of godly leadership among the kings who took the thrones of Israel and Judah. In that light, it is also striking that Elijah was directed to anoint Elisha as a prophet (1 Kings 19:16). We may be more accustomed to hearing of kings and clergy anointed as leaders, but when both these classes failed in leadership, we find this sacred designation performed on the prophet Elisha.

Divinely anointed leaders did not always live up to their high calling. Consequently, we encounter a growing expectation regarding one who will be anointed and serve as the ultimate leader of God's people. Though this special "Anointed One" will face grave opposition from the kings of the earth (Dan. 9:25–26; see also Ps. 2:2), his victorious kingdom will endure. The anticipation of such a leader

Worship furniture and objects used during worship were separated for special service by anointing.

becomes real when Jesus is called the Christ, the Anointed One. We may have expected him to be anointed with sacred oil, but instead he was anointed by the Holy Spirit on the day of his baptism (Isa. 61:1; Luke 4:18). Subsequently, he accepted the title of Christ (Matt. 16:16–17; John 4:25–26 NASB) and lived the life and died the death that allow us to be anointed by the Holy Spirit (1 John 2:20, 27).

Israel's clergy was ceremonially marked for lifelong service through anointing.

ARMOR-BEARER

hink of someone in whom you have absolute confidence, someone into whose hands you are willing to entrust your very life, and you are on the way to understanding the armor-bearer of the ancient world. Whether named or unnamed, the armor-bearers of the Bible were always attached to people who held significant leadership positions. Kings, princes, and generals had one or more armor-bearers in their company when going into battle (Judg. 9:54; 1 Sam. 14:1; 16:21; 2 Sam. 18:15). Typically, the Bible mentions only one armor-bearer at a time, but in the case of the general Joab, we read that ten armor-bearers accompanied him (2 Sam. 18:15 NASB).

As Saul's armor-bearer, David would normally play a supporting role, but contrary to expectation, he assumed the lead role in fighting Goliath and freeing the Elah Valley (below) of Philistine control.

Three specific duties were attached to the armor-bearer. As the name suggests, the first responsibility of the armor-bearer was to carry extra weapons so he could replace a leader's weapon that was either damaged or lost in combat.[4] The second role of the armor-bearer was to use those weapons himself. As the leader battled against enemy soldiers, leaving a trail of wounded fighters in his wake, the armor-bearer was entrusted with the grisly task of following behind to finish them off (1 Sam. 14:13; 2 Sam. 18:14–15). The third and most important responsibility of the armor-bearer was to protect the principal from harm. This was clearly the role of the shield-bearing armor-bearer who accompanied Goliath onto the battlefield against David (1 Sam. 17:7, 41).

The Baker Illustrated Guide to Everyday Life in Bible Times

With weapons in hand, these armor-bearers stand ready to protect and assist their king.

Because kings and generals quite literally entrusted their lives into the hands of their armor-bearer, leaders were very careful in selecting men for this vital role. They looked for the kinds of qualities we see in the armor-bearer who accompanied Jonathan in his assault on a Philistine outpost that was located at the top of the high, inaccessible ridge described in 1 Samuel 14. This man was Jonathan's sole companion during the assault (v. 6). He displayed absolute loyalty to Jonathan, responding to the invitation to participate in an exposed climb to the enemy with these words, "Do all that you have in mind. . . . Go ahead; I am with you heart and soul" (v. 7). And we observe that his courage paralleled that of Jonathan as they climbed the near-vertical cliff face toward the outpost, weapons idle because both hands and feet were required to sustain the perilous climb (v. 13).

Undoubtedly armor-bearers were present in battle scenarios much more frequently than is mentioned in the biblical accounts. Thus the reported presence of this assistant invites our consideration. Generally speaking, we can say that the presence of an armor-bearer marked an individual as a person of importance and that being an armor-bearer cast a complimentary light on the person given that honorary position. Thus when David was enlisted as an armor-bearer of King Saul, we are invited to see him as worthy of our admiration (1 Sam. 16:21)—an admiration that grows as we see this armor-bearer of Saul refusing to take up his weapons against the Lord's anointed (1 Samuel 24 and 26).

Armor-bearers play a more important role in three biblical narratives. In each case, the armor-bearer functions in a way that counters our expectation. First is the role of Abimelek's armor-bearer. There are many things that are disturbing about Abimelek, the first Israelite to claim the title of king (Judg. 9:6). His subjects eventually revolted against him, and in his efforts to reestablish his authority over them, Abimelek put one of the rebellious cities under siege. Mortally wounded when a woman hurled a millstone from above, cracking his skull, Abimelek asked his armor-bearer to play an unexpected role. Rather than killing enemy soldiers left in the wake of the king, the armor-bearer was asked to kill the king so no one could say that a woman had killed him (Judg. 9:54).[5]

The second time we see an unexpected turn in the role of armor-bearer comes in 1 Samuel 17, the well-known story of David and

Goliath. Just a few verses earlier, in 1 Samuel 16:21, King Saul was so impressed with a young man named David that he invited him to be one of his armor-bearers. This created an expectation regarding their roles that was completely reversed in what followed. When Goliath and the Philistines made their presence felt in a valley critical to Israel's national security, we would expect the king to take the lead in ridding Israel of this threat, with David's role limited to being a weapons supplier, follow-up executioner, and faithful assistant. But in a shocking role reversal, Saul offered weapons to David (1 Sam. 17:38), and David initiated the fight against the Philistine champion. This reversal in expected roles lifted David to prominence, while Saul drifted to the remote corners of the narrative.

The third time an armor-bearer plays a sustained role is in 1 Samuel 31. Many chapters earlier, the Lord had rejected Saul as king. The slow, downward spiral met the ground when Saul took his own life on Mount Gilboa after being mortally wounded by Philistine archers.

An Assyrian armor-bearer.

He then asked his unnamed armor-bearer to finish him off (see v. 4). In asking his loyal assistant to play this very unexpected role, he not only signaled just how horribly wrong things had gone that day but also linked himself rhetorically to Abimelek, the failed king who also made this unusual request of his armor-bearer (Judg. 9:54). In each of these three accounts, it is the reversal in the expected role of the armor-bearer that helps mark transpiring events as so noteworthy.

When Saul asked his armor-bearer to kill him on the heights of Mount Gilboa (below), he linked his failed rule to that of Abimelek, who had made a similar request.

ARROW
(TO SHOOT)

The basic tools and the techniques for hurling an arrow at its mark have evolved over the centuries, but the appearance of the bow and arrow of the past is nearly identical to the bow and arrow of the present. The arrows of Bible times consisted of a wood or reed shaft that was approximately thirty inches in length. An arrowhead made of bone, bronze, or iron was at one end of the shaft and the fletching composed of feathers was at the opposite end. The latter helped stabilize this nimble missile in flight. Ancient bows ranged from the simple convex arc to the composite bow that increased the killing range of the archer to more than two hundred yards and was already in the hands of hunters and soldiers by the time of Abraham.[6]

The physics behind shooting an arrow remains the same today as it was in Bible times. The potential energy housed within the muscles of the archer is transferred to the drawn bowstring and then released as kinetic energy when the bowstring recoils to its neutral position. Anyone with sufficient strength can make it work, but regular practice with bow and arrow is required to fire this weapon accurately. When Jonathan needed to deliver a message to David about the attitude of his father toward David without drawing undue attention, he engaged in an activity that was a normal part of his weekly routine. He took his bow and arrow outdoors to practice (1 Sam. 20:19–21, 35–37). Everyone who understood the skill required to shoot an arrow accurately also knew the risk of putting a fighter into the field without sufficient practice. The inspired poet of Proverbs 26 took it a step further in this simile: "Like a maniac shooting flaming arrows of death is one who deceives a neighbor and says, 'I was only joking!'" (Prov. 26:18–19 TNIV).

Apart from target practice, ancient artwork shows and the Bible mentions the shooting of an arrow in two settings: during the hunt and during war (Gen. 27:3; 1 Sam. 31:3; Jer. 50:14). We encounter the latter most frequently in

This bow allowed an archer to fire lethal volleys of arrows while remaining safely outside the range of most other ancient weapons.

the Bible. And when the biblical authors take special pains to mention the fact that Israelite soldiers were equipped to fire arrows, it is meant to portray an Israelite fighting unit as fully capable of effective combat, whether that be the rebel band of David or the army of King Uzziah (1 Chron. 12:1–2; 2 Chron. 26:11–15).

Two connotations are linked to shooting an arrow. First, those who fired arrows in combat did so from a relatively safe position compared with others who had to expose themselves while wielding sword, mace, or spear. When defending a city, soldiers fired arrows from above while using the city walls for protection (2 Sam. 11:20, 24), and when attacking a city from the outside, they shot arrows over the walls of the city while safely out of range of other weapons (Jer. 50:14), unseen in the "shadows" (Ps. 11:2; see also 64:4). Second, the flip side of that coin is the terror and panic that flying arrows could generate for those on the receiving end. A hail of arrows arrived unexpectedly and with lethal consequences. Only when we appreciate the terror they caused can we appreciate the peace that came

with the assurance that arrows would not be shot. When the Assyrian Sennacherib was threatening to attack Jerusalem, King Hezekiah received this reassurance: "He will not enter this city or shoot an arrow here" (2 Kings 19:32; Isa. 37:33).[7] What a blessing to live in a setting where "you will not fear the terror of night, nor the arrow that flies by day" (Ps. 91:5).

In the Bible we also find instances when the arrow being shot is metaphorical rather than literal. In the first instance, the biblical authors put a metaphorical bow in the Lord's hands and note that he is shooting people instead of arrows. In Exodus 15:4 the best of the Egyptian military is "hurled"—that is, fired like an arrow—into the Red Sea. And in Job 30:19, the unfortunate Job says that the Lord "throws" him—again, fired like an arrow—into the mud. In both instances, it is not just the forceful delivery of the bow shot but the helplessness of the arrow that is in view.

The advance of God's kingdom on earth was and is destined to meet opposition felt by God's people. In this second instance, that opposition can come in the form of words or actions that are likened to the assault of arrows in the inspired poetry of the psalms: "For look, the wicked bend their bows; they set their arrows against the strings to shoot from the shadows at the upright in heart" (Ps. 11:2). "They shoot from ambush at the innocent; they shoot suddenly, without fear" (Ps. 64:4).

Finally, it is the Lord who also shoots metaphorical arrows that are emblematic of the victory he

Assyrian arrowheads made of iron were fired on the besieged Israelite city of Lachish.

The Baker Illustrated Guide to Everyday Life in Bible Times

Arrows were used not only in support of a military operation but also when hunting big game.

will win over all opposition. Though this action cannot be commended to our readers for replication, Elisha opened the window of his bedroom and fired an arrow through it. The firing of this arrow represented the victory of God's people over Aram (2 Kings 13:17). Arrows shot by an unseen divine hand are even more effective than literal arrows in taking out opposition to God's people and his kingdom. "But God will shoot them with his arrows; they will suddenly be struck down" (Ps. 64:7; see also 144:6 and 2 Sam. 22:15).

Arrows were fired not only at a city under siege but also from within its walls by defenders on the ramparts.

AUTHORITY
(TO HOLD OR TO EXERCISE)

For many in the West, the notion of holding or exercising authority is linked to our democratic ideals. The person wielding authority has the right to make decisions that affect the lives of others because the leader was given that right by the people whom he or she governs. Furthermore, the authority given to the elected official is limited in scope by some form of constitution. Within the culture in biblical times, however, the right to exercise authority was often held by the one who seized that right by force; it was might, not popular elections, that imbued a person with authority—authority that often had few, if any, limitations. A more down-to-earth image of what it meant to have authority in the biblical world is offered by the Capernaum centurion who asked Jesus for help on behalf of his ailing servant: "For I myself am a man under authority, with soldiers under me. I tell this one, 'Go,' and he goes; and that one, 'Come,' and he comes. I say to my servant, 'Do this,' and he does it" (Luke 7:8).

In the Bible the idea of authority is discussed most often and directly in three categories: political, religious, and messianic. The biblical authors formally link the word *authority* with leaders of nations-turned-empires such as Egypt, Babylon, Persia, and Rome (Gen. 41:35; Neh. 3:7; Esther 9:29; Dan. 4:28–31; Luke 20:20; see also John 19:10 NASB). A blend of accumulated wealth and military competence gave the empires a striking amount of authority. But the Bible goes on to note that such political authority is not fully autonomous. In fact, it is only the dominion of the Lord that is fully autonomous and enduring. As the psalmist says, "Your kingdom is an everlasting

In advance of bestowing on their students the authority to teach, rabbis were known to teach them on these steps, which were the main entry to the temple in Jerusalem.

The Baker Illustrated Guide to Everyday Life in Bible Times

kingdom, and your dominion endures through all generations" (Ps. 145:13). Furthermore, the Lord was the one who ultimately manipulated the strings of history to allow one nation to rise and become the dominant empire of the ancient world at the expense of another. When Nebuchadnezzar failed to recognize that his authority was dependent on the authority of the Most High, this Babylonian king was temporarily removed from his throne until he got it right (Dan. 4:28–37). Shortly afterward, Daniel's dream about the four beasts not only pointed to the succession of world empires to come but also affirmed the fact that it is the Lord who orchestrates the giving and removing of political authority (Dan. 7:1–8). It naturally follows that those who submit to the authority of God will also submit to the authority of political powers to which he has given authority to rule. "Let everyone be subject to the governing authorities, for there is no authority except that which God has established" (Rom. 13:1).

At Jesus's baptism, God the Father declared that his Son had full authority to speak for him.

The notion of religious authority became a matter of importance in New Testament times because Jesus was frequently challenged by Jewish religious leaders in that regard. For example, the chief priests and elders accosted Jesus in the temple courts with these two questions: "By what authority are you doing these things? . . . And who gave you this authority?" (Matt. 21:23). In order to understand why this was such a sticking point for them, we need to understand that there was no social principle more firmly established within first-century Judaism than this. In order for a person to teach with authority as a rabbi, it was necessary for him to have been trained and formally authorized to teach by someone already recognized to possess such authority.[8] Students who wished to teach with the authority of a rabbi first completed a prescribed course of study that culminated in something akin to ordination; this formally marked a man as authorized to teach.[9] Thus Jesus was challenged repeatedly to either provide evidence of this pedigree or quit holding himself out as an authorized teacher.

Of course Jesus was authorized to teach, because he fulfilled the messianic prophecy of Daniel 7:14. A revolving set of empires would give way to the establishment of an eternal kingdom led by one unique figure. The Ancient of Days would give this man authority to rule an empire that would include "all the peoples, nations and men of every language," a kingdom that "will not pass away; and . . . will not be destroyed" (NASB). Jesus did not have to attach himself to a rabbinic school to obtain authorization to teach because he was ordained, so to speak, in a very unusual ceremony on the day of his baptism.[10] The declaration of none other than the heavenly Father authorized him to teach. "This is my Son, whom I love; with him I am well pleased" (Matt. 3:17).

The Gospel writers were careful to report that despite the reservations of certain Jewish leaders, the common people who heard Jesus teach recognized that he did so with authority. "The people were amazed at his teaching, because he taught them as one who had authority, not as the teachers of the law. . . . The people were all so amazed that they asked each other, 'What is this? A new teaching—and with authority!'" (Mark 1:22, 27).

While Jesus acknowledged that all authority resides in him, he shared a portion of that authority with his followers, who were charged with advancing the kingdom of God to its ultimate realization. We see this occurring in a limited, local way during Jesus's time on earth (Luke 9:1; 10:19) and then exploding into an international effort at the time of his ascension. "All authority in heaven and on earth has been given to me. Therefore go and make disciples of all nations" (Matt. 28:18–19). It is this divinely given authority that lies behind the teaching we meet in the Epistles (2 Cor. 10:8; 13:10; Titus 2:15; Heb. 13:17).

A funeral mask of King Tut's mummy. Rulers such as King Tut of Egypt often sustained their authority through the use of military power.

BAKE BREAD

When the biblical authors formally mention the baking of bread or make strong allusion to this activity, they are directing our attention to the most ordinary of all the daily tasks in Bible times. The bread made from wheat provided the majority of carbohydrates and proteins consumed by those living at that time.[1] Because their bread was baked without preservatives and so would spoil more quickly than the processed bread of today, it generally was baked daily and was intended for consumption on the day it was baked.

Three different methods were used to bake this daily bread. The first did not require an oven but only a flat rock, making it the easiest method for baking bread when traveling. The baker built a fire on the upper surface of the rock, and once the fire burned down to hot embers, the coals were swept from the surface and replaced by raw bread dough. Because the rock retained the heat long after the embers were removed, its surface became the rack on which the bread baked.[2] The second method for baking bread used a clay oven called the *tabun*, which was shaped like a beehive with an opening on the top. A fire

built around the exterior of the *tabun* heated the interior of the oven, and the temperature was controlled by adjusting the lid that fully or partially closed the opening on top of the beehive. Stones placed on the floor of the *tabun* became the baking surface on which the dough was placed. The third method for baking bread was also in an oven. This one was called the *tannûr*, and it was also shaped like a beehive. But in the *tannûr* the fire was built inside the oven and the bread dough was slapped on the curved sides of the oven to bake.[3]

Bread was baked on a daily basis.

We can divide the instances in which the biblical authors formally mention the baking of bread into two categories: (1) baking that occurred in ordinary and expected settings, and (2) baking that is noteworthy because it was unusual in some way. We can safely say that no activity was more ordinary in Bible times than the baking of bread. It was done on a daily basis for one's family whether the family was lingering around the family compound or preparing for an extended journey (Exod. 12:39). It was also customary to bake and offer bread to recently arrived guests, who would naturally be hungry after walking a long distance (Gen. 14:18; 18:6; 1 Sam. 28:24). Bread was also baked and brought to the Lord as an offering, honoring the premise that there would be no grain without the blessing of the Lord. This offering could consist of raw grain, but it was more often prepared and presented before the Lord

A first-century AD bread stamp used to impress a design into the bread dough before baking.

as baked goods (Lev. 2:4; 6:17). Baked loaves of bread were also used as symbolic representatives of God's people; twelve loaves resided in the presence of the Lord within his sanctuary (Lev. 24:5–9).

In contrast to these ordinary instances involving baked goods, we find six instances in which baking or not baking receives special mention because the circumstances were unusual: (1) Moses taught the Israelites that this fundamental task was to be suspended on the Sabbath. Any baked goods eaten on the Lord's Sabbath had to be baked the day before (Exod. 16:23). (2) The normal rhythm of baking was also interrupted by Israel's demand that they be led by a king. Monarchs of Bible times had their own full-time baking staff (Gen. 40:1–2). Consequently, Samuel warned that Israel's request for a change in political structure would result in daughters being removed from their family household and put to work baking daily bread not for their own families but for their king (1 Sam. 8:10–11, 13). (3) The smell of baking bread was as pleasant an aroma in Bible times as it is today. But in at least two instances, these pleasant

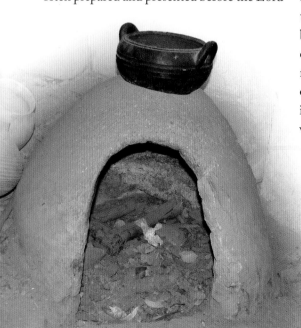

An oven for baking bread was included in the plan of every home.

The Baker Illustrated Guide to Everyday Life in Bible Times

aromas were used in a nefarious way, disarming those about to be taken advantage of. Jacob presented Esau with freshly baked bread as he set the stage for extracting the birthright from his brother (Gen. 25:34), and Amnon, who was feigning illness, requested that Tamar prepare and bake bread in his presence as part of his plan to sexually assault her (2 Sam. 3:8).

In the fourth and fifth instances the horror of a siege is amplified or illustrated by a description of unusual baking. God called his Old Testament people to live a unique life that honored him in all its dimensions; punishment, including foreign invasion and siege of the cities, would follow failure to honor their commitment. (4) In Leviticus the Lord warned of a punishing siege with this vivid language: "When I cut off your supply of bread, ten women will be able to bake your bread in one oven" (Lev. 26:26). (5) The disobedience of God's people during the days of Ezekiel meant that just such a siege was imminent. The Lord commanded Ezekiel to bake *siege food* for himself and eat it in front of the people even before the siege of Jerusalem had begun in order to symbolically warn them of the events about to transpire (Ezek. 4:9–13). (6) Finally, we would expect travelers to bake their own bread while traveling, to replenish their energy levels. But the highly stressed Elijah was so exhausted by his flight that he had not made any food for himself. Consequently, the Lord illustrated his ongoing concern for his prophet by sending an angel to rouse him from sleep and offer him "bread baked over hot coals" (1 Kings 19:6).

Art pieces from many ancient Near Eastern cultures depict the process of bread making.

BELT
(TO WEAR OR TO TUCK)

The belt of our Western world is very different in appearance and function from the belt of the ancient world. What is more, modern Bible translations have used the word *belt* for two different articles of clothing that looked and functioned in very different ways from each other. For example, in the case of Elijah, a shift in Hebrew vocabulary signals that we are no longer talking about the true belt that was worn around the tunic. In fact, it was not a belt at all but an undergarment worn beneath the tunic. Typically made of linen and less commonly of leather (2 Kings 1:8), this garment resembled a kilt wrapped around the waist that extended to mid-thigh.[4]

By contrast, the true belt (or sash) was a long cloth approximately six to ten inches in width that wrapped around the waist, worn over the tunic.[5] Ordinarily such belts were made from wool or linen, so the one wearing "a belt of fine gold" was marked as unique (Dan. 10:5; see also Prov. 31:24). The belt's role was intimately linked to the tunic, the primary garment worn by average men and women living in Bible times. The tunic was a rectangular, sack-like garment that reached all the way to the ankles. It was sewn so as to be open at the bottom and had openings cut in the appropriate places for the head and arms. The belt gathered the tunic around the waist during the day and was loosened or removed at night when the tunic became loose-fitting sleepwear.

This true belt functioned in a number of ways. First, it provided a place into which the owner could tuck his garment when its length interfered with walking or working. The biblical authors mention this tucking most

While staying in Caesarea Maritima (below), Paul was bound by his own belt to symbolize his coming arrest (Acts 21:11).

The Baker Illustrated Guide to Everyday Life in Bible Times

frequently in connection with long or urgent trips during which an untucked garment would have impeded the legs (Exod. 12:11; 1 Kings 18:46; 2 Kings 4:29; 9:1). Second, because the ancient belt was a wider piece of cloth with folds in it, the belt also became a convenient place to put things one wanted to carry, such as a weapon or coins (2 Sam. 20:8; Matt. 10:9; Mark 6:8). Third, the type of belt worn might be used to mark one's place in society. For example, we read about a belt that marked the special accomplishment of a warrior (2 Sam. 18:11), belts worn by the clergy (Exod. 29:9; Lev. 8:7, 13; NIV "sashes"), and a special leather belt that helped mark Elijah as a divine messenger (2 Kings 1:8).

The belt and actions associated with it carry two important connotations that are exploited by the biblical authors. First, lifting the tunic and stuffing it into the belt indicates readiness for action and willingness to engage the task ahead. This connotation is clearly seen in Exodus 12:11 as the Lord calls the Israelites to leave Egypt with "your cloak tucked into your belt." But this imagery is lost for the English readers of 1 Peter 1:13. Here the inspired author urges the reader to "prepare your mind for action" (NASB). The Greek verb translated as "prepare" is the verb that urges the tucking of one's garment into the belt. Thus Peter urges believers to do with their minds what they typically did with their tunics in order to prepare for action. Ironically, the belt that symbolizes the enabling of action was used by Agabus to depict the restrictions Paul was about to encounter. As Paul was on his way to Jerusalem, Agabus "took Paul's belt [and] tied his own hands and feet with it" before announcing that the owner of the belt would be bound by the Jews of Jerusalem and delivered into the hands of the Gentiles (Acts 21:11).

The second connotation associated with the belt is great intimacy. When David was anointed by Samuel to succeed Saul as king of Israel, it was Saul's son Jonathan who had everything to lose politically since he would have been regarded as Saul's likely successor. Our concerns over competition for the throne are removed as we observe David and Jonathan making a covenant in which Jonathan affirmed David as Saul's successor.[6] Jonathan gave David a variety of personal items to confirm this agreement. The list terminates with the most intimate item of all: Jonathan's belt. Intimacy

In days without elastic or Velcro, a belt held a loose-fitting garment in place around the waist.

is also in view during the enacted message of Jeremiah 13. Here the Lord urged Jeremiah to purchase a linen belt, wear it for a time, and then leave it in the crevice of a rock. After many days, the Lord sent Jeremiah to retrieve the belt. When he dug it up, the linen belt was completely ruined and useless. In this case the belt stood for the people of Israel and Judah, whom the Lord bound to himself as a belt (Jer. 13:11). But despite the intimacy of this connection, God's people failed to listen to him and so were destined for the same ruin as Jeremiah's belt.

Finally, we see the intimate relationship between belt and owner used in two metaphors in which the belt symbolizes a quality that is as closely linked to a person as the belt is linked to the one who wears it. Isaiah described the Messiah in this way: "Righteousness will be his belt and faithfulness the sash around his waist" (Isa. 11:5). And Paul encouraged us all

The long belts of royal officials added style and distinction to an otherwise ordinary piece of apparel.

to have our lives so intimately linked to truth that we walk with the "belt of truth buckled around [our] waist" (Eph. 6:14).

Most people wore belts made from cloth, so a belt made of bronze helped distinguish this belt's wearer as a warrior.

BIRTH

After God called our world into being and personally made the first man and woman in the Garden of Eden, he invited them to "be fruitful and increase in number" (Gen. 1:28). Thus the Lord empowered and invited husbands and wives to join sexually in order to give birth to sons and daughters who would fill his new world. That power did not cease with the fall into sin but was changed dramatically by it. The process of giving birth that had been pain free was now beset by the horrific pain associated with contractions and the compression of nerve endings (Gen. 3:16). God linked this most fundamental human experience with a reminder of sin—a link affirmed in subsequent passages of Scripture (Lev. 12:2, 5; Ps. 51:5; John 3:6).

Despite the pain associated with childbirth, people during Bible times honored God's command to bring children into the world. And within the culture of the biblical world, giving birth to children became an economic necessity.[7] Having a large number of children improved the economic well-being of a family by allowing that household to farm more acres of land, increase the number of animals under their care, and maintain the water resources needed to survive. When the senior members of the family were no longer able to contribute labor to these tasks, the children provided their parents with the fundamentals needed so that they could enjoy more comfortable years at the end of their life. But the efforts to grow a large family and its attending security came with a physical and emotional price. High infant and child mortality rates rocked the world of God's people, where only one in two children lived to adulthood.[8] It was a great blessing to have a large family (Ps. 127:3–5), but the loss of children and the death of mothers in

Having children was an economic necessity that permitted growing sufficient grain to feed the family and to ensure the well-being of aging parents.

childbirth became all-too-familiar realities for families in Bible times.

Childbirth not only played a role in economic security but also paved the way for eternal security because childbirth was intimately linked to God's plan to redeem the world from sin. Adam and Eve were told that one of their children would be the key to this rescue (Gen. 3:15). This means that biblical authors were particularly attuned to the birth of children in the larger context of this promise. In Genesis that starts with attention given to the first sons of Eve (Gen. 4:1–2) and then ramps up into long genealogies that repeat the Hebrew verb for giving birth 170 times. (Unfortunately this refrain is muted by many contemporary English translations.) The intimate link between childbirth and God's plan to save the world made childbirth a target of those demonic forces that sought to undo the plan of salvation. We meet women like Sarah, Rebekah, Rachel, Hannah, and Elizabeth who were at first unable to bear the children necessary to advance the divine cause (Gen. 17:17; 18:11; 25:21; 29:31; 1 Sam. 1:2; Luke 1:7). But in each case, the Lord intervened and allowed these women to give birth to the children who played a pivotal role in advancing the plan of salvation. This created an expectancy and a trajectory that led to the great miracle of the virgin birth of Jesus (Isa. 7:14; Matt. 1:18–25; Luke 1:26–38; 2:1–20); the child promised to Adam and Eve was born of a woman and so born under the law so that he could become the Savior-substitute for all those born of a woman (Gal. 4:4–5).

The biblical authors also tapped into the imagery of childbirth metaphorically. The great intimacy created between a mother and child is the kind of intimacy we expect to see between the Lord and the people to whom he gave birth. But all too often we find just the opposite: "You deserted the Rock, who fathered you; you forgot the God who gave you birth" (Deut. 32:18). What is worse, God's people acted as though wood and stone idols gave them birth. "They say to wood, 'You are my father,' and to stone, 'You gave me birth'" (Jer. 2:27).

The transition between the deep pain of childbirth and the pure joy of a child's birth also becomes a metaphor in the Bible. Jesus told his disciples that the roller coaster of pain and pleasure experienced in this world would parallel that of a woman in labor. "A woman

Adam and Eve were immediately encouraged to have children so that their world might be filled with family life.

In order to fully qualify as our Savior and substitute,
Jesus had to be born as a mortal.

giving birth to a child has pain because her time has come; but when her baby is born she forgets the anguish because of her joy that a child is born into the world. . . . Now is your time of grief, but I will see you again and you will rejoice" (John 16:21–22). And we read in Romans that the creation itself is struggling due to the presence of sin. It is "groaning as in the pains of childbirth" (Rom. 8:22) but waiting for the time of its restoration and the joy to follow.

The difficult process of childbirth, however, does not always result in the joy of a healthy child. This image also appears in the Bible when sinful behavior and attitudes give birth to disillusionment (Ps. 7:14), wind (Isa. 26:18),

straw (Isa. 33:11), evil (Isa. 59:4), and death (James 1:15).

In the New Testament, the trajectory of physical births listed in the Old Testament culminates in the birth of the Savior. This language is complemented by the use of birth as an image of entering into the family of God. "Yet to all who did receive him, to those who believed in his name, he gave the right to become children of God—children born not of natural descent, nor of human decision or a husband's will, but born of God" (John 1:12–13). In his dialogue with Nicodemus, Jesus spoke of this special birth as being "born of the Spirit" (John 3:6–8; see also James 1:18; 1 Pet. 1:3).

BLIND

*B*lindness was much more common in the biblical world than in our contemporary Western setting due to the fact that people endured harsh environmental conditions and did not have access to the early medical intervention that could have spared the eyesight of newborn infants. Fortunately, today we enjoy both fewer instances of blindness and a more enlightened view of those who live with a visual disability. But being blind in Bible times carried harsh connotations regardless of whether this disability was congenital, the result of an accident, or intentional maiming (1 Sam. 11:2; 2 Kings 25:7; John 9:1–2).

The Bible alludes to these connotations without endorsing them. Generally speaking, those living in the biblical world perceived the blind as less capable and highly vulnerable.[9] That connotation comes through loud and clear in language like this: "At midday you will grope about like a blind person in the dark" (Deut. 28:29). This stigma is preserved in the troubling language of the Jebusites, who had this to say when they wanted David to know just how impregnable their fortress was: "Even the blind and the lame can ward you off" (2 Sam. 5:6). Reflecting the misinformed views of their contemporaries, the disciples of Jesus asked, "Who sinned, this man or his parents, that he was born blind?" (John 9:2). And Jesus himself acknowledged the impoverished social status of the visually impaired when he included the blind in a list of those who were least likely to receive an invitation to a banquet (Luke 14:13, 21).

The legal code of the Old Testament reflects some of this stigma together with a passion to protect the more vulnerable members of society. For example, a descendant of Aaron who was blind could not serve as a priest (Lev. 21:17–18). Similarly, an animal that had any defect, including blindness, could not be offered as a sacrifice to the Lord (Lev. 22:22; Deut. 15:21; Mal. 1:8). On the other hand, divine law made it clear that no one was to take advantage of those who were visually impaired (Lev. 19:14; Deut. 27:18).

Ultimately, the Bible puts the Lord in control of this matter. He is the one who gives or withholds the

Within Israel today, the visually impaired may still face challenges. This man is soliciting gifts of mercy from those who pass by.

ability to see (Exod. 4:11; Ps. 146:8). For example, he removed sight from those who threatened the advance of his kingdom (Gen. 19:11; 2 Kings 6:18; Acts 13:11). He struck the persecutor Saul with temporary blindness as part of his conversion experience (Acts 9:4–9). And he permitted a man to be born blind so that the work of God could be revealed in his life (John 9:2–3).

Blindness is also used as a figure of speech. The law in the Old Testament forbade the use of a bribe because it "blinds those who see and twists the words of the innocent" (Exod. 23:8; see also Deut. 16:19). Blindness is also used as a metaphor for the willful failure to honor God's Word as truth. This notion of spiritual blindness occurs with some frequency, particularly in the prophetic books. "Hear, you deaf; look, you blind, and see! Who is blind but my servant, and deaf like the messenger I send? Who is blind like the one in covenant with me, blind like the servant of the Lord?" (Isa. 42:18–19; see also 56:10; Zeph. 1:17). In the New Testament, Jesus seized on this metaphor when he criticized the Jewish leaders of his day who were nothing more than "blind guides" (Matt. 15:14). In the sustained criticism Jesus leveled against the teachers of the law and the Pharisees in Matthew 23, repeated mention of their blindness rings like a refrain in verses 16 through 26.

Finally, the healing of both physical and spiritual blindness is linked to the work of the promised Messiah. In speaking of the Servant of the Lord, God himself said, "I will keep you and will make you to be a covenant for the people and a light for the Gentiles, to open eyes that are blind" (Isa. 42:6–7). As we read the Gospels, it

Jesus's miracles restoring sight to the blind also identified him as the promised Messiah.

is striking how often Jesus came into contact with those who were visually impaired and subsequently restored their sight. Whether those who were blind called out to Jesus themselves (Mark 10:46–47) or were brought to him by friends and family members (Matt. 15:30–31), time after time Jesus chose to interact with such spurned members of society and touched them with his healing power. Given the Old Testament anticipation of such acts (for example, Isaiah 42), Jesus's repeated interaction with the blind became a strategic part of the way in which he identified himself as the Messiah. The man born blind whom Jesus healed gave voice to the popular perspective on such miracles: "Nobody has ever heard of opening the eyes of a man born blind. If this man were not from God, he could do nothing" (John 9:32–33).

In addition to the accounts that describe Jesus restoring sight, we also have two instances in which Jesus specifically referred to such healing acts as evidence that he was the Messiah. In the first, John the Baptist's disciples inquired if Jesus was the one to expect or if they should look for another. In response, Jesus explicitly linked those acts of healing to Isaiah 42 (see Matt. 11:5). In the second, we catch up with Jesus in the synagogue at Nazareth. When it was time for the Scripture reading, he was handed the scroll of the prophet Isaiah and read the portion from Isaiah 61 that describes the Messiah as one who provides "recovery of sight for the blind" (Luke 4:18 TNIV). With healing miracles in his wake, Jesus declared, "Today this scripture is fulfilled in your hearing" (Luke 4:21).

The importance of vision is suggested by the emphatic depiction of the eyes in ancient art.

The steep climb from the Kidron Valley to the ridge (left) led the Jebusites to boast that even the lame and blind could defend their city against David (2 Sam. 5:6).

BORROW/LEND

People applied for and received both commercial and personal loans during Bible times.[10] When the biblical authors speak of borrowing and lending, however, they are generally referring to the personal loans sought by those facing difficult times. In this light, the Lord challenged those capable of lending to do so not in the interest of generating income but in the interest of helping those who were less fortunate.

The need to borrow became important when the poor, who were already living on the edge of financial exhaustion, faced famine that depleted their food supply or a government that demanded taxes at an exorbitant rate (Neh. 5:3–4). While at times it became necessary to borrow a tool (2 Kings 6:5) or an animal (Exod. 22:14–15) to accomplish a specific task, the most perilous kind of borrowing required the less fortunate to borrow a consumable product like grain (Neh. 5:3).

Like a contemporary loan, the terms of an ancient loan included a rate of interest, a lending period, and some form of collateral.

This old Babylonian loan document states that repayment of the loan with attending interest will occur at harvesttime.

In records from ancient history we find that the interest rate for a loan varied from 12 percent to as much as 33 percent.[11] While the Israelite lender could charge a non-Israelite a reasonable rate of interest on a loan, a loan made by one Israelite to another who was impoverished was to be interest free (Exod. 22:25; Lev. 25:35–37; Deut. 23:20). God also limited the time of such a loan to just six years. At the seventh year, all debts were forgiven. While this might seem to discourage the practice of providing loans to those in

In the Bible, borrowing can involve something as simple and familiar as tools (2 Kings 6:5).

need, God promised that those honoring this directive would enjoy material blessings that more than compensated the lender for the apparent loss (Deut. 15:1–6). Furthermore, God's law permitted the taking of property or persons as collateral, though with limitations. It was the debtor, not the creditor, who picked the property to guarantee the loan, and lest the creditor attempt to influence the choice of collateral, he was required to remain outside the residence while the debtor selected the item (Deut. 24:10–11). The use of a poor person's outer garment as collateral also receives special mention. Because this garment doubled as the blanket that helped keep the wearer warm on cold winter nights, the cloak could be kept for only one night before it was returned to the debtor (Deut. 24:12–13).[12] Sadly, this principle was not always honored (Amos 2:8). In dire circumstances, either the debtor or a member of the family could be offered as collateral for the loan (2 Kings 4:1; Neh. 5:5). Although such persons were called "slaves" and their labor was used to pay off the loan, the Lord called for them to

be treated as "hired workers" who were to be released from service in the Year of Jubilee (Lev. 25:39–40).

In addition to this legislation designed to eliminate the abuses of the borrowing-lending process, the book of Proverbs offers very practical advice when it comes to guaranteeing the loan made by another: "One who has no sense shakes hands in pledge and puts up security for a neighbor" (Prov. 17:18). Those who had already done so were strongly urged to free themselves from that circumstance as quickly as possible (Prov. 6:1–5).

The expected connotations follow the realities of the borrowing described above. Lenders were perceived as powerful while borrowers were perceived as lacking power. "The rich rule over the poor, and the borrower is slave to the lender" (Prov. 22:7). Thus the ideal life was one in which the person always played the role of lender. The Lord used this image to describe the blessings that covenant obedience would bring to his people, including obedience to his laws regarding proper lending habits. "For the LORD your God will bless you as he has promised, and you will lend to many nations but will borrow from none" (Deut. 15:6).

When speaking in broader strokes about the borrowing and lending of money, the biblical authors roundly criticize those who abuse the system. It is the wicked who borrow money but then fail to repay it (Ps. 37:21), who lend and charge interest rates in violation of God's direct instructions (Neh. 5:6–11), or who fail to show leniency to their debtors. Uncharitable lenders who themselves have been forgiven a

The Old Testament allows the creditor to take collateral for a debt but limits what that security can be. For example, it does not allow the taking of a millstone (Deut. 24:6).

The Baker Illustrated Guide to Everyday Life in Bible Times

larger debt are likened to those who refuse to forgive others in the same way the Lord has forgiven them (Matt. 18:23–24). Jesus closed the parable of the unmerciful servant with these words: "This is how my heavenly Father will treat each of you unless you forgive your brother or sister from your heart" (Matt. 18:35).

By contrast, the righteous are characterized as those who lend to the poor as if they were lending to the Lord (Prov. 19:17). They lend freely and without giving undo attention to the repayment schedule (Deut. 15:8–9; Pss. 37:26; 112:5). Jesus took these notions another radical step when he challenged his followers to examine their way of living: "And if you lend to those from whom you expect repayment, what credit is that to you? Even sinners lend to sinners, expecting to be repaid in full. But love your enemies, do good to them, and lend to them without expecting to get anything back" (Luke 6:34–35).

A Palestinian man processing wheat. At the time of Nehemiah, family economics had become so dire that people were borrowing money and mortgaging their personal property to purchase grain (Neh. 5:3–4).

BOW DOWN
(TO KNEEL)

The formal and intentional act of bowing down played an important cultural role in the ancient Near East. The physical act is easily pictured: it meant falling to one's knees, head down, while fixing one's eyes on the ground (for example, 2 Kings 1:13). But under certain circumstances, it also included bending to touch one's face to the ground. When a meeting took place, the act of bowing down was initiated by the person regarded as socially inferior. It was a physical demonstration of the respect and deference offered to the one who occupied a higher station in life.[13] Consequently, Moses bowed down to his father-in-law, Ruth bowed down to Boaz, and an unnamed servant bowed to Joab (Exod. 18:7; Ruth 2:10; 2 Sam. 18:21). Subjects of the kingdom also acknowledged royal figures by bowing. This bow became very important in Bible stories in which there was a lurking question about the loyalty of the subject to the king (1 Sam. 24:8; 2 Sam. 9:6–8; 14:33).

The Bible notes two enhancements to this social custom, both of which intensify the deference being accorded to the other by the one bowing down. In some instances, we read that people exceeded expectations by bending so deeply that they touched their face to the

The defeated king Jehu bows before his Assyrian overlord to show political submission.

ground (for example, Gen. 42:6; 1 Sam. 24:8). A second way of intensifying the deference was by repeating the act of bowing multiple times. Jacob bowed before Esau seven times, and Jonathan bowed before David three times (Gen. 33:3; 1 Sam. 20:41).[14]

Bowing down was also linked to worship. To bow down before the Lord, whether physically or metaphorically, was the equivalent of worship (Gen. 24:26; Deut. 26:10; Rom. 14:11; Phil. 2:10). In that light, the Lord ordered his people never to bow down to fraudulent deities (Exod. 20:5). But soon after this command was given, the Israelites bowed down to a golden calf (Exod. 32:8). Despite repeated warnings shaped with the same language, God's people continued to bow down to both idols and celestial bodies (Deut. 4:19; 5:9; Josh. 23:7; 2 Kings 17:16, 35). Ever merciful, the Lord never lost hope, anticipating a time when all nations of the earth will bow before him. "All the ends of the earth will remember and turn to the LORD, and all the families of the nations will bow down before him" (Ps. 22:27; see also 66:4; 72:11; Isa. 66:23).

The biblical authors mention this act of deference frequently because it was very much a part of the fabric of everyday living. But there were certain instances of bowing down that became more powerful, particularly because they reversed expectation in one way or another. Such instances often involved the bowing of one who was socially superior to one who was regarded as socially inferior. As Bible readers, we have a high regard for Abraham. But his true social status in Canaan was marked by his bowing before the Hittite "people of the land" from whom he wished to purchase a cave in which to bury Sarah (Gen. 23:7, 12). In another instance, as the second youngest of his family, Joseph would have been expected to occupy a lower social status than his living parents and older brothers. But that expectation was turned upside down by the prediction and then reality of his father and brothers bowing down to him (Gen. 37:7, 9–10; 42:6; 43:28). And before Genesis closes, we find one more instance of unexpected bowing. In a culture in which the elder brother was expected to receive the greatest honor, it was Jacob's son Judah who was told that he would be the leader of the clan: "Your father's sons will bow down to you" (Gen. 49:8; compare 35:23).

Another way in which expectations regarding bowing are undone by the biblical authors is when someone expected to bow either completely failed to do so or did so in a less deferential manner. Moses told the Egyptian officials that despite his more humble origins and appearance, they would be the ones who would bow down before him (Exod. 11:8). Later we

In these fields outside Bethlehem, Ruth bowed with her face to the ground before Boaz, showing she recognized his superior social station (Ruth 2:10).

see Absalom bowing deeply before his father, King David. We think this should settle the ill will between this father and son, but an ironic reversal was at hand. When anyone tried to bow down before Absalom, he was quick to arrest their act of deference, thus beginning to steal the hearts of the people in advance of stealing the throne from David (2 Sam. 15:5). Years later, it was David's son Adonijah who had his eye on his father's throne. After his initial bid for the throne collapsed, his bow before Solomon was not the deep bow that indicated full submission to Solomon (1 Kings 1:53). This seemingly innocent omission looms larger in view of his subsequent attempts to position himself for the throne. And a failure to bow became the catalyst for the plot in Esther. This time it was the Jew Mordecai who refused to bow before the Persian official Haman (Esther 3:2–6). This so vexed Haman that he sought to eradicate the Jews from the kingdom.

The Magi prepare to bow as they present their gifts to the Christ child.

Finally, bowing plays a very important literary role in the early chapters of Matthew. When the Magi came to see the newborn King of the Jews, "they bowed down and worshiped him" (Matt. 2:11). But with a turn of the page we meet quite a different story when the tempter confronted Jesus with a mission-ending invitation. Showing Jesus all the kingdoms of the world he was destined to rule, he said, "All this I will give you . . . if you will bow down and worship me" (Matt. 4:9).

On the flanks of Mount Hermon (below), within sight of the international trade passing below, Satan offered Jesus all the kingdoms of the world and their splendor in exchange for a bow of submission (Matt. 4:8–9).

BREAD
(TO EAT)

When a family sat down to eat, they ate bread prepared by the loving hands of the women of the family, who baked bread for them on a daily basis (Lev. 26:26; Jer. 7:18). The recipe and process were well practiced. After the grain was ground into flour, that flour was mixed with water, salt, and a small amount of fermented bread dough (leaven). This dough was kneaded and then shaped into flat, round loaves resembling pita that were left to rise before baking.[15]

People ate bread in both mundane and religious contexts. Bread was eaten on a daily basis with virtually every meal because it provided the bulk of the carbohydrates and protein people required in order to complete a full day of physical labor or overland travel.[16] But the Bible also speaks of bread eaten in connection with religious observance. Prior to leaving Egypt, God directed the Israelites to prepare unleavened bread and consume some of it in advance of the long-distance traveling they were about to do

(Exod. 12:8). This special eating of bread became part of Passover—an annual feast that commemorates the exodus of God's people from Egypt (Exod. 12:18–20; Lev. 23:6; Deut. 16:3). The week before his death, Jesus hosted the Passover meal, fittingly incorporating the eating of bread into the new meal designed for those living in the new era (Mark 14:22; 1 Cor. 11:23–28). "While they were eating, Jesus took bread, and when he had given thanks, he broke it and gave it to his disciples, saying, 'Take and eat; this is my body'" (Matt. 26:26).

The eating of bread that was a standard feature of daily living was formally mentioned

Bread lovingly baked at home was a staple food eaten on a daily basis.

by the biblical authors when something special was associated with eating or not eating bread. Sometimes the preparation and eating of bread was mentioned because it was one way a host signaled the acceptance of a traveler who was passing through (Gen. 14:18; 18:6; 1 Sam. 28:24–25). Note that the connotations of welcome and acceptance accompanied the bread that Jesus offered to Peter and the other disciples as he sought to restore them to service in his kingdom following his resurrection (John 21:9, 13).

The biblical authors also mentioned the eating of bread when it occurred following the miraculous appearance of that bread. The Israelites ate bread made from manna—a mysterious food provided by the Lord during their travel in the wilderness (Exod. 16:8, 15, 32). Elijah was refreshed by bread brought to him by ravens during a famine (1 Kings 17:6). Elisha took a small amount of bread and fed hundreds (2 Kings 4:42). And Jesus himself took an even smaller amount of bread and fed

After Jesus spent forty days in this forbidding Judean wilderness without eating, Satan tempted him to make bread from stones (Matt. 4:1–4).

thousands on at least two occasions: (1) the feeding of the five thousand is the version of this miracle done for Jews (Matt. 14:13–21), and (2) the feeding of the four thousand is the parallel miracle done for Gentiles (Matt. 15:32–38). The biblical authors formally mentioned the eating of bread in each of these instances because they provided evidence of a divine, caring power among us.

The biblical authors also took pains to mention those periods when people were not eating bread. This may have been a way of showing just how horrible a time of siege or famine had become or would be (Lev. 26:26; 1 Kings 17:12; Jer. 38:9). The failure to eat bread may also be a sign that one's life had become disturbed in some way or other. For example, David's refusal to eat bread accentuated the pain he felt over Abner's death at the hands of Joab (2 Sam. 3:35). And Job had no appetite for bread when faced with the multiple personal challenges that God allowed into his life (Job 3:24; NIV "food"). Finally, the refusal to eat bread might signal that a divine mission was in process. Moses ate no

During the last week of his life on earth, Jesus invited his disciples to eat Passover bread while initiating a new meal for the New Testament era.

Satan's temptation to make bread for himself from the stones that surrounded him (Matt. 4:1–4).

Eating bread also appears as a metaphor in the Bible. Because eating bread was such an ordinary part of everyday living, it can be synonymous with a regularly occurring activity. "Do all these evildoers know nothing? They devour my people as though eating bread; they never call on the Lord" (Ps. 14:4; see also 53:4). "They eat the bread of wickedness and drink the wine of violence" (Prov. 4:17). But perhaps the most striking metaphor linked to the eating of bread is the one found in John 6. Here eating bread is symbolic of believing in Jesus. "Then Jesus declared, 'I am the bread of life. Whoever comes to me will never go hungry, and whoever believes in me will never be thirsty'" (v. 35). This amazing discourse culminated in these memorable words: "I am the living bread that came down from heaven. Whoever eats this bread will live forever. This bread is my flesh, which I will give for the life of the world" (v. 51).

bread during his forty days on Mount Sinai (Exod. 34:28). When God sent the prophet of Judah to condemn the altar of Jeroboam at Bethel, he ordered him not to eat any bread while executing his mission (1 Kings 13:8–9). This seemingly incidental detail was repeatedly mentioned and closely woven into the fabric of the story (1 Kings 13:16–18, 22) because this prophet of Judah paid with his life for failing to obey this directive. Finally, Jesus did not eat bread during his forty-day fast in the wilderness. Despite his hunger pangs, Jesus maintained his fast in the face of

The grain for making daily bread was ground using wheat mills such as these.

BRIDEGROOM

To this day, family and marriage remain very important dimensions of the value system of those living in the Middle East. In Bible times getting married and having children was the norm. Young people considered it their obligation to participate in the system that provided economic and physical security for their clan. Thus the journey from bachelor to bridegroom was made as quickly as possible so that each young man could find his place in fulfilling this important role.

The process began in earnest during the teenage years when a variety of responsibilities related to getting married fell on the shoulders of the prospective groom.[17] Though his parents formally arranged the marriage on his behalf, the bridegroom typically was involved in the discussions that led to the selection of his mate. It was also the bridegroom's responsibility to secure the *mohar* or bride-price. This fee, agreed on in advance with the bride's family, was paid either in cash or in service (Gen. 29:15–30; 1 Sam. 18:23–27) and was designed to compensate the bride's family for the loss of a family member who contributed to the well-being of their social unit.[18] Once the *mohar* was paid, the betrothal was formally under way. Then it became the duty of the bridegroom to woo his bride-to-be, building a relationship with her while forgoing any type of sexual intimacy. Toward this end, the bridegroom enlisted the aid of a trusted friend who helped him negotiate these new and challenging waters. In addition to relationship building, the bridegroom also began constructing an additional room in the family living compound in which he and his bride would raise their family (John 14:2). The responsibilities and the time needed to accomplish these social obligations were so great that a young man was excused from military service during the betrothal period (Deut. 20:7).

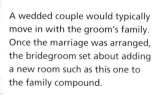

A wedded couple would typically move in with the groom's family. Once the marriage was arranged, the bridegroom set about adding a new room such as this one to the family compound.

All this preparation culminated in the wedding day itself when the groom traveled to the family home of his bride to bring her in festive procession to the wedding celebration that lasted from seven to fourteen days. During this time the bride and groom were excused from any other responsibilities and dressed in ways that marked them as the special focus of the celebration. Following the first day of the celebration, they retired to a special chamber where they enjoyed the sexual union they had long anticipated (Ps. 19:5).

The formal mention of the bridegroom in the Bible nearly always occurs within a figure of speech. At times the image builds on the connotations of joy and celebration. For example, the people of Zion are likened to the ornately dressed and royally treated bridegroom (Isa. 61:10). Conversely, the Lord is represented as the bridegroom who "rejoices over his bride" (Isa. 62:5).

When the prophets formally mentioned a bridegroom, however, it was frequently in judgment speeches that foretold this joy going away. Jeremiah repeatedly called for God's people to abandon their rebellious path. And he warned that if they failed to do so, the most fundamental elements of life would change. "I will bring an end to the sounds of joy and gladness and to the voices of bride and bridegroom in the towns of Judah and the streets of Jerusalem, for the land will become desolate" (Jer. 7:34; see also 16:9; 25:10; Rev. 18:23). The need to repent was so great that bridegroom and bride were urged to abandon their first night of romantic pleasure in their marriage chamber in order to participate in seeking God's favor (Joel 2:16). Only many years after the exile did God remove the consequences of his judgment, and that change is marked in Jeremiah with a reversal of the metaphor, promising that the celebratory voice of the bridegroom and bride will return to the land (Jer. 33:11).

In the New Testament Jesus is pictured as the bridegroom. When the less sober demeanor of his disciples was called into question, he observed that the time of his presence on earth was a time for celebration because the bridegroom was among them. All too soon that would change, introducing a time when pensive fasting would be appropriate (Matt. 9:15; Mark 2:19–20; Luke 5:34–35). Jesus is also pictured as the bridegroom in the eschatological parable of the

This statue from the thirteenth century BC captures the posed Egyptian family of Ptahmai. Wedded life was the norm in all cultures of the ancient Near Eastern world.

ten virgins (Matt. 25:1–10). Traditionally the bridegroom made his way to the bride's home to take her to the wedding celebration, and Jesus's second coming is likened to that journey. The parable calls for the church—the bride's attendants—to remain ever attentive for his arrival.

The image of Jesus as bridegroom was also used by John the Baptist and Paul to help define their role in comparison to Jesus. In each case they described themselves as the faithful friend who was pledged to assist the bridegroom during the betrothal period. John said, "The bride belongs to the bridegroom. The friend who attends the bridegroom waits and listens for him, and is full of joy when he hears the bridegroom's voice. That joy is mine, and it is now complete" (John 3:29). And Paul said, "I promised you to one husband, to Christ, so that I might present you as a pure virgin to him" (2 Cor. 11:2).

The connotations of bridegroom as protector are ironically reversed in two instances. In Judges 15:6 Samson baited the Philistines into ever deeper aggression against himself, his intended bride, and her family. Rather than bringing benefits to this Philistine family, he brought increasing harm to them en route to the increasing harm he eventually brought to many Philistines. The most striking appearance of this ironic image, however, comes in the difficult verses of Exodus 4:24–26. After Moses accepted God's call to lead the Israelites out of Egypt, the Lord was going to execute him on his way to fulfill the assignment. Zipporah, Moses's wife, interceded on his behalf, ironically playing the role of his protector. She then attached a stinging title to her husband, calling Moses her "bridegroom of blood" (v. 25).

The connotation of protection linked to bridegrooms is turned upside down in the story of Samson. Among the disasters that befell his intended bride's family was the loss of their grain fields in the Sorek Valley (below).

The Baker Illustrated Guide to Everyday Life in Bible Times

BURY THE DEAD

*I*n our culture, soon after a loved one passes away we place his or her mortal remains in the hands of a mortician, who prepares the body and superintends the final steps toward burial or cremation. In Bible times the care of the deceased fell firmly into the hands of loving family members and friends. The Israelites did not practice the art of embalming or cremation[19] (the exception being the special circumstances associated with Jacob and Joseph in Genesis 50:2–3, 26). Consequently, the family found itself in a race with decomposition, forcing them to grieve and give attention to the details of the burial at the same time. There was also a theological reason for haste. According to Old Testament law, the link between sin and death meant that a dead body desecrated the Promised Land and made those who came into contact with it ritually unclean (Num. 19:11–16; Deut. 21:22–23).

The death of a family member set into motion a well-practiced set of rituals. The body was washed (Acts 9:37) and aromatics were applied to the body (2 Chron. 16:14; Mark 16:1; John 19:39) before the family dressed their loved one in familiar clothing or wrapped the remains with strips of linen (John 11:44; 20:6; Acts 5:6). Then the body was taken to the specially prepared cave or tomb cut out of rock where the loved one's remains were interred. These burial chambers could be simple and unadorned or complex and ornate depending on the person's station in life and financial means.[20]

When the biblical authors mention someone's burial, the rhetorical importance is most often associated with either the location of the burial or the failure of that person to be buried. The intimate connection between Canaan and the expectation of the coming Messiah is frequently reinforced in the book of Genesis, but it takes on new depth when Abraham

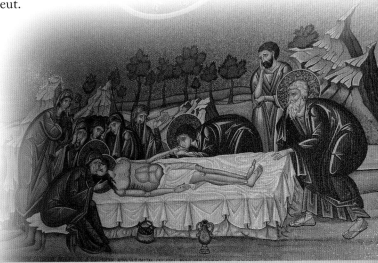

The death of a family member set into motion a well-rehearsed set of rituals enacted during the burial of Jesus (right).

purchases property there. Prior to the death of Sarah, Abraham roamed about this promised real estate without holding the deed to a single parcel of land. That changed when Sarah died and Abraham purchased a cave from the local Hittites in which to bury Sarah (Gen. 23:4–19). We come back to this tomb frequently as one family member after another is buried there (Gen. 49:31). And lest we miss the point, the book closes by reinforcing the important connection between the Promised Land and God's people. Although both Jacob and Joseph died outside this land, they insisted that their remains be transported back to Canaan for burial there (Gen. 47:29–30; 50:25).

Jewish culture in the first century practiced second burial. Once flesh and muscle had decayed away, the bones were gathered and put into a limestone box called an ossuary.

Honor and burial location are also linked. As the Israelites settled into towns and cities within the Promised Land, the tombs themselves always remained outside the community living areas for the ritual reasons noted above. The exception was the royal house of Judah. David, Solomon, Rehoboam, and others were singled out for special treatment; they were buried within the City of David (1 Kings 2:10; 11:43; 14:31). Honor also went to those who were buried with their families (Judg. 8:32; 16:31; 2 Sam. 2:32; 17:23; 21:14). This informs the remarkable promise extended by Ruth to Naomi. Although her biological family was in Moab, she promised Naomi, "Where you die I will die, and there I will be buried" (Ruth 1:17).

Failure to be buried was a great disgrace—one that often came in connection with divine judgment. When people rebelled against the Lord, they might hear of this impending punishment: "They will be exposed to the sun and the moon and all the stars of the heavens. . . . They will not be gathered up or buried, but will be like dung lying on the ground" (Jer. 8:2). The despicable Jezebel was not buried, and this judgment also fell on other political leaders, prophets, priests, and ordinary citizens who chose to reject God's call to repent (1 Kings 14:13; 2 Kings 9:10, 35–37; Jer. 14:16; 16:4, 6; 22:19; 25:33).

Three special instances of burial deserve mention because of their uniqueness. First, we read at the close of Deuteronomy that

The indignity of not being buried was furthered by being consumed by wild animals.

The Baker Illustrated Guide to Everyday Life in Bible Times

the Lord himself buried Moses (Deut. 34:6). Given that the immediate family typically performed the burial, this loving action of the Lord's shows the close relationship he enjoyed with this prophet.

The second unique mention of burial comes from Jesus. When one of his followers expressed the desire to follow him but only after a delay to bury his father, Jesus responded, "Follow me, and let the dead bury their own dead" (Matt. 8:21–22; see also Luke 9:59–60). The apparent harshness in Jesus's response is muted somewhat when we understand this man's request in light of first-century Jewish burial culture. The deceased loved one was placed in a tomb and left undisturbed for a year. Once the soft tissues and flesh had decomposed, the bones were gathered and put into a special bone box called an ossuary. If we understand this person's request within this larger context of burial, he was asking for up to a yearlong sabbatical from service. Jesus was telling him that this lengthy delay was not appropriate.[21] To paraphrase, he said, "Let the dead bodies in the tomb take care of such matters." This hyperbolic statement is designed to drive home the importance of engaging with Jesus without delay. Finally, there is the metaphorical burial mentioned in both Romans 6:4 and Colossians 2:12. In each case the experience of Christian baptism is likened to burial. As real burial paves the way for resurrection, so baptism paves the way for a new life of obedience.

In this Iron Age tomb, the deceased was laid on the slab, where recesses for the head can be seen. Once the flesh and muscle had decayed away, the bones were placed in a chamber beneath this bench.

CAST METAL

The process of casting was used to transform molten metal into both decorative and utilitarian objects. Before the metal was cast, the artisan had to construct a mold made from stone, sand, or clay (1 Kings 7:46)[1] that could withstand the tremendous temperatures required to melt various metals. Stone molds were carved with a metal tool that scraped away at the stone until the appropriately shaped depression appeared. Then the molten metal was poured into the stone mold.

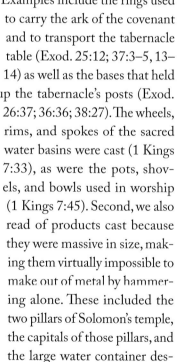

The sand or clay molds involved another step. The metalworker had to create a positive model of the object using beeswax. This wax model was either pressed into wet sand or layered with clay to create the negative mold or cast for the product. If the mold was of the open type, the wax could simply be pried from the mold. If the mold was enclosed, the wax would be melted away as the molten metal took its place.[2] With the mold completed, it was necessary to heat the metal until it changed into a pourable, liquid state. This required heating the metal to very high temperatures—gold to 1,063°C, copper to 1,083°C, and silver to 961°C. After the

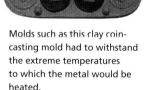

Molds such as this clay coin-casting mold had to withstand the extreme temperatures to which the metal would be heated.

molten metal had cooled within the mold, the mold was broken apart and the cast product was removed for final shaping and finishing.

A variety of products made by casting are mentioned in the Bible. First, we read about products cast to obtain high durability goods that could endure many duty cycles. Examples include the rings used to carry the ark of the covenant and to transport the tabernacle table (Exod. 25:12; 37:3–5, 13–14) as well as the bases that held up the tabernacle's posts (Exod. 26:37; 36:36; 38:27). The wheels, rims, and spokes of the sacred water basins were cast (1 Kings 7:33), as were the pots, shovels, and bowls used in worship (1 Kings 7:45). Second, we also read of products cast because they were massive in size, making them virtually impossible to make out of metal by hammering alone. These included the two pillars of Solomon's temple, the capitals of those pillars, and the large water container destined for use in the temple courtyard, which was called "the Sea of cast metal" (1 Kings 7:15–16, 23). The third category of cast items mentioned by the biblical authors are those cast with special decorations. In this case, rather than having the decorative components of a product made separately and then attached to the primary product, the decorative elements such as gourds, wreaths, or bulls were included in the mold and so made one with it (1 Kings 7:24, 29–30; 2 Chron. 4:3). Finally, products were cast when the artisan desired to create exact replicas. In this case, use of the same mold ensured precise duplication (1 Kings 7:37).

Two connotations are associated with products that were cast in molds. The first is that they were extremely hard and durable. In the book of Job we encounter this connotation a number of times. When speaking to a man whose body had been ravaged, Zophar told Job that if only he would devote his heart to the Lord, he would be "cast solid" and so be without shame (Job 11:15; NIV "stand firm"). Later the Lord is pictured as a metal-worker who made the heavens "a mirror of cast bronze" (Job 37:18). And the soil after the summer drought is pictured as hardened like cast metal (Job 38:38; NIV "becomes hard").

The second connotation that attends passages that mention a cast product is uniqueness. When we consider that most products used by the Israelites were made either from animal skin or from clay, we can begin to appreciate how very special a metal object was. That is even truer of a metal object made by casting. Not everyone possessed the skills or the necessary tools to create effective molds, heat the metal to one thousand degrees centigrade, and do the finishing work on a cast product. It is no wonder that when major castings had to be made for the temple, King Solomon turned to someone with expertise in the field (1 Kings 7:13–14, 45–46).

An Egyptian vessel cast in gold.

The casting of so many items associated with the temple helped to make that place stand out as unique, which was fitting for the place God had chosen to meet his people (1 Kings 7:40–45).

A unique object obtained by the casting process, however, could also be put to work in the service of false gods. The first time we read about such an object in the Bible, it is a pagan worship object built by Aaron. As Moses was receiving directions from the Lord about how various items were to be cast for use in the tabernacle, Aaron yielded to the pressure of impatient people and made a cast or molten calf toward which they directed their worship (Exod. 32:4, 8). This rebellion is memorialized and decried repeatedly when the molten calf is mentioned in subsequent books (Deut. 9:16; Neh. 9:18; Ps. 106:19).

The Canaanites also used this special process of casting to make idols for themselves. And before the Israelites entered the Promised Land, the Lord warned them to destroy all the "cast idols" they found (Num. 33:52). This brought the Israelites to a crossroads in their history. They could either return to the days of making and worshiping their own molten idols or make sure that all molten idols were eliminated from their land. Sadly, it was the former course they followed. The failure

of the northern kingdom of Israel was linked to the two molten calves placed at Bethel and Dan (2 Kings 17:16). Those molten idols spawned a culture of molten images commissioned for use by ordinary Israelites and roundly criticized by Isaiah (Isa. 40:19; 44:10).

The carrying rings for this incense altar, as well as its associated shovels and basins, were cast out of metal in order to endure repeated use.

CIRCUMCISE

*M*ale circumcision requires the amputation of the foreskin in order to expose the glans of the penis. The Bible mentions that this procedure was common not only among the Israelites but also in Egypt, Edom, Ammon, Moab, and among "all who live in the wilderness" (Jer. 9:25–26); conspicuous by its absence is any mention within Mesopotamian cultures. Consequently, when the Lord spoke with Abraham about circumcision (Gen. 17:1–14), any familiarity he had with the procedure probably was gleaned during his Egyptian stay rather than from his experience in his former homeland.

Western Semitic people apparently practiced circumcision as a rite of passage into manhood prior to marriage.[3] But it had special meaning for the Israelites. As the Lord confirmed his covenant promises to Abraham, he directed Abraham to circumcise himself and every male member of his household, slave or free, blood relation or

not (Gen. 17:10–14). This surgery was likely done with a flint knife (Josh. 5:2) and was henceforth to be done on every male child eight days after his birth (Lev. 12:3). From this time forward, circumcision became a "sign of the covenant" and a "covenant in your flesh" for the descendants of Abraham (Gen. 17:11, 13), showing one's allegiance and commitment to the divine agenda. Though this procedure was limited to the male members of the community, females were not left out. Culturally among God's Old Testament people, no act was perceived as an individual act but had ramifications for the entire clan. So it was that the implications of circumcision extended to all the female members of the clan as well.[4]

The many acts of circumcision during the time of the Old Testament are largely unmentioned; those that are usually involve some misuse of the procedure. For example, the shadow of the Lord's disapproval hung

Jesus joined a long line of Bible notables when he was circumcised, linking himself to the promises given to Abraham about the coming Messiah.

over the act of Jacob's sons when they persuaded the males of Shechem to undergo circumcision, luring them with the hope that they would enjoy economic advantages when their real intention was to disable the men of the city before attacking them (Gen. 34:13–27). We also sense the Lord's disapproval of the Israelites' failure to be circumcised when we learn that many Israelites had to be circumcised again because they either had been improperly circumcised in Egypt[5] or were never circumcised at all during their stay in the wilderness (Josh. 5:2–5). This is a remarkable omission given the Lord's statement that those who ignored this rite were to be cut off from the people (Gen. 17:14). A third misuse of circumcision was found in the perception that circumcision was merely skin deep. Things were to change on the inside as well. If the external act did not change the inner convictions, then the biblical authors began to address the malady metaphorically: "Circumcise yourselves to the LORD, circumcise your hearts" (Jer. 4:4; see also Deut. 10:16; 30:6).

The matter of circumcision became a contested issue as the early Christian church was finding its feet. To

appreciate why, we first need to understand that this had grown to be a most important element within Judaism. Between the time of the Old and New Testaments, Seleucid King Antiochus IV attempted to stamp out Judaism, in part by forbidding the practice of circumcision among the Jews. This rite had become so vital to the identity of God's people that they chose to die rather than yield to this pagan order.[6] Similarly, in the days of the New Testament the Sabbath was guarded very aggressively by the Jewish rabbis. Nothing resembling work was to be done. But if the eighth day after a boy was born was a Sabbath, circumcision was permitted (John 7:22). So it follows that New Testament notables with deep roots in Judaism, like John the Baptist, Jesus, and Paul, were circumcised (Luke 1:59; 2:21; Phil. 3:5).

Given the importance of circumcision, Jews who became believers in Jesus were slow to relinquish the practice. And given the nature of the rite, Gentile believers in Jesus were slow to adopt it unless required to do so. Consequently, there was a cultural divide among those who came to know Jesus as their Savior in the first century—Gentile believers and "circumcised believers" (Acts 10:45). This brought the early Christian church to an uneasy crossroads that required the wise council of senior Christian leaders in Jerusalem (Acts 15:1–5). The options were clear: (1) all Christians could be required to undergo circumcision, (2) all

The simple flint knife was the traditional tool used for performing the rite of circumcision.

The Baker Illustrated Guide to Everyday Life in Bible Times

Christians, including Jews, could be directed to remain uncircumcised, or (3) the matter could be left to personal discretion. While certain directives were put into a letter from this council of Christian leaders for distribution to the churches at large, there was no demand for circumcision (Acts 15:23–29). The council left the matter to the discretion of each believer. Paul seems to capture the essence of their thoughts in 1 Corinthians 7:18–20. Liberty and expediency guided Paul, who called for the circumcision of Timothy but not of Titus (Acts 16:3; Gal. 2:3).

But the matter did not go away and had to be addressed in the Epistles to the Romans, Corinthians, Galatians, and Colossians. The circumstances varied a bit in each case, but the bottom line was that certain Jews insisted that faith in Jesus as the Savior from sin was not saving faith unless accompanied by the rite of circumcision (Rom. 4:9–12; 1 Cor. 7:18–20; Col. 2:11; 3:11). The language of the Bible against this premise takes its strongest tone in Galatians: "Mark my words! I, Paul, tell you that if you let yourselves be circumcised, Christ will be of no value to you at all" (Gal. 5:2; see also 2:3–5; 6:12–13).

The question about circumcising Gentiles who had converted to Christianity was taken up by the council in Jerusalem (below) in Acts 15.

CLAP HANDS

When we communicate with each other, we do so not just with our words but also with the gestures we make, such as clapping our hands. Within the culture of the Western world of our day, this single gesture of clapping our hands together can send many and even contrasting messages. For example, we clap our hands to show our approval and appreciation of what has been said or done. But we also can clap our hands together in a mock show of approval and appreciation when we intend to send just the opposite message. A single clap of our hands together may indicate anger or surprise. Consequently, it requires more than just seeing the gesture but also knowing the context in order to correctly interpret the message. That is equally true of interpreting the gesture of clapping in the Bible.

Studies of hand clapping in the ancient Near Eastern world have not always led scholars to a consensus on what an individual occurrence means whether in written form or as depicted in ancient art. There is, however, general

The Jordan River. "Let the rivers clap their hands" (Ps. 98:8).

agreement that hand clapping sends one of four messages. It can be used: (1) to mark a time of joy-filled celebration, (2) to mock or scoff at someone's misfortune, (3) to express grief or anger, or (4) to play a part in a magical incantation.[7]

When the clapping of hands is mentioned, Bible interpreters must honor two premises. First, formal hand clapping mentioned in the text increases the importance and intensity of the message being communicated. And second, because the gesture of hand clapping can have a variety of meanings in the ancient Near East, the interpreter must carefully look at the context for clues as to which of the specific nuances applies.

In a number of instances, the connotation of celebration and approval attends the clapping of hands, particularly in contexts of a change in political leadership. This is aptly illustrated in the accession of Joash to the throne. Following her son's death, Queen Athaliah had systematically eliminated members of the royal family who might challenge her passion to sit on the royal throne. She ruled for six years unaware that one prince, Joash, had escaped her purge. In the queen's seventh year, Jehoiada, the high priest, took the risky step of revealing this hidden prince at the temple and anointing him as king. The enthusiastic acceptance of this royal coup is reported with these words: "The people clapped their hands and shouted, 'Long live the king!'" (2 Kings 11:12; see also Ezek. 25:6; Nah. 3:19). This is the gesture that the psalmist called for when the Lord himself assumes his rightful throne. "Clap your hands, all you nations; shout to God with cries of joy. For the Lord Most High is awesome, the great King over all the earth" (Ps. 47:1–2).

By contrast, fierce clapping of the hands might attend the scoffing or deriding of the words, actions, or circumstances of another.[8] Elihu took offense at the way Job had clapped his hands at his critics. "To his sin he adds rebellion; scornfully he claps his hands among us and multiplies his words against God" (Job 34:37). The ruins of Jerusalem faced the same response from those who walked by. "All who pass your way clap their hands at you; they scoff and shake their heads" (Lam. 2:15).

The hand clapping gesture could also signal anger and disgust. Balak's anger at Balaam's failure to curse the Israelites, as he had been hired to do, caused this king to strike his hands together in disgusted anger just before sending Balaam home (Num. 24:10). But it is in Ezekiel that we find this aspect of hand clapping mentioned most frequently. The Lord directed his prophet to announce his displeasure with his people both in words and in actions. "Strike your hands together and stamp your

An Egyptian ivory hand clapper.

The clapping of hands depicted in this Assyrian relief could be communicating celebration or sorrow.

feet and cry out 'Alas!' because of all the wicked and detestable practices of the people of Israel" (Ezek. 6:11; see also 21:14). And as the Lord directed Ezekiel to strike his hands together in anger over the constant rebellion of Israel, the Lord used that same gesture himself. "I too will strike my hands together, and my wrath will subside" (Ezek. 21:17). "I will surely strike my hands together at the unjust gain you have made and at the blood you have shed in your midst" (Ezek. 22:13).

In addition to these literal instances of hand clapping, there were several instances of hand clapping in figures of speech in which wind, river, and trees were personified with hands they clapped together. The first example from Job carried the connotation of derision as he discussed the fate of the wicked who would be punished for their sins. In this case, he mentioned the "east wind" (Job 27:21)—the hot dry wind that exits the desert and generally makes everyone uncomfortable. In Job's language, the east wind became a symbol of the troubles that would infiltrate the lives of the wicked, and it "claps its hands in derision and hisses him out of his place" (Job 27:23).

The two other instances involve rivers and trees that were invited to clap their hands in celebration. As the psalmist invited the entire earth to break forth in joy at the news of the Lord's salvation, the rivers were invited to clap their hands (Ps. 98:8). And as the Lord returned his people from exile, all the trees of the field were invited to clap their hands at the sight (Isa. 55:12).

CLEAN/UNCLEAN

The Old Testament concept of being clean can be difficult to grasp. The basic idea sounds foreign to modern ears, and the legislation that describes how that state is achieved and maintained can overwhelm us, making books like Leviticus, Numbers, and Deuteronomy much more difficult to understand. But when we acquire a clearer understanding of the notion, we find that the image of being clean is a helpful one that spreads its influence from Genesis through Revelation.[9]

As we enter the Bible and meet the world that came from God's creating hand, we are reminded repeatedly that it was "good" (Gen. 1:4, 10, 12, 18, 25, 31). We may say that it was *clean*—not in a hygienic sense but in the sense that it resonated at every level with the Creator. Sadly, that changed when the creation broke stride with its Creator; it stopped being *good* or *clean*. As the Lord set about the restoration of the world and its people, he chose one family that would become the one nation to take the lead. They would care for and advance the plan to restore holiness to a now unholy place. God sought to separate this nation from the other nations of the world, calling them to be distinct or holy (Lev. 11:44–45; 19:2). Furthermore, the Lord himself promised to reside among them in a way he did not reside with other people on earth (Exod. 25:8; 33:1–6).[10]

Because of God's special presence among them and in order to mark them as a unique people with a unique mission, God directed them to see the world through his eyes. This was a world in which things, places, behavior, and people were labeled either as clean or unclean. "You can distinguish between the holy and the common, between the unclean and the clean" (Lev. 10:10). The law given on Mount Sinai added detail to this general worldview. Animals, vessels, natural processes, places, and behaviors were all placed in one of two categories: clean or unclean (Lev. 4:12; 11:1–47; 14:53; Josh. 22:17; Isa. 66:20). What is more,

The rock hyrax (coney) is listed among the unclean animals (Lev. 11:5).

people could now move between the states of clean and unclean. The goal for God's people was to remain ritually clean.

It would have been virtually impossible for anyone to honor that command for very long because there was so much in the world that made a person ritually unclean, such as: eating an animal that was defined as unclean (Lev. 11:4–23), touching or carrying something that was defined as unclean (Lev. 11:24–25; 15:9–10), natural processes like childbirth or a bodily discharge (Lev. 12:1–5; 15:2–13), contracting an infectious skin disease (Lev. 13:3), as well as acts and thoughts that God had defined as immoral (Lev. 18:20; Ps. 51:2–7). When Israelites became ritually unclean, they were required to use the appropriate method(s)

to restore themselves to a condition of ritual purity. This might mean waiting for a given period of time (Lev. 12:2; Num. 31:19–20), washing with water (Lev. 15:5, 16–24; Num. 19:17; 31:24), or offering a sacrifice (Lev. 12:8). So it was that this matter required the constant attention of God's people in the Old Testament. And as they gave it their attention, they were reminded of their special calling and the special presence of God among them.

Then we come to the time of Jesus when the idea of being ritually clean began to change. He made it his business to respond to the pleas of those who had become unclean and were not capable of correcting their situation on their own (Matt. 8:2–3; Mark 1:40–42; Luke 5:12–13; 17:14, 17). And he directed

The ibex (wild goat) met the definition of a clean animal and so could be eaten by the Israelites.

The Baker Illustrated Guide to Everyday Life in Bible Times

Ceremonial washing was one method of obtaining ritual cleansing.

surprisingly, the book of Hebrews invites us to see the link between Old Testament shadow and New Testament reality, presenting Jesus as the one who ultimately cleanses the human race: "The blood of goats and bulls and the ashes of a heifer sprinkled on those who are ceremonially unclean sanctify them so that they are outwardly clean. How much more, then, will the blood of Christ . . . cleanse our consciences from acts that lead to death" (Heb. 9:13–14). John puts it so simply and yet so elegantly when he says, "The blood of Jesus, his Son, purifies us from all sin" (1 John 1:7).

This same inspired author lifts our eyes to the world to come in order to confirm that it will be a place where cleansing comes to its fullest maturity. Surveying the many who have already arrived, John is told by his heavenly docent, "These are they who have come out of the great tribulation; they have washed their robes and made them white in the blood of the Lamb" (Rev. 7:14). And so the world that was called "very good" in Genesis becomes clean again in the book of Revelation (Rev. 15:5–6; 19:8, 14; 22:14).

sharp criticism at those who sustained (even expanded) the purity laws but failed to see them as marking the need for a greater change from within (Luke 11:39–41). Jesus's life was following a trajectory that would result in the ultimate cleansing. He declared all food formerly defined as unclean to now be clean (Mark 7:19; see also Acts 10:10–16; Rom. 14:20). And he marched to the cross where his ultimate act of substitutionary cleansing restored humans to the state they had lost in Eden. Not

As in the Garden of Eden, some foods were approved for consumption and others were forbidden. The pomegranate was approved.

CONCUBINE

Mentioned in numerous Old Testament passages, the concubine was not a prostitute but an auxiliary marriage partner who was both similar to and different from the wife. She was similar in that the Bible describes her marriage partner as her "husband" and includes her along with sons, daughters, and wives as a member of the ancient household (Judg. 20:4–6; 2 Sam. 19:5). Like the wife, she enjoyed the economic support of her husband (2 Sam. 20:3), and like a full-status wife, she was to have sexual relations only with her husband (Judg. 19:1–2). Given the other wives and concubines in the household, she could not expect the same fidelity from him.

At the same time, the life of the concubine and her children was also different from that of the full-status wife. The differences started with the economic exchanges that attended the marriage. The concubine did not have to secure a dowry to bring with her into the marriage. Her status was also different. Within the hierarchy of the household that included full-status wives as well as slaves, the concubine fell short of the wife in rank but above the female slaves.[11] Her children felt the brunt of this lower social status. The children of a concubine were not scheduled to receive a portion of the inheritance unless the husband chose to make special allowance for them. Sarah was worried that Abraham would do this for Ishmael, so she urged that he be sent away (Gen. 21:10). In the end, Abraham graciously provided gifts for all of the children of his concubines before he passed away (Gen. 25:6).

The reasons for seeking a concubine in marriage varied from person to person, but we can safely make the following observations. As with the full-status wife, the man seeking a concubine could expect to enjoy sexual pleasure in this relationship as well as enjoy the blessing of additional children.

Even among the most conservative cultures of the Middle East, where women are required to dress modestly whenever they are in public, the practice of keeping a concubine is no longer employed.

Given the importance of children in extending the economic and physical security of a household, it is not surprising that concubines are frequently mentioned in connection with the children to whom they gave birth (for example, Gen. 22:24; 2 Sam. 5:13; 1 Chron. 2:46, 48).

Of course a full-status wife also brought advantages to her husband, but there were economic incentives that made the marriage to a concubine more desirable. The groom did not have to pay the bride-price that was required for marriage to a full-status wife.[12] In addition, the husband could add children to the household without complicating the inheritance since the concubine and her children were not included in the calculation. Concubines were sought by kings for an additional reason. When alliances were struck, the partner nations exchanged young women who married the respective kings as a symbol of the pact that had been made. The more alliance-born concubines one had, the more prestigious one looked as a leader in the ancient world. Although the Lord warned the Israelites about buying into this worldview (Deut. 17:17), Solomon had three hundred concubines and Rehoboam had sixty (1 Kings 11:3; 2 Chron. 11:21).

Yet another reason for seeking a concubine was to demonstrate control over the assets and legacy of a father or king.

Royal marriages to foreigners included marriages to concubines. They were carefully negotiated, as evidenced by this Mittani letter addressed to the Egyptian leader Amenhotep III.

Reuben attempted to force the hand of Jacob into declaring him the primary heir of the family by sleeping with his father's concubine (Gen. 35:22). The same happened in royal circles. Abner, Absalom, and Adonijah all either slept with a king's concubine or attempted to do so in order to advance their legitimacy as a royal figure (2 Sam. 3:7; 16:21–22; 1 Kings 2:17, 21–25).

Concubines have a more extended presence in two Bible stories. The first comes at the

The foundation of David's royal palace in Jerusalem. During his attempt to seize the throne, Absalom pitched a tent on top of this building and slept with his father's concubines.

close of the book of Judges as the climax to a series of events that illustrate the depths to which the morality of God's people had sunk. A Levite from the hill country of Ephraim had married a concubine from Bethlehem. She was unfaithful to him and then left him and returned to her paternal home. Four months later, her husband went to resolve the matter and brought his concubine home with him. On the way back, they stopped at Gibeah, an Israelite city where they could expect a respectful and warm reception. Instead they found themselves threatened by the local residents. To save himself, the Levite offered his concubine to the men pounding on the door of the home in which they were staying. The concubine was sexually assaulted throughout the night by the men at the door and died as a result. The Levite took her body, cut it into twelve pieces, and sent them throughout the land to call for retribution against Gibeah (Judg. 19:1–30).

The second story takes us to a time when David ruled all Israel. The Gibeonites asked David to execute seven of the male descendants of Saul for the crimes that the king of Israel had committed against them. Included among those executed were two sons of Rizpah, the concubine of Saul. After their execution, their bodies were intentionally left unburied. Rizpah stayed near the bodies of her two sons the entire summer, keeping the birds and predators from further dishonoring the decomposing bodies of her sons. This striking act of family devotion motivated David to secure the remains of Saul and Jonathan from Jabesh Gilead so they could be buried with honor in the family tomb (2 Sam. 21:2–14).[13]

As a full-status wife, Nofret, wife of the Egyptian high priest at Hierapolis, would have enjoyed marriage benefits that were unavailable to concubines.

CROSS THE JORDAN RIVER

*T*oday as we walk or drive, we move quickly and easily over flowing rivers, giving little thought to our crossing and never pausing to contemplate the deeper significance of the moment. In order to capture all the Old Testament has to offer, we need to pay special attention to those instances when the Jordan River was crossed so we can appreciate both the realities of the crossing and the connotations linked to it.

Both bridges and ferries were available to cross rivers in Mesopotamia and Egypt during the time of the Old Testament. There is no evidence, however, that such devices were used in Israel and no mention of them within the

pages of the Old Testament.[14] So we presume that when people crossed the Jordan River, they did so using natural fords. Fords typically occur where tributaries join the river, making the riverbed shallow with the silt they contribute. At such natural fords, one can more easily wade across the river or, if necessary, inflate a goatskin and float past those segments too deep to wade.[15] Natural fords on the Jordan occur opposite Adam, Beth Shan, and Jericho. During Bible times, those locations favored travelers except during the spring floods. Then the fords of the Jordan were susceptible to problems like those of other fords of the ancient world.[16] The water became more turbid, the approaches muddy, the water deep, and the current strong. The perils associated with

As the Israelites prepared to cross the Jordan River from the plains of Moab (below), Moses could only glimpse the Promised Land from the ridge on the horizon.

When a river was too deep to wade through, people could cross it by using inflated animal skins such as the ones depicted here.

crossing a ford during flood stage made heroes of those who successfully accomplished this feat (1 Chron. 12:14–15).

Certainly people crossed the Jordan River many times during the course of conducting family visits and business, but when such crossings are mentioned by the biblical authors, we need to consider their importance and connotations. Those connotations flowed from the first crossing of the Israelites into the Promised Land. The link between the land of Canaan and God's plan to save the world is made early in the book of Genesis (12:1–3, 6–7). But by the time of Joshua, Abraham's family had been out of the land for four hundred years. The anticipation of reentry fills the pages of Deuteronomy. Moses repeatedly urged the people to anticipate crossing the Jordan because it meant entering the land God had promised (Deut. 4:14, 21–22, 26; 6:1; 9:1; 11:8, 31; 12:10; 27:2–3; 30:17–18; 31:3, 13; 32:47). This refrain is quickly resumed in the book of Joshua: "Moses my servant is dead. Now then, you and all these people, get ready to cross the Jordan River into the land I am about to give to them—to the Israelites" (Josh. 1:2). When anticipation gives way to reality, the author of Joshua dedicates two full chapters to the actual crossing (Joshua 3–4). And what a crossing it was. God's people stood before a very inhospitable ford brimming with deep, turbulent, muddy water caused by the spring runoff. As the crossing began, the Lord miraculously cut off the flow of the water, allowing the Israelites to cross on dry ground (Josh. 3:15–17).[17]

The significance of this crossing of the Jordan River lends interpretive energy to many others. The actual crossing still lay

Iron Age fortifications at Beth Shan (left) provide an unrestricted view of the Jordan Valley and particularly of the important ford that lies in the valley floor below the distant ridges.

in the future when the three Transjordan tribes sought permission to make their homes east of the Jordan. Technically this would preclude crossing the Jordan River to come into their homeland. The request for land east of the Jordan was granted, but Moses insisted that these three and a half tribes be part of the momentous river crossing (Num. 32:6–7, 20–22, 27–32; Deut. 3:18; Josh. 1:14; 4:12–13). When the time came, they crossed but Moses did not. He and Aaron had failed to honor the Lord in the Desert of Zin, so they were not given that privilege (Num. 20:12). Moses, not one to surrender easily, longed to be part of this defining moment in Israel's history so he pleaded with the Lord, but to no avail (Deut. 3:25–27; 4:21–22). Thus the somber moment of Moses's passing is further tinged by the prohibition that prevented him from fording the Jordan into the Promised Land (Deut. 34:1–3).

Subsequent exits and reentries via a Jordan River crossing must also be viewed in light of this first momentous crossing of the Jordan. Consider the negative connotations associated with those who forded the river in order to exit the land of Canaan, essentially reversing the direction of the momentous crossing at the time of Joshua. During the time of Saul, Israelites were fording the river eastward in order to escape the Philistine invasion (1 Sam. 13:7). The defeated Abner crossed the Jordan en route to Mahanaim (2 Sam. 2:29). And David forded to the east as he fled from Absalom, who was intent on wresting the kingdom from his father's hands (2 Sam. 17:16, 22).

In each case, the events of the narrative are made all the more dramatic by the fact that they reverse the entry into the Promised Land.

Those exits make the reentries even more spectacular—recapturing the spirit and excitement of Israel's entry into the land. Perhaps the most striking example is that of David. After Absalom was defeated, the path was clear for David to return to his capital city via the ford that took him across the Jordan River. The crossing itself would have been a rather simple matter to execute and report, but the biblical author spends some time there with David on the east side of the river. And the longer we linger, the more people show up to make the ceremonial crossing with David—his personal reentry into the land (2 Sam. 19:15–40). For Bible readers, it is important to weigh into our interpretation not only when someone is crossing the Jordan River but also the direction of that crossing.

Tributaries of the Jordan River such as the Wadi Qilt (right) carry silt to the river channel, which shallows the river, creating fords.

CROWN
(TO WEAR)

Three different types of crowns are mentioned in the Bible: royal crowns, wedding crowns, and athletic crowns. They all serve the purpose of distinguishing someone as unique from others around him or her; however, each has its own distinctive appearance and connotations that impact the way we understand its role in real and metaphorical mention in the Bible.

Royal crowns were worn by Israelite, Ammonite, Egyptian, and Mesopotamian royalty (2 Sam. 1:2–10; 12:30; 2 Kings 11:12; Esther 1:11; 2:17).[18] The royal crowns pictured in ancient Near Eastern art differ from each other in size and shape but have this in common: the style of headdress distinguishes royals from their subjects, and the height afforded by the crown makes the royal figures appear taller. The Bible mentions that some such crowns were made of gold and inset with precious stones (1 Chron. 20:2; Esther 8:15; Ps. 21:3; Zech. 9:16). Whether the royal crown was granted voluntarily or seized by force from the rightful owner (2 Sam. 12:29–30; Esther 8:15; Isa. 23:8), possession of the royal crown was symbolic of a ruler's political authority.

The Bible also mentions wedding and athletic crowns. As the name suggests, the wedding crown was the one that a bride or groom wore during the marriage celebration (Song of Sol. 3:11; Ezek. 16:12). This seems to have been a garland woven of plants and flowers that distinguished the bride and groom from their guests. Its mention always conjures the connotation of joy that surrounded the nuptials. The athletic crown had no intrinsic value of its own and was made

A statue of King Tut wearing his royal crown. Such crowns varied in style and size but always sent the same message: the one wearing it was in control.

The Baker Illustrated Guide to Everyday Life in Bible Times

from bent twigs interwoven with flowers. Although it would fade quickly, it was pursued aggressively by athletes because it marked one as the victor in an athletic contest (1 Cor. 9:25; 2 Tim. 2:5).

While physical crowns are mentioned by the biblical authors, it is metaphorical crowns that are most often referred to in their writings. The key to the interpretation of such texts requires us to correctly identify the type of crown in view and its attending connotations. Many of the figurative crowns mentioned in the Old Testament are royal crowns. When a person or people lost a war, the loss of the crown became a symbol of their defeat. Job implied that he was at war with the Lord who had "removed the crown from [his] head" (Job 19:9). And when God's people and their leaders were unfaithful to the covenant the Lord made with them, they could expect to be defeated—a defeat symbolized by the removal of the crown from their leaders (Ps. 89:39; Jer. 13:18; Lam. 5:16; Ezek. 21:26–27).

In the New Testament we see a mocking reversal of this procedure. The Roman soldiers who prepared Jesus for execution mocked his claim to be a king not by removing a royal crown but by putting a crown of thorns on his head (Matt. 27:27–29; Mark 15:17; John 19:2, 5). This of course was not the end of that story. The book of Revelation describes the final struggle between Christ and those who challenge his authority. Many of the entities participating in this struggle are pictured wearing crowns: the woman who wears a crown with twelve stars, the red dragon with seven heads and seven crowns, the beast that comes out of the sea sporting ten crowns, as well as Christ himself, whose crown of thorns will be replaced by a golden crown (Rev. 12:1, 3; 13:1; 14:14; 19:12).

The wedding crown appears as a metaphor in Proverbs and Isaiah, and in each case there is a connotation of joy and celebration. Wisdom provides a "glorious crown" (Prov. 4:9), "blessings crown the head of the righteous"

David seized the weighty crown of Ammon's king when he captured the Ammonite fortress built on this peninsula of land (2 Sam. 12:29–30).

(Prov. 10:6), "a wife of noble character is her husband's crown" (Prov. 12:4), "the prudent are crowned with knowledge" (Prov. 14:18), and "the wealth of the wise is their crown" (Prov. 14:24). Both gray hair and grandchildren, which are symbolic of long life, are also described as celebrative crowns (Prov. 16:31; 17:6).[19] The prophet Isaiah also uses the image of the wedding crown. The Lord himself is likened to this headwear as he is the joy of the redeemed. "In that day the LORD Almighty will be a glorious crown, a beautiful wreath for the remnant of his people" (Isa. 28:5). The ransomed of the Lord "will enter Zion with singing; everlasting joy will crown their heads" (Isa. 35:10).

In many New Testament locations, it is the athletic crown that is in view. Paul alludes to the sense of victory he feels in seeing people come to know Christ through his ministry; he calls them his "joy and crown" (Phil. 4:1; see also 1 Thess. 2:19). Eternal life is also pictured as a crown of victory; the victory of Jesus over sin and death makes it possible for every believer to wear a crown that signals their victory. "Everyone who competes in the games goes into strict training. They do it to get a crown that will not last, but we do it to get a crown that will last forever" (1 Cor. 9:25; see also 2 Tim. 4:8). Trials may come, but "blessed is the one who perseveres under trial because, having stood the test, that person will receive the crown of life that the Lord has promised to those who love him" (James 1:12). This is the "crown of glory that will never fade away" (1 Pet. 5:4); it has already been won by the saints who reside at the Lord's side in heaven (Rev. 4:4). We who remain live with this encouragement: "Be faithful, even to the point of death, and I will give you life as your victor's crown" (Rev. 2:10).

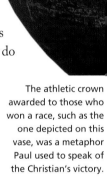

The athletic crown awarded to those who won a race, such as the one depicted on this vase, was a metaphor Paul used to speak of the Christian's victory.

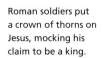

Roman soldiers put a crown of thorns on Jesus, mocking his claim to be a king.

CRUCIFY

The sights, sounds, and smells of any form of public execution are never pleasant, but it is hard to find a method of execution more disturbing than crucifixion. The notion of crucifixion seems to have grown from the practice of impaling lifeless or living persons on a post. This practice morphed into crucifixion and was employed by the Persians, Phoenicians, Greeks, Jews, and eventually Romans.[20]

The execution itself was conducted by attaching a person either to a tree or to a wooden post in one of several postures but always with arms extended.[21] The victim could be either tied or nailed in this position to await death, which might take several days. Death was most likely caused by asphyxiation when the muscles of the thorax controlling exhalation failed and victims could no longer rid themselves of the carbon dioxide building up in their lungs.[22] Given the nature of this painful and humiliating death, the Romans reserved it for punishing criminals like robbers, deserters, and political insurrectionists. Consequently, it was available to Pilate as a way of punishing Jesus for the crimes with which he had been charged (Luke 23:2).

When the Gospel writers describe the execution of Jesus, they spare us many of the more horrific details.[23] But they want us to be absolutely clear on the fact that Jesus was crucified. The message is not just repeated, it is delivered by a wide variety of reporters as if to confirm the fact. Well before the soldiers took nail in hand, Jesus announced that this was going to happen to him when he went

The Church of the Holy Sepulchre has marked the location of Jesus's crucifixion since the fourth century AD.

to Jerusalem (Matt. 20:17–19; 26:1–2; Luke 24:7). And in the reports of Jesus's passing, the word *crucify* is spoken by a variety of witnesses with widely ranging interests, including Pilate, the hostile crowd, Jewish leaders, an angel, the disciples on the road to Emmaus, and the narrator (Matt. 27:22–23, 26, 31, 35; 28:5; Mark 15:13–15, 20, 24–25, 27; 16:6; Luke 23:21, 33; 24:20; John 19:6, 10, 15–16, 18, 20, 23, 41). The variety of reporters and the repetition of the term leave us certain of the fact that Jesus was crucified.

Jesus's death on the cross receives so much attention because it is so shocking that he should die in this way and, at the same time, so necessary. If we were to design a Savior of the world whose death for our sins would be welcomed by Jews and Gentiles, we would choose some other means than crucifixion. Paul noted the difficulty: "For the message of the cross is foolishness to those who are perishing. . . . But we preach Christ crucified: a stumbling block to Jews and

Execution by crucifixion meant attaching a person either to a tree or to a wooden post in one of several postures, with arms extended.

No matter how ornate or simple, the cross remains the symbol of hope and salvation for believers in Jesus.

foolishness to Gentiles" (1 Cor. 1:18, 23). Jews saw the crucified person in terms of God's declaration in Deuteronomy that those impaled on a post died under the curse of divine rejection (Deut. 21:22–23). Gentiles saw the crucified person as a social outcast and enemy of society. Thus a crucified hero was a very hard sell in either cultural setting.

But it was just this kind of ignominious death that was required for Jesus to complete his mission on earth and to pay the sin debt that we owe. Paul in particular created the important link between salvation and the crucified Christ, who reconciled the world to God by his death (Eph. 2:16; Col. 1:20). He observed that the law that called for the punishment of sinners was nailed to the cross: "Christ redeemed us from the curse of the law by becoming a curse for us, for it is written: 'Cursed is everyone who is hung on a pole'" (Gal. 3:13; see also Col. 2:13–14). It is no wonder that Paul insisted that this was the most fundamental and important information he had to share with his listeners: "For I resolved to know nothing while I was with you except Jesus Christ and him crucified" (1 Cor. 2:2; see also Gal. 3:1; 6:14). Thus while we would never have designed a rescue plan that involved crucifixion, it was the only way to ensure that the rescue mission achieved its goal.

The act of crucifying also appears in two figurative settings. First, in his letter to the Galatians Paul notes that he has been "crucified with Christ" (Gal. 2:20) and that those who have come to know Christ have "crucified the sinful nature" (Gal. 5:24 TNIV). Here Paul addresses one of the dramatic changes that occur within Christians when they come to faith in Jesus as their Savior. The sinful nature—that part of us that actively pursues rebellion against God—is metaphorically executed so that we no longer are obligated to follow the lead of our sinful nature in pursuing a life of sin.

The second figurative use of this image comes in Jesus's insistence that those who follow him as disciples must be ready to "take up their cross" (Matt. 10:38; 16:24; Mark 8:34; Luke 9:23; see also 14:27). This crucifixion imagery is drawn from the Roman practice that required the condemned man to carry the crossbeam to which his arms would be attached (Matt. 27:32; Mark 15:21). Just as the condemned man had no choice but to surrender his will, deny his own passions, pick up the instrument of his own death, and carry it to the place of execution, so believers are called to surrender their own will, deny themselves, and accept the life God places in their path, no matter how austere or difficult it may be.

Byzantine- and Crusader-period columns stand side by side in the Church of the Holy Sepulchre—witnesses to the centuries of Christian worshipers who have come to this place to recall the event that changed their lives forever.

DANCE

ancing is an art form through which a person gives external expression to feelings by using rhythmic movement. Whether choreographed or spontaneous, the descriptions and illustrations from the ancient Near East illustrate that dance was an important component of ancient culture. The Bible also reflects this importance, employing more than fourteen different words to present the idea of dancing to its readers. When we assemble the artistic images and descriptions of dancing that come to us from the ancient Near East, we get the following picture: Both men and women of every social station danced individually and in groups. There is no evidence, however, that men and women ever danced together either in Egypt or in Mesopotamia.[1] Within these cultures, people danced in connection with worship, marriage rites, and funeral rites. They danced vigorously to celebrate a military victory and spontaneously to express deep feelings of joy.[2]

The dancers we meet in the Bible are almost always women, sometimes dancing individually and at other times in groups.[3] The one

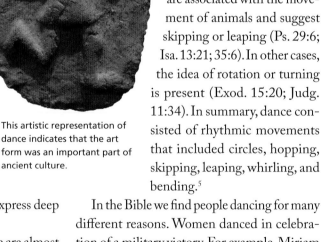

This artistic representation of dance indicates that the art form was an important part of ancient culture.

glaring exception is King David, who appears "leaping and dancing before the Lord" as the ark of the covenant is brought to Jerusalem (2 Sam. 6:16). David's exuberant, spontaneous dancing thoroughly embarrassed his wife (2 Sam. 6:20). Apparently this sort of thing was not done, for among all the ancient Near Eastern evidence we have for dancing, this is the only mention of a king engaged in this form of artistic expression.[4]

The Bible does not include a formal description of dancing, but the verbs used in connection with dancing give us an idea of how it may have looked. Some of those verbs are associated with the movement of animals and suggest skipping or leaping (Ps. 29:6; Isa. 13:21; 35:6). In other cases, the idea of rotation or turning is present (Exod. 15:20; Judg. 11:34). In summary, dance consisted of rhythmic movements that included circles, hopping, skipping, leaping, whirling, and bending.[5]

In the Bible we find people dancing for many different reasons. Women danced in celebration of a military victory. For example, Miriam led the Israelite women in celebrative dance after the Lord's victory over the Egyptians

(Exod. 15:19–20). In the same fashion, the Israelite women celebrated David's victory over the Philistines by dancing and singing as he returned home (1 Sam. 18:6–7; see also Judg. 11:34; 1 Sam. 21:11; 29:5; 30:16; NIV "reveling"). Dance also accompanied religious celebrations whether pagan or orthodox. The people danced before the molten calf at the time of Moses (Exod. 32:19), and the prophets of Baal attempted to manipulate Baal through their ritualized dance steps (1 Kings 18:26).

On the other hand, dance was also part of orthodox worship of the Lord, used in connection with giving thanks for the harvest (Judg. 21:21), moving the ark to Jerusalem (2 Sam. 6:16), and worshiping in the temple: "Let them praise his name with dancing and make music to him with timbrel and harp" (Ps. 149:3; see also 150:4). And lest we think that dancing was reserved for adults, we have examples that children danced as well (Job 21:11; see also Matt. 11:16–17). In all these examples of dancing, the connotation of joyful celebration is always in view. This stands in contrast to the Egyptian practice that favored dancing in connection with their funeral rites.[6]

We also have one example of dance assuming a more nefarious role in a Bible story. Herodias, the wife of

People of the past danced both as individuals and in groups, as depicted on this vase.

Herod Antipas, did not like the criticism that John the Baptist had been directing at their family (Matt. 14:3–5). On Herod's birthday, Herodias apparently directed her daughter to dance for him in a highly sexual fashion. Herodias used this dance to leverage Herod's libido and his gratitude, setting the stage for the girl's request to have her mother's nemesis, John the Baptist, executed (Matt. 14:6–11).

The biblical authors also mention dance that does not necessarily include physical dancing. In these cases the word *dance* is used as a symbol for happiness. In the list that describes the opposing experiences of life, Ecclesiastes notes that there is "a time to mourn and a time to dance" (Eccles. 3:4), using dance as a symbol

Verbs used to describe dance movements were often associated with the movement of animals, such as the leaping of an ibex.

for joy. David was celebrating that season of life when he sang, "You turned my wailing into dancing; you removed my sackcloth and clothed me with joy" (Ps. 30:11). Jeremiah lamented the destruction of Jerusalem by calling it a time when "joy is gone from our hearts; our dancing has turned to mourning" (Lam. 5:15). But this same prophet lifted the hope of his readers with news of better times to come: "Again you will take up your timbrels and go out to dance with the joyful" (Jer. 31:4; see also 31:13).

Dance as a symbol of joy was also employed by Jesus as he criticized the people of his day

This basalt relief depicts a woman dancing for joy.

who did not seem to know what they wanted. They perceived John the Baptist and his followers to be pursuing a more somber way of life while Jesus appeared to them as the purveyor of unbridled joy. Because they found neither appealing, Jesus said they were like children playing games and calling to each other: "We played the pipe for you, and you did not dance; we sang a dirge, and you did not mourn" (Matt. 11:17).

This Jerusalem home destroyed by the Babylonians is emblematic of the destruction that led Jeremiah to lament that times of dancing had turned into times of mourning (Lam. 5:15).

DESTROY
(HEBREW, *HRM*)

Cultural practices mentioned in the Bible can be quaint, amusing, interesting, and in rare cases repulsive. The notion of *total destruction* discussed here will likely cause us to take a step back in horror. In Hebrew, the total destruction of places, people, animals, and personal possessions during warfare is called *hrm*. The verb is translated in a number of different ways, including "devote to the Lord," "completely destroy," "destroy totally," and "set apart for destruction." The practice itself is known in other ancient Near Eastern cultures, including those of Moab, Assyria, Babylon, and Egypt,[7] but here our focus will be on the distinct nature of this practice in Israel and its rhetorical use in the Bible.

Among the Israelites, this extreme warfare was to be practiced only when the Lord specifically called for it and only to the degree he authorized. In its most extreme form, this destruction was directed against a location, its residents regardless of age or gender, its animals, and all personal possessions (Deut. 13:15–17; Josh. 6:18, 21; 1 Sam. 15:3). The only

Extreme acts of violence, including impaling, were used outside a besieged city in order to encourage the city's early surrender.

things spared in such extreme cases were the fruit trees (Deut. 20:19–20). Alternatively, the city and its citizens were sometimes destroyed while the livestock and personal possessions were taken as plunder by the conquering Israelites (Deut. 2:34–35; 3:6–7; Josh. 8:25–27).

As distasteful as this form of warfare sounds to modern ears, the application of *hrm* served a couple of grisly purposes within the larger strategy of military conquerors. First, in a location where natural resources including water were scarce, it eliminated competition for those resources by reducing the population. Second, as a military strategy, the horrific nature of this destruction could be used against future cities as leverage to shorten otherwise lengthy sieges. Sennacherib attempted to induce Hezekiah, king of Judah, into an early surrender by reminding him of all the cities that had fallen victim to the Assyrian form of this total destruction, which they would also experience if they did not surrender (2 Kings 19:11).

When the Lord put this military technique into operation, it served a very different purpose. To understand it, we must enter the mind-set of the biblical authors, who invite us to see that all the people, places, animals, and things in this world belong to the Lord. They were created to serve him, honor him, and glorify his name. But when people, places,

The divine direction to totally destroy a city, including killing the people within, was shocking.

animals, and possessions were put into service to other gods, they became a violation of the most basic divine command. Egregious cases that literally threatened the maturing of God's plan to redeem the world from sin and death were treated with an equally aggressive form of warfare: *hrm* (Deut. 7:1–6).

We now consider the rhetorical role of this destruction in Bible history as God commanded that *hrm* be executed during the time of Moses, Joshua, and the judges. There is frequent mention of this principle in Deuteronomy and Joshua, where obedience to the command demonstrates the trust and faithfulness of Israel and its leaders. Note that there is no attempt by any of the biblical authors to soften the notion or make us comfortable with this form of warfare. When God called for the total destruction of a city and all living things within it, including men, women, children, infants, and animals, that command was as shocking and as distasteful then as it is now. We suspect that even the most hardened soldiers would have paused at the notion. Consequently, this extreme warfare called for an extreme act of trust and obedience. We see it in the days of Moses (Num. 21:2–3; Deut. 2:34; 3:6; Josh. 2:10). We also see it in the days of Joshua (Josh. 6:17–18; 10:1, 28–40; 11:11–12, 20–21), with the exception of Achan's violation of this command in Joshua 7.

Repeatedly the mention of *hrm* is associated explicitly or implicitly with obedience. "He totally destroyed all who breathed, just as the Lord, the God of Israel, had commanded" (Josh. 10:40; see also 11:20). That makes what follows in Judges so striking. There as the Israelites were supposed to be consolidating their hold on Canaan using the same method of warfare, the practice of *hrm* is conspicuous by its absence. It is mentioned only twice: once in the first and once in the last chapter (Judg. 1:17; 21:11). It is a subtle but powerful way of contrasting the rebellious period of the judges with the more honorable period of Moses and Joshua.

The next time we find frequent mention of *hrm* is in 1 Samuel 15, where another leader was asked to do the uncomfortable. King Saul was told to "attack the Amalekites and totally destroy all that belongs to them. Do not spare them; put to death men and women, children and infants, cattle and sheep, camels and donkeys" (1 Sam. 15:3). Saul had the chance to lead and obey as Moses and Joshua had, but instead his obedience was only partial in the face of this faith-demanding directive (1 Sam. 15:8–9, 18–21). Because Saul failed to obey this difficult divine command, the Lord withdrew Saul's right to lead.

Pomegranates. At times, the only living things allowed to survive a divinely directed attack against a city were its fruit trees.

Mention of this divine form of extreme warfare is less frequent in the books of the prophets. But its presence recalls that there is a much bigger war going on: the war against those who oppose the coming of God's kingdom. The Lord told the rebellious children of Israel that he was bringing the Babylonians to wage this kind of war against them because the Israelites had become opponents rather than allies in establishing an eternal kingdom (Jer. 25:8–10; see also Deut. 13:12–16). Babylon not only would dish out *hrm* but it would also be on the receiving end when it failed to honor the Lord as the true King of this world (Jer. 50:21, 25–26; 51:1–3). Finally, as the world moves to its close, all nations that take the wrong side in this eschatological fight will experience *hrm* delivered by a divine hand (Isa. 34:2; Dan. 11:44; Mic. 4:13).

Hazor (below) was one of three cities destined for total destruction by the forces of the Lord under Joshua.

DIVINATION
(TO PRACTICE)

The Lord created humans to live within the constraints of time. We are bound to the present and our knowledge is ordinarily limited to what is happening at the moment or what has happened in the past. But this does not prevent us from being curious about what the future holds. It is this desire to know the future that drives the practice of divination.

Divination was a common component of all ancient Near Eastern cultures,[8] growing from the belief that the disposition and actions of the gods had a direct impact on future events. Thus the goal of divination was to tap into the mind-set of the gods to acquire from them the insights that could reveal the course of future events. This knowledge was obtained in a wide variety of ways, often in conjunction with a professional who was willing to interpret the data for a fee (Num. 22:7; Mic. 3:11). Insights into the future were gained by observing the position of the heavenly bodies, the organization of birds in flight, the swirling shape of incense smoke, or the shape of oil floating on the top of water in a cup. Future events were made known by casting lots, observing the shape of a slaughtered animal's liver, consulting the deceased through a medium, as well as interpreting dreams.[9]

The biblical authors maintain that the one true God controls future events and that only he can make the future known to humans. But they also make it very clear that divination was part of a pagan worldview that God's people were commanded to avoid. Its use was characterized as a detestable practice of the nations the Lord had driven out ahead of them, and it was listed among the most heinous sins (like the sacrifice of one's own

Facing a crucial battle, Saul went to Endor, located at the base of Mount Moreh (below), in order to learn his fate from a medium.

The Baker Illustrated Guide to Everyday Life in Bible Times

child) and so was strongly forbidden (Deut. 18:9–12; 2 Kings 21:6; see also Lev. 19:26). Nevertheless there were times when the Lord elected to use the trappings of pagan divination in order to communicate information about future events. Consider the use of dreams, the mysterious Urim and Thummim, the casting of lots, and even the manipulation of dew on a fleece (Gen. 37:5–11; Exod. 28:30; Judg. 6:36–40; Acts 1:23–26). These rare exceptions, however, in no way reverse the legal directives designed to separate Israel from the all-too-common practice of pagan divination.

Dice could serve as lots, which were thrown to divine information inaccessible through normal channels.

When the biblical authors mention the practice of divination, it is being practiced by pagans in the nations around Israel. They speak of kings, royal advisers, and professional diviners from among the Canaanites, Moabites, Ammonites, Philistines, and Babylonians all practicing divination (Num. 22:7; Deut. 18:9–10; 1 Sam. 6:2; Isa. 2:6; 47:12–13; Ezek. 21:18–21, 29; Dan. 2:27; 4:7; 5:7–12). Given the ubiquitous nature of the practice, this is not surprising.

It is quite another story that we find the apparent practice of divination among the Israelites. As an Egyptian ruler, Joseph had a special cup used for divination (Gen. 44:5); he even implied that he could use the cup to discover things otherwise unknown (v. 15). We do not know if Joseph merely held the cup as part of the trappings of his office or actually used the cup for divination. What we can know is that this cup played an ironic role in the story. Joseph wanted to know if his brothers had really changed since the day when they ruthlessly sold him as a slave. He set up a scenario that made it easy for the brothers to again turn on one of their own by making it appear as though Benjamin had stolen Joseph's special cup. The irony naturally follows. Though there was not a drop of liquid in this diviner's cup, it allowed Joseph to see that his brothers had really changed in a wholesome way.

Another ironic use of divination occurs within the narrative that traces King Saul's demise and ruin. The Lord had given Saul very specific instructions regarding a war to be waged against the Amalekites. Saul did not follow those instructions and later insisted his changes to the plan were for the good of all, including the Lord. Samuel castigated this notion by observing that Saul's "rebellion is like the sin of divination" (1 Sam. 15:23). Perhaps

This model of a sheep's liver guided the interpretation sought by a diviner, who compared it to the real liver extracted from a sheep slaughtered specifically for this purpose.

Seeking knowledge of the future could involve observing the position of heavenly bodies in the night sky.

in response to this strong language and in a bid to put himself back on good terms with the Lord, Saul expelled professional diviners from the land (1 Sam. 28:3). But in the end this man, whose rebellion was like the sin of divination and who had removed diviners from the land, went to a practitioner of the dark arts to learn what his future held (1 Sam. 28:5–7).

The mention of divination occurs again as the demise of the northern and southern kingdoms is recounted. As the author of 2 Kings explains the reason for the defeat and exile of the northern kingdom of Israel, he mentions the people's strong affinity for the practice of divination (2 Kings 17:16–17). We may have hoped this lesson would not be lost on the sister kingdom to

Astrological symbols often appear in ancient art.

the south, but it was. King Manasseh "practiced divination, sought omens, and consulted mediums and spiritists" (2 Kings 21:6). The practice of divination became widespread particularly among Israelite false prophets. Thus the Lord's prophets directed fiery rebukes at them, often branding them as liars (Jer. 14:14; 27:9–10; 29:8–9; Ezek. 13:6, 7–9; 22:28; Zech. 10:2; see also Ezek. 12:24; 13:23; Mic. 3:6–7). The frequency with which these diviners are mentioned suggests that they played an influential role in shaping public opinion. Their crime was so heinous because by softening the message of impending exile, they removed the motivation to repent, which could have saved God's people from experiencing exile.

DIVORCE

When sin entered the world, marital discord was quick to follow. Confronted by an angry God about eating the forbidden fruit, Adam blamed his wife for their problems. From that time on, the passion of marriage has lived in tension with the challenges of being married. Sometimes those challenges so overwhelm a couple that their relationship becomes irreparably broken—a circumstance recognized by divorce. The cultures that surrounded the Israelites in the Old Testament had divorce laws that sought to regulate this matter. Generally they spoke only of men divorcing their wives, with only a few exceptions noted. The primary goal of the laws was to deal with the finances of the two parties, particularly regarding the restoration of the bride-price paid by the husband and the disposition of the dowry the bride had brought into the marriage.[10]

God's perspective on the topic is clear: "'I hate divorce,' says the LORD God of Israel" (Mal. 2:16 TNIV). This sin-induced wrinkle in the divine plan left a trail of pain, sadness, and complexity in its wake. While it was not part of God's plan for this world, he sought to regulate its practice and minimize the fallout. The law was generally written from the husband's perspective, suggesting that the wife's only option was to leave the family compound. By contrast, the husband was empowered to declare the marriage terminated and then write "a certificate of divorce" for her (Deut. 24:1). The woman then returned to her parents' home. Lest we dress those divorced in too dark a garb, we should note that the divorced daughter of a priest was not shunned or regarded as spiritually unclean; she was even permitted to eat the food that came from the sanctuary (Lev. 22:13). Generally there was no prohibition against remarriage of either husband or wife, the major exception being that a divorced husband could not remarry his former wife if in the meantime she had married another man, even if the second husband died or divorced her

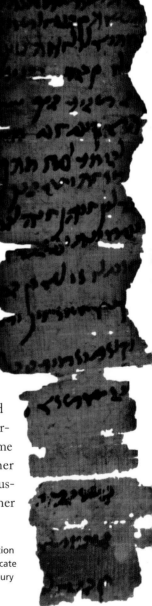

God sought to regulate the notion of divorce by requiring a certificate of divorce such as this first-century example (Deut. 24:1).

(Deut. 24:1–4). Given the strong penalty for adultery, the certificate of divorce became the tangible evidence that the earlier marriage had terminated. This safeguarded both the woman and her second husband against the charge of sexual misconduct (v. 2).

Jesus was drawn into a conversation concerning divorce by the Pharisees (Matt. 19:3–10), who wanted to know his position on the topic in view of the ongoing debate between the Jewish interpretive schools of Shammai and Hillel. The language of Deuteronomy 24:1, which gives legitimate grounds for a husband to divorce his wife, is somewhat vague and requires interpretation. The school of Shammai interpreted it to mean that a man could divorce his wife only if she was proven to be sexually impure. The school of Hillel interpreted the language very broadly, allowing a husband to divorce his wife for nearly any reason—even the failure to adequately complete household duties.[11] In this context, the Pharisees asked Jesus, "Is it lawful for a man to divorce his wife for any and every reason?" (Matt. 19:3). Jesus enlarged the discussion by first noting that when God established marriage, he intended that there never be divorce. He described the Old Testament legislation as a concession required to regulate the practice

A Greek vessel with a wedding scene. Since the fall into sin, the passion to be married lives in tension with the challenges of being married.

in a sin-ruined world. He then reiterated the position he had taken on this debate in the Sermon on the Mount (Matt. 5:31–32; 19:9). In both cases and in contrast to the lax interpretation of Roman divorce practice and the interpretation of Hillel, Jesus urged that divorce be avoided in all but the most extreme circumstances, naming the sexual unfaithfulness of the wife as an example of such a circumstance.[12]

Because marriage was often used figuratively to describe the relationship between the Lord and Israel, divorce also could be considered when disaffection was felt in this figurative marriage. The prophets are particularly noted for use of this imagery. "This is what the LORD says: 'Where is your mother's certificate of divorce?'" (Isa. 50:1). The implication here is that the Lord's wife, Israel, had been so unfaithful in her relationship with him that it justified a formal divorce. On the other hand, the fact that no certificate was written suggests that there was still hope for reconciliation. Jeremiah's image takes things a step further in this rhetorical question: "If a man divorces his wife and she leaves him and marries another man, should he return to her again?" (Jer. 3:1). The laws of Israel required a negative answer (Deut. 24:4). Jeremiah continued by indicating that

When Israel proved unfaithful to the Lord by worshiping pagan deities such as this one, the Lord threatened to terminate their metaphorical marriage with a metaphorical divorce.

the faithless northern kingdom of Israel had already been given "her certificate of divorce" and had been sent away (Jer. 3:8). Hope of reconciliation appeared lost. And the southern kingdom of Judah faced the same fate (Jer. 8–10), making this image a powerful call to repentance.

But God's grace was so much larger than the law that even the issuing of the divine divorce certificate did not prohibit the hope of restoration for Israel (Jer. 3:12). This grace was prophetically enacted in the life of the prophet Hosea, who received a most strange directive. As a living symbol of what was going on between the Lord and his people, God directed his prophet, "Go, marry a promiscuous woman" (Hosea 1:2). While Hosea would have had every right to divorce her, there is not a single word about divorce, only of love and reconciliation. "The LORD said to me, 'Go, show love to your wife again, though she is loved by another man and is an adulteress. Love her as the LORD loves the Israelites'" (Hosea 3:1).

The Church of the Beatitudes (below) marks the traditional location for Jesus's Sermon on the Mount, in which he spoke directly to the topic of divorce.

DREAM
(TO HAVE OR TO INTERPRET)

With a full day of work and recreation behind us, bedtime is a welcome prospect. We long to give our weary bodies and minds a rest, but our minds do not always get the message. Sometimes they continue to churn and process the data we have collected through our waking hours, turning some of the data into dreams. Researchers do not agree on what causes us to dream or even how those dreams are created. By all accounts, the ancients were less interested in answering scientific questions about dreaming than they were in learning what their dreams meant.

Many living in Bible times saw dreams as windows into the unseen world of the gods where future events were forged. While they did not regard every dream as significant, they pursued the meaning of vivid dreams and even tried to stimulate

An Egyptian woman processing grain. In dreams, ordinary household activities were thought to have symbolic meanings.

the occurrence of meaningful dreams. Temples both inside and outside Canaan are known to have had special rooms in which worshipers could sleep in the hope of incubating revelatory dreams.[13] Revelatory dreams often contained images that required interpretation, and this gave birth to the so-called dream books that come to us from the ancient cultures of Egypt and Mesopotamia. These books paired images with stock interpretations of those images. For example, if you dreamed of entering a city, it was a sign that your desire would be fulfilled.[14] Seals were symbolic of children. If you were given a seal of red stone in your dream, this was a sign that a child would be born. If the dream showed a seal worn by the dreamer being taken away, it signaled that a child would die.[15] Furthermore, the ancients did not believe that the future forecast in such dreams was assured; it could be altered by the performance of a ritual. Of course all this suggests that people in Bible times took dreams and their interpretation very seriously. That explains why Joseph's older brothers were willing to execute him based on the message delivered in his vivid dreams (Gen. 37:19–20); and that is why kings employed advisers to assist them in interpreting dreams (Gen. 41:8; Dan. 2:1–2).

God used dreams to communicate words of warning, direction, and reassurance throughout the Old and New Testaments. At times dreams were used to warn individuals about changes they needed to make in their thinking or actions. For example, Abimelek was warned about making advances on Sarah, Nebuchadnezzar was warned about his irreverent attitude, the Magi were warned in a dream not to go back to Herod, and Pilate's wife was warned about her husband's efforts to convict an innocent man (Gen. 20:3–6; Dan. 4:4–37; Matt. 2:12; 27:19; see also Gen. 31:24; 41:1–32; Matt. 2:13).

God also used dreams to mark changes in personal destiny. Two Josephs—Jacob's son and Mary's husband—received such destiny dreams (Gen. 37:5–10; Matt. 1:20; 2:19–22; see also Gen. 31:10–11; 40:5–11). We also see the Lord using dreams to deliver reassurance to individuals. Gideon was reassured regarding the outcome of a specific battle (Judg. 7:13–15), and Daniel was reassured that the turbulent and troubling events of history were steadily marching toward a divinely appointed goal (chapters 2, 7, and 8 of the book of Daniel).

Because dreams were regarded so highly in the ancient world, the biblical authors invite us to see those who frequently received such communication from God or who were given the capacity to interpret dreams in a more favorable light. This is particularly true of Jacob's son Joseph, Daniel, and

Pagan sanctuaries such as the ones depicted here often contained special rooms for the incubation of meaning-filled dreams.

Joseph (right) was informed about the special nature of Mary's pregnancy via a dream.

Mary's husband, Joseph. In an ironic extension of this notion, Moses was distinguished by the fact that God did not speak to him in dreams. When Miriam and Aaron challenged Moses's leadership, the dream revelations other prophets received were contrasted with the face-to-face revelation that marked Moses as unique (Num. 12:1–8).

This distinguished culture of dream revelation was subsequently leveraged by false prophets. The Lord warned about the coming of such prophets who would claim to speak for him, using their dreams as evidence of their validity (Deut. 13:1–5). They were present at the time of Jeremiah: "I have heard what the prophets say who prophesy lies in my name. They say, 'I had a dream! I had a dream!'" (Jer. 23:25). The Lord denounced them and their message in no uncertain terms despite their efforts to bolster their bogus claim by the fact that they had a dream (Jer. 23:27–28; Zech. 10:2; Jude 1:8).

Dreaming also appears in the Bible within figures of speech in which the content of dreams is disparaged as unreal and the process of dreaming is disparaged as a waste of good time. In his debate with Job, Zophar observed that the wicked would go away: "Like a dream he flies away, no more to be found" (Job 20:8). The psalmist had a similar perspective on the wicked: "Like a dream when one awakes, when you arise, Lord, you will despise them as fantasies" (Ps. 73:20). The biblical authors further criticized those who waste time dreaming: "Much dreaming and many words are meaningless" (Eccles. 5:7). Isaiah called those charged with alerting the people to the spiritual danger that surrounded them sleeping dogs who "lie around and dream" (Isa. 56:10).

But dreaming was redeemed from false prophets and habitual daydreamers. Joel predicted that the coming age would be one in which the Spirit would so fill people that "your sons and daughters will prophesy, your old men will dream dreams, your young men will see visions" (Joel 2:28). Here dreaming again is linked to the idea of inspired revelation from God. Peter saw this prophecy being fulfilled around him on the day of Pentecost (Acts 2:14–17).

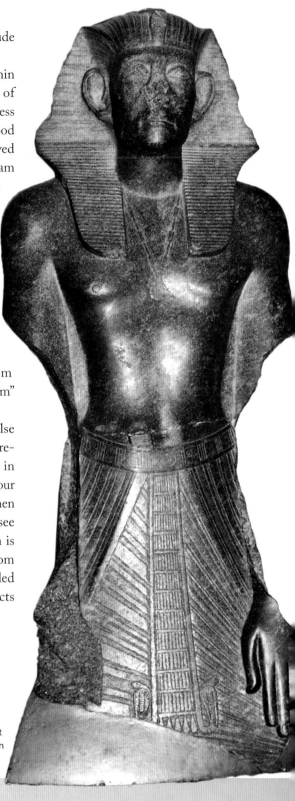

Sesostris III (right) was a young man when Joseph interpreted the dreams of his father, Sesostris II. Egypt would enjoy seven years of bumper crops before seven years of famine threatened.

The Baker Illustrated Guide to Everyday Life in Bible Times

DRUNK
(TO BECOME)

Intoxicating beverages were readily available throughout the ancient Near East, including Israel. The alcoholic beverage of choice in Egypt and Mesopotamia was beer, in contrast to Israel, where it was wine.[16] While grape juice is fermented today in order to produce wine for those who enjoy it, the fermentation process served a very practical purpose in Canaan. Without refrigeration or fermentation, the grape juice would spoil, an unthinkable notion in a land where this juice was consumed on a daily basis in order to supplement a meager water supply.[17] The presence of these intoxicants in the culture of God's people created the opportunity to misuse these beverages and become drunk. Consequently, the biblical authors both address the topic of overconsumption of alcoholic beverages and employ images of drunkenness within figures of speech.

The most sustained picture of inebriation is found in Proverbs 23:29–35, leading to these words of warning: "Do not gaze at wine when it is red, when it sparkles in the cup, when it

goes down smoothly!" (v. 31). There is nothing in the picture this divinely inspired poet presents that suggests getting drunk has redeeming value. What one can expect is a litany of misfortune: sadness, strife, bruises, bloodshot eyes, physical instability, hallucinations, and the risk of dependency.

The biblical authors corroborate this description in Proverbs with the real-life experiences of those who overindulge. In situation after situation, those who are drunk meet very unfortunate consequences. The first case mentioned in the Bible is that of

Ripening grapes were a divine blessing but were sometimes misused by those who fermented their juices to become drunk.

The so-called Mona Lisa of the Galilee adorns a Roman dining room mosaic that champions drunken revelry.

Noah, whose drunkenness leads to a case of embarrassing immodesty (Gen. 9:20–23). The law identifies routine drunkenness as a characteristic of a perennially rebellious son who could be publicly executed (Deut. 21:20–21). Public leaders and members of the royal family are assassinated or defeated in battle when drunk (2 Sam. 13:28–29; 1 Kings 16:9–10; 20:16). We look in vain within these pages to find any redeeming value in the practice of getting drunk. Whether applied to those who are drunk or thought to be drunk, public opinion of those in this condition is uniformly negative (1 Sam. 1:13–14; Ps. 69:12; Prov. 23:21; Eccles. 10:17; Matt. 11:19; Acts 2:15).

While the Old Testament tends to teach on this topic by example, the New Testament is prone to address the topic of drunkenness more directly, often including it in lists of behaviors and attitudes that God's people should avoid. For example, consider this directive to the Christians in Rome: "Let us behave decently, as in the daytime, not in carousing and drunkenness, not in sexual immorality and

debauchery, not in dissension and jealousy" (Rom. 13:13; for similar lists see 1 Cor. 5:9–11; 6:9–10; Gal. 5:19–21; 1 Tim. 3:3; Titus 1:6–8; 1 Pet. 4:3). Given this characterization of inebriation, it is no wonder that Paul was deeply distressed by the abuse of alcohol that he heard was occurring during the banquet that accompanied the celebration of the Lord's Supper (1 Cor. 11:20–21).

When drunkenness is mentioned in figures of speech, it is nearly always employed negatively. The one exception is found in the poem of Moses in which the Lord says, "I will make my arrows drunk with blood" (Deut. 32:42). Just as an inebriated person is saturated with alcohol, so the Lord's arrows will be saturated with the blood of his enemies. The remaining figures are negative, addressing the various forms of impairment that accompany overconsumption of alcohol. Alcohol impacts the drinker's fine motor skills and sense of balance, so the psalmist describes sailors struggling to keep their balance

A Greek drinking vessel. "Do not gaze at wine when it is red, when it sparkles in the cup" (Prov. 23:31).

on a storm-tossed vessel as reeling and staggering like drunken men (Ps. 107:23, 27). No one would want to be close to an inebriated person who was wielding a thornbush, given the drunk's erratic movements and the risk imposed on anyone nearby. "Like a thornbush in a drunkard's hand is a proverb in the mouth of a fool" (Prov. 26:9).

Impairment in judgment also puts the inebriated person at risk of being abused. The Lord told the Edomites that their days of rejoicing in the misfortune of Israel would come to an end: "But to you also the cup will be passed; you will be drunk and stripped naked" (Lam. 4:21). The metaphor of drunkenness was also used to tell the people of Babylon to expect trouble: "Woe to him who gives drink to his neighbors, pouring it from the wineskin till they are drunk, so that he can gaze on their naked bodies! You will be filled with shame instead of glory. Now it is your turn! Drink and let your nakedness be exposed!" (Hab. 2:15–16). And Isaiah foresaw a time when the earth would sway as one incapacitated by too much alcohol (Isa. 24:20).

Drunken swaying can produce the nausea that results in the drunkard wallowing about in his or her vomit. This disgusting image was used to describe those who opposed the Lord and were forced to drink from the cup of his wrath. This judgment fell broadly and without discrimination on Egypt, Moab, Babylon, Edom, and Assyria (Isa. 19:14; Jer.

48:26; 51:37–39, 57; Lam. 4:21; Nah. 1:10). God's chosen people were not safe from this judgment either. Jeremiah delivered this pointed message from the Lord: "This is what the LORD says: I am going to fill with drunkenness all who live in this land, including the kings who sit on David's throne, the priests, the prophets and all those living in Jerusalem" (Jer. 13:13). "Drink, get drunk and vomit, and fall to rise no more because of the sword I will send among you" (Jer. 25:27; see also Isa. 29:9; Ezek. 23:33). This incapacitation would come; but a time of restoration was foretold as well: "Therefore hear this, you afflicted one, made drunk, but not with wine. This is what your Sovereign LORD says, . . . 'See, I have taken out of your hand the cup that made you stagger; from that cup, the goblet of my wrath, you will never drink again. I will put it into the hands of your tormentors'" (Isa. 51:21–23).

Paul was deeply distressed at the people in Corinth (below) who had been misusing alcohol at the banquet that preceded the celebration of the Lord's Supper.

DRY
(TO BE OR TO EXPERIENCE DROUGHT)

The notion of being dry or of dryness is mentioned more than one hundred times in both literal and figurative settings by the biblical authors. Their attention to this topic is propelled at least in part by the importance of water to the human experience in general and to the experience of living in the Promised Land in particular. Human beings require water to maintain their health through such fundamental processes as digesting food, transporting nutrients throughout the body, removing waste, and regulating body temperature. It has been estimated that to maintain one's health a person ought to drink two-and-a-half liters of water per day and that for a country's citizens to live comfortably, each person requires access to approximately one thousand liters of water per year. The modern state of Israel is able to produce less than half of that; the ancient Promised Land offered only a fraction of that amount.[18] All that is to say that living in the Promised Land was to live with dryness. This dearth of water had a direct impact on how people who lived in the land thought, so when the biblical authors speak of life and living, they often characterize places as either wet or dry (for example, Gen. 1:9–10; Deut. 29:19; Hag. 2:6). There were seasons of the year with moisture and those without (Deut. 11:13–17). There were dry roads that were easier to travel and wet roads that were nearly impossible to travel (Matt. 24:20).

The biblical authors formally mention dryness in their communication with us. The uniqueness of the God who compelled that communication is depicted in images of the Lord turning wet places into dry places.[19] The three most prominent by position in the canon or repetition are: (1) the emergence of dry land from the chaotic waters of creation (Gen. 1:9–10; Ps. 95:5), (2) the drying of the Red Sea to create a pathway for Moses and the Israelites (Exod. 14:16, 21–22, 29; 15:19; Josh. 2:10; Pss. 66:6; 74:15; 106:9; Isa. 50:2; 51:10), and (3) the drying of the Jordan River to create a path into the Promised Land for Joshua and the Israelites (Josh. 3:17; 4:22–23; 5:1). In each case the Lord demonstrates his unique power by making something wet become dry.

Potsherds. "My mouth is dried up like a potsherd" (Ps. 22:15).

The biblical authors also mention the drying up of the world, seas, and rivers as symbols of a new beginning.[20] The roiling waters that covered the globe made for a most uninviting place until the Lord's hand swept the sea to the side and allowed dry land to appear (Gen. 1:9–10). This process was reversed in Genesis 7:22 when the waters returned to wipe out "everything on dry land that had the breath of life in its nostrils." A new beginning was marked by the reemergence of dry ground to sustain Noah and his family (Gen. 8:6–7, 13–14). With this paradigm firmly set in Genesis, we can see it more easily in Exodus and Joshua. New segments in Israel's history were marked by the drying of the Red Sea (Exodus 14) and the drying up of the Jordan River (Joshua 3–4). We can also trace this motif into the transfer of prophetic leadership from Elijah to Elisha and the drying up of the Jordan River (2 Kings 2:8, 13–14).

The Lord did not just dry up bodies of water, he also dried up the land. While the aforementioned examples of drying up a body of water are surrounded with very positive connotations, the drying up of the land is filled with negative connotations and predictions of judgment on those who sought to obstruct the advance of God's plans on earth. A variety of prophecies foretold that the Lord would dry up the pastures and agricultural fields of nations and empires like Moab, Egypt, Babylon, and Assyria (Isa. 15:5–6; 19:5–6; Jer. 50:3, 12, 38; 51:35–36, 43; Ezek. 30:11–12; Zeph. 2:13). The Lord also delivered on his promise to "reward" his own people's covenant disloyalty with the devastating impact of withered crops, dry wells, and emaciated pastures (Lev.

Divine acts of judgment included the drying up of agricultural fields before harvesttime.

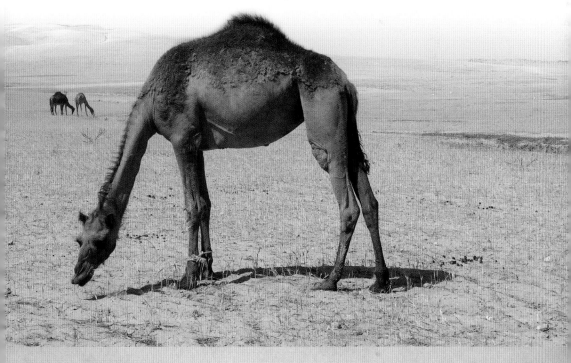

26:19; Deut. 11:17; Hosea 13:15; Joel 1:10–12, 17–20; Amos 1:2).

The negative connotations that attach themselves to the notion of dryness also inform the figurative uses of this idea. When people died, their remains became a pile of lifeless, dry bones. Ezekiel saw the exiled Israelites as such a pile of dry bones (Ezek. 37:1–4, 11), and then he was led to preach to them: "Dry bones, hear the word of the LORD! . . . I will make breath enter you, and you will come to life" (Ezek. 37:4–5). The loss of a person's ability to procreate was described as having "his roots dry up below and his branches wither above" or as becoming a "dry tree" (Job 18:16; Isa. 56:3). Generally, any kind of deprivation in life could be described in connection with the process of becoming dry. Job described his erstwhile friends as the seasonal streams that "cease to flow in the dry season, and in the heat vanish from their channels" (Job 6:17 TNIV). A person's strength could be "dried up like a potsherd" (Ps. 22:15), and the search for the comforts that only God can afford became like a search for water "in a dry and weary land where there is no water" (Ps. 63:1 NASB). Finally, the fragile nature of life itself was likened to dryness. It became like water that disappeared from the sea, a riverbed that dried up, or new grass that sprang up in the morning and by evening was dry and withered (Job 14:11–12; Ps. 90:5–6).

Dry places and wet places stand in close proximity to one another in the Middle East.

The Baker Illustrated Guide to Everyday Life in Bible Times

EAT

*E*ating is a normal human function. Adam and Eve ate food in the Garden of Eden, and it is what some people will be doing at the moment Jesus returns (Gen. 1:29; Matt. 24:38–39). Full satisfaction in life cannot be achieved without it (Deut. 6:11–12), a fact elegantly summarized in Ecclesiastes 2:24–25: "A person can do nothing better than to eat and drink and find satisfaction in their own toil. This too, I see, is from the hand of God, for without him, who can eat or find enjoyment?" Obviously, people in Bible times ate much more often than is formally mentioned in the Bible; here we will focus on the special circumstances that surround the mention of eating in the Bible.

There are examples in the Bible of people who demonstrated their trust in the Lord through what they ate. Shortly after Adam and Eve were placed in the garden and hunger pangs pushed them toward the fruit trees, God placed a restriction on what they could eat, and they could demonstrate their trust in him by adhering to his instructions. Every plant and tree was approved with the exception of the

The types of food sold in the markets of the Old City in Jerusalem may look strange to us, but they provide families with the basics every person needs to eat.

fruit growing on the tree of the knowledge of good and evil (Gen. 2:16–17). Their faith failed when the serpent invited them to trust him rather than God (Gen. 3:1–11), and their inappropriate eating was followed by penalties, for both the serpent and the humans, that also involved eating (Gen. 3:14, 17–19, 22).

But this is not the last time the Lord linked eating with faith. The miraculous provision of manna in the wilderness was an invitation to know "that man does not live on bread alone but on every word that comes from the mouth of the Lord" (Deut. 8:3; but see Num. 11:13). He further called for the Israelites to demonstrate their faith by following the restrictions of the kosher food laws (Lev. 11; 17:10–14; Deut. 14:3–21). And when the kosher food restrictions were relaxed, believers

were invited to honor God by recognizing that change (Acts 10:11–15; Col. 2:16). Jesus honored the fundamental necessity of eating at the same time he wrapped it into the topic of trust. He placed the reality of hunger pangs next to the reality of divine provision—even miraculous provision should it be deemed necessary. His conclusion was that worry over eating was something that pagans had to do. But if we seek God's kingdom and righteousness first, then we can escape the vortex of worry about having food to eat (Matt. 6:31–33). Eating as a demonstration of faith translates very easily into the figure of speech in which eating becomes a metaphor for believing what God has said. The invitation of wisdom in Proverbs 9:1–6 and the invitation of Jesus in John 6:50–58 are examples of the use of this metaphor (see also 1 Cor. 3:1–2; Heb. 5:11–14).

Eating was not just a sign of faith in God; it also became a way of enacting a

In this Sumerian record of food supplies, the verb *to eat* is communicated by the image of a head before a triangular piece of bread.

social connection that implied acceptance.[1] This is why the meals Jesus ate with social outcasts met with such criticism from his opponents (Matt. 9:11), and it is why eating at the king's table was considered such an honor (2 Sam. 9:7; 1 Kings 2:7). Within the culture of Bible times, this premise was applied in various ways. Those who were making agreements with one another might eat a meal together to commemorate the consummation of the agreement (Gen. 26:30; see also Exod. 24:8–11). This connotation of acceptance also cast its shadow over the ritual meals, from the celebration of Passover to the eating of the Lord's Supper (Exod. 12:4–11; Matt. 26:26). But this connotation of unity also had a more sinister side when ritual eating was used to show affiliation with pagan deities. In the mind-set of the ancient world, food sacrifices were offered to provide food for the pagan deities, who had to eat to sustain themselves (Deut. 32:37–38; Ps. 50:12–13).

Humans who participated in eating some of the sacrifice were showing their acceptance of and association with the deity, which is why the Lord vigorously warned against eating such a meal (Exod. 34:15; Ezek. 18:6, 10–11, 15; 1 Cor. 8:4, 7–10, 13).

There are many figures of speech associated with eating. It was a necessary and wholesome activity for which both positive and negative connotations are mentioned in the Bible. For example, when a person was

The Old Testament limited the diet of believers by taking animals such as this rock hyrax off the menu (Lev. 11:5).

forced to eat something disgusting, it became a symbol of a deeply troubled time. When ancient cities were under a siege, their residents could be pressed into eating unthinkable things: their own excrement, their neighbors, even their children (2 Kings 18:27; Isa. 49:26; Lam. 2:20). Not even Jerusalem would escape such horrific times. "I will make them eat the flesh of their sons and daughters, and they will eat one another's flesh because their enemies will press the siege so hard against them to destroy them" (Jer. 19:9). Difficult times were also in view when people ate "ashes" or when they chose an ungodly path that led to eating "the fruit of their ways" (Ps. 102:9; Prov. 1:31). The otherwise positive connotations of eating are also reversed when it is the people who are eaten rather than doing the eating. The wicked are pictured as consuming God's people in the same way that people eat bread (Ps. 14:4). In a vivid metaphor that uses images of food preparation, Micah pictures the harm misguided leaders bring to God's people with the vivid image that they "eat my people's flesh" (Mic. 3:3).

As the Bible begins with the notion of eating, so it comes to a glorious close with people eating as well. Jesus promised his disciples that they would participate in a grand eschatological feast at the close of all time (Luke 22:30). The book of Revelation whets our appetite for this feast: "Blessed are those who are invited to the wedding supper of the Lamb!" (Rev. 19:9; see also 3:20).

When the Israelites were in the Wilderness of Zin (below), the Lord solicited the trust of his people, promising to provide miraculous food called manna.

ENGRAVE

rtisans of the past were occasionally commissioned by their benefactors to create works of art that delivered messages and captured beauty. One mode of delivery was engraving: the incising of words or images into clay, wood, stone, or metal. The process of engraving began with the purchase or production of the necessary tools for the job. The engraving tool could be a reed stylus, metal chisel, or flint point (Job 19:24; Jer. 17:1), depending on the hardness of the medium to be inscribed and the amount of detail expected in the finished piece.[2] But the tools alone could not produce art apart from the hands of the artist. Only when such tools were skillfully wielded by practiced hands did the most refined pieces of art appear from the raw materials (Exod. 35:30–35). This process was painstakingly slow as snippets of debris were removed from the raw materials. In most cases, if any error occurred, the artisan had two options: either incorporate the error into the design or start over.

Not just anyone was well versed in the art of engraving and not just anything was engraved. This process was reserved for special items. In the archaeological record from Bible times, we have examples of stamp seals that were engraved. Most of these are stone seals that called for special visualization skills by the artist. Stamp seals were designed to leave an impression in wet clay or wax; consequently the seal itself had to be incised in reverse so the stamp impression would appear properly oriented. Such stamp seals were used to authorize documents in the same way we may give authorization via a signature today.[3] We also have examples of stone stelae that are inscribed with the images and exploits of ancient kings—sort of an ancient blog left for posterity to read. The common connotations

The Treasury at Petra (left) demonstrates the expert carving skills of the Nabateans, who engraved such structures in living stone.

The Baker Illustrated Guide to Everyday Life in Bible Times

that underlie these and other cultural examples of engraving are their special status, value, and enduring nature.

In the Bible, specific mention of engraved items is rare, but all of them are intimately linked to worship of the Lord. The uniform of Israel's high priest had a number of components; three of them contained engraving. The *ephod*

A steady hand was joined with a creative eye in the artisan who executed the unique design in this signet ring.

was a robe or apron that covered the upper body of the high priest. Two onyx stones were attached to this garment and were inscribed with the names of the twelve tribes (Exod. 28:9–12; 39:6–7). Similarly, the small cloth breast piece that the high priest wore over the ephod had twelve precious and semiprecious stones attached to it, each engraved with the name of one of Israel's tribes (Exod. 28:21; 39:14). On the priest's turban a gold plate was slung so that it faced forward. It was engraved with the phrase "HOLY TO THE LORD" (Exod. 28:36; 39:30). Solomon's temple was also filled with handiwork that called for the skill of the engravers. The panels of the ten moveable basins and the structure of the temple itself were filled with engravings (1 Kings 6:18, 29, 35; 7:18–20, 36, 42). Clearly all this engraving helped set apart the clergy and the temple in a way that lifted them above the mundane things of life, as was fitting of their purpose. But the most striking example of engraving is one that was lost nearly as soon as it was created. That was the engraving God

A gold plate engraved with the words "HOLY TO THE LORD" adorned the head of Israel's high priest.

himself did as he etched his will into two stone tablets (Exod. 32:15–16).

In four instances the idea of engraving is used as a metaphor by Job, Jeremiah, Isaiah, and Zechariah. The physical and emotional pain endured by Job shook him to his very core. There was one premise to which he lifted his eyes and found some measure of comfort: "I know that my redeemer lives, and that in the end he will stand on the earth. And after my skin has been destroyed, yet in my flesh I will see God" (Job 19:25–26). This notion is so powerful that Job expressed his desire for this hope to be "inscribed with an iron tool on lead, or engraved in rock forever!" (Job 19:24). There it could sustain him and others facing intense challenges of life.

That is the kind of message we want preserved for all time. At the other end of the spectrum, however, is sin. That is not something we want anywhere near us because where sin abounds a divine response is sure to follow. Yet that is exactly what had happened to God's

people prior to their exile in Babylon. "Judah's sin is engraved with an iron tool, inscribed with a flint point on the tablets of their hearts and on the horns of their altars" (Jer. 17:1). The circumstances grew so grave in Israel that the Lord permitted his holy city of Jerusalem to be destroyed. Nevertheless, the Lord had a plan for its restoration; a new Zion would arise. The hope that lived in the hearts of the faithful was propelled in part by this amazing image: "See, I have engraved you on the palms of my hands; your walls are ever before me" (Isa. 49:16).[4]

The image on this cylinder seal had to be engraved in reverse so that its likeness would appear correctly oriented when rolled into soft clay.

Forgiveness and restoration are ultimately linked to one day—Good Friday—when the sins of all people of all time would be poured out on Jesus. Zechariah anticipates that day and summarizes it in one powerful phrase that he says is worthy of being inscribed in stone: "I [the LORD] will remove the sin of this land in a single day" (Zech. 3:9).

Enduring messages such as the one on this funeral stela were engraved in stone to preserve their message.

The Baker Illustrated Guide to Everyday Life in Bible Times

EXILE

To experience exile was far from taking a trip to an exotic destination. If you experienced exile, it meant you were the victim of a successful military conquest and now faced deportation from your home and marked changes in your life that would carry you far from anything you had previously known as normal.

Here we consider the concept of exile from the perspective of both the empire and the exiled citizen. For the ancient empires, exile became a tool with which to disrupt the potential for revolt in far-away conquered territories. The goal was not to empty the land of its population entirely but to selectively and strategically remove the political leaders, nobles, soldiers, religious leaders, craftsmen, and artisans who gave the conquered country its identity (2 Kings 24:14; 1 Chron. 6:15; Jer. 20:6; 27:20). A small number of impoverished families were left behind to tend the agricultural fields and vineyards. These inconsequential citizens were considered too

This Assyrian siege ramp at Lachish provides evidence of the powerful force that defeated this city and exiled its citizens.

small in number to create a risk of revolt and too culturally unsophisticated to preserve the old national identity. Those deported were expected to make contributions to the health and well-being of their new homeland, whether as promising leaders, artisans, or part of the general labor force that produced goods and commodities.

From the perspective of the exile, this was anything but an advantageous event. While a few of the best and brightest were selected for advanced education and eventual leadership positions in the new country (Dan. 1:3–5), most functioned in less dignified ways.[5] It is hard for us to imagine just how devastating and disorienting the experience of exile was. The descriptions offered by the biblical authors give us some sense of what exiled people faced (Deut. 28:63–68; Isa. 20:4; Ezek. 12:18–19). After being conquered, they were uprooted from their homes, stripped naked, and marched in the direction of an unknown land and an uncertain future. There were no moments of rest and repose but rather days and nights filled with fear. Anxiety was never softened by hope; it was only complicated by growing feelings of hopelessness. "In the morning you will say, 'If only it were evening!' and in the evening, 'If only it were morning!'—because of the terror that will fill your hearts and the sights that your eyes will see" (Deut. 28:67).

This Assyrian relief depicts Israelites forced from their homes as they are driven into exile.

When the biblical authors write about exile, it is almost exclusively in regard to the tens of thousands of Israelites who experienced exile at the hands of the conquering Assyrians or Babylonians. The repeated mention of these exiles is disturbing because of the theological tension that it creates. The God who had promised the Israelites that they would occupy and hold the Promised Land in connection with their role of bringing the Messiah into the world became the God who sponsored their removal from that land. People like Habakkuk were genuinely puzzled over what this could mean (Hab. 1:12–17). For it was not political happenstance but divine instigation that brought about these exiles—a point confirmed repeatedly in the Bible (1 Chron. 6:15; Jer. 27:6; Ezek. 39:28; Amos 5:27).

It is not that the Lord was incapable of keeping them in their homeland; he sponsored their departure because they had failed to hold up their end of the covenant. The promise of a national homeland was conditioned on the Israelites' obedience to divine law. And among all the life-disrupting consequences of disobedience, the most earthshaking was God's promise to remove the Israelites from the Promised Land (Deut. 28:36, 63–64; 2 Kings 17:7–23; 18:9–12). This was among the most devastating messages delivered by the prophets, and it was the most traumatic theological experience endured by God's Old Testament people.[6] The event of the exile was so significant that it continued to be a way of marking the passage of time even at the dawn of the New Testament era (Matt. 1:11–12, 17).

But ultimately the Lord used the exile of the Israelites as a tool to reshape them. The harsh realities of exile took their toll both physically and emotionally on God's people, breaking down their prideful resistance and leading them to acknowledge the spiritual damage caused by their sin. The voice of Ezekiel, an exile himself, echoed throughout Babylon calling God's people to repentance (Ezek. 1:1; 3:11; 11:15; 39:23). And the voice of God also came from outside Babylon with words of encouragement and direction. The prophet Jeremiah wrote a letter to the exiles in Babylon telling them how they ought to live in order to maximize their time of displacement (Jer. 29:1–14). Rather than scheming ways to disrupt the government or seeking ways to escape, the exiles were directed to build houses, plant gardens, marry, and have families. "Also, seek the peace and prosperity of the city to which I have carried you

The striking Ishtar Gate in Babylon symbolizes the foreign environment that became the Israelites' home in exile for seventy years.

into exile. Pray to the LORD for it, because if it prospers, you too will prosper" (Jer. 29:7). As the hardship of the exile and God's words of encouragement softened and changed the Israelites' hearts, a new kind of people began to take shape—so that the ones who would return to the Promised Land would not be like those who left. Those returning exiles would have a rehabilitated faith and exhibit a renewed faithfulness that would advance the plan of God (Jer. 24:5–7).

The Lord likens the Israelites' errant behavior to bad grapes found in a well-cared-for vineyard (Isa. 5:4). Such sustained behavior led to the unthinkable exile of God's people from the Promised Land.

Exile

FAMINE

There are many things we may want in life but only two things we really need to sustain life: food and water. A famine takes both away. The famines mentioned in the Bible were typically initiated by a change in climate or a declaration of war. The food and water resources of the Promised Land were based on predictable climatic patterns that brought rain and dew into the region during expected seasons (Deut. 11:10–15). This moisture recharged the springs and wells, filled the cisterns, made the pastures green, ripened the grain fields, and matured the summer fruit. If the weather pattern was interrupted, then both water supply and food production were imperiled. Given the slim margins that enabled the land to produce food, we read about famines occurring somewhat regularly from the time of Abraham through the reign of Claudius (Gen. 12:10; Acts 11:28).[1] That is why those living in Canaan developed the habit of eating the grain harvested in the previous year and storing away the harvest of the current year as a buffer against famine (Lev. 26:10). But if the famines lasted more than two years, the situation became grave (Gen. 45:11; 2 Sam. 21:1; 24:13; 1 Kings 17:1; 2 Kings 8:1). This is also why we see people migrating from Canaan when a sustained famine occurred (Gen. 12:10; Ruth 1:1).

Another cause of famine was war. Rather than expose its soldiers to withering fire while attacking a fortified city, an enemy army could blockade the city and wait for its residents to run out of food and water. The famine caused by such a siege meant that those within would "eat their food in anxiety and drink their water in despair" (Ezek. 12:19). All civility was abandoned as the strong seized food from the weak.[2] In extreme cases, we even read of cannibalism occurring in cities under siege (2 Kings 6:25–29).

Small changes in the amount of annual precipitation could turn a full threshing floor such as this one into an empty floor, which quickly translated into a food crisis in the fragile ecosystem of the Promised Land.

Whether in connection with climate or siege, famine was clearly one of the worst experiences in the ancient world (1 Kings 8:37). The purchase of food would first consume all a person's precious metal, then livestock, and finally even the land they relied on to produce food, putting its former owners into virtual servitude (Gen. 47:13–22). Jeremiah vividly describes the circumstances in which hunger pangs could no longer be endured in silence but were given voice in the moans and groans emanating from the starving people who staggered from one location to the next looking for water with the little strength they had left (Jer. 14:1–3; Amos 4:7–8). "Those killed by the sword are better off than those who die of famine; racked with hunger, they waste away for lack of food from the field" (Lam. 4:9).

When the Bible emphasizes the experience of famine, it does so in two settings. First, God used the rigor of famine to see if those experiencing it would trust him (Ps. 33:18–19; Rom. 8:35). In Genesis, three members of the same family line were confronted by famine and a faith decision. Abraham, Isaac, and Jacob—father, son, and grandson—had been told that the spiritual survival of their world depended on them remaining in the Promised Land; yet each was confronted by a famine that threatened their lives if they stayed (Gen. 12:10; 26:1–2; 43:1–3). Should they stay or should they go? While Abraham and Isaac both trusted the hope that water-rich Egypt offered, it was Jacob who demonstrated true faith in the face of famine. Driven from Canaan by famine and drawn to Egypt with the hope of reunion with Joseph, he hesitated at the border of Canaan until the Lord signaled his approval for departure (Gen. 46:1–5).[3]

Famine drove Jacob to this location at the threshold of the Promised Land. But he refused to leave Beersheba (below) and walk toward Egypt without the Lord's direct approval.

Invasion of powerful armies and the siege of Israel's cities, as depicted here, precipitated horrible famine.

of his people, but he declared that he would permit its presence if they failed to live up to his clear commands (Deut. 11:13–17; 32:19, 24). A number of the instances of famine mentioned by the biblical authors were punitive (1 Kings 18:2; 2 Kings 25:3), and later prophets continued to raise the threat of famine repeatedly as they warned God's people that their ungodly attitudes and behavior were bringing this trouble their way (Isa. 51:17–19; Jer. 14:11–16; Ezek. 5:16–17). And finally, as horrible as real famine was, there was one metaphorical famine that topped them all. Amos warned of such a famine to come that would be "not a famine of food or a thirst for water, but a famine of hearing the words of the LORD" (Amos 8:11).

Because there were always some who suffered more quickly and more deeply from the onset of famine, it also tested the willingness of God's people to show charity to those who were less fortunate. Believers living at the time of both Nehemiah and Paul responded positively to this faith challenge (Neh. 5:1–13; Acts 11:28–30). And lest we think that those tests are a thing of the past, we need to remember that the final days of this world's history will also be marked by famine (Matt. 24:7; Mark 13:8; Luke 21:11; Rev. 6:8), giving us our opportunity to trust the Lord and care for those in distress when the days become difficult.

The second setting in which the biblical authors frequently mentioned famine was in regard to God using it to punish covenant violation. God could prevent famine from ever tarnishing the lives

Famine impacted not only the agricultural fields but also the pastures that sustained the health of Israel's livestock such as these goats.

FAST

*T*oday intentional abstention from food and drink for a given period of time is more likely associated with preparation for a medical test or in conjunction with a weight-loss plan than with spiritual development. But in the Bible, the physical act of fasting was employed in order to enrich an awareness of mortal vulnerability and to sharpen awareness of the Lord's ability to provide.[4]

Fasts of any duration will cause the body to react in predictable ways. After four to eight hours our bodies naturally seek to replace the glucose needed to maintain brain function by tapping into stored reserves. We first tap into the raw materials produced by the liver; then after about twelve hours we pursue the proteins available in the muscles and then the energy stored in the fat. Our metabolism generally slows during a prolonged fast, leaving us where David found himself: "My knees give way from fasting; my body is thin and gaunt" (Ps. 109:24). The typical fast reported by the biblical authors lasted for only one day, with food and drink shunned only during daylight hours (Judg. 20:26; 1 Sam. 14:24; 2 Sam. 1:12; 3:35). That makes fasts of three, seven, and even forty days exceptional and worthy of special notice (Exod. 34:28; 1 Sam. 31:13; 2 Sam. 12:16–21; 1 Chron. 10:12; Esther 4:16; Matt. 4:2).

In the Bible, fasting is associated with several occasions. People fasted as they reflected on their own sin, the sins of their community,

Moses fasted prior to receiving the Ten Commandments on Mount Sinai (below).

and the need of all to repent. Such penitential fasts were sometimes enacted spontaneously in response to special circumstances (1 Sam. 7:6; Ezra 10:6; Dan. 9:3; Joel 1:14; 2:12, 15). In addition, God's people were required to fast on the Day of Atonement when all Israel sought forgiveness. Here the directive to "deny yourselves" included fasting (Lev. 16:29–31; 23:27–32).

People also fasted in advance of special experiences or in connection with prayerful inquiry. Moses fasted prior to receiving the tablets of stone containing the Ten Commandments on the two separate occasions they were given (Exod. 34:28; Deut. 9:9). Immediately after his baptism, Jesus retreated into the wilderness where he too fasted as he initiated his public ministry (Matt. 4:1–2). Fasting also accompanied special inquiry of the Lord, whether interceding on behalf of a dying child,

seeking direction in the face of an advancing army, requesting safe travel, or commissioning church workers (2 Sam. 12:16; 2 Chron. 20:3; Ezra 8:21, 23; Acts 13:2–3; 14:23).

Fasting was also practiced in connection with mourning those who had died (2 Sam. 1:12; 3:33–35; 1 Chron. 10:12). This is the category in which the fasting of Nehemiah 1:3–4 and Esther 4:3 seems to fit. In the first case, Nehemiah sat before the ruined walls of Jerusalem to mourn for a dead city. In Esther, when the Jews across the provinces of Persia heard the king's annihilation order, they enacted mourning rituals on behalf of their nation, which seemed as good as dead.

The fasts mentioned in connection with each of these occasions appear to have had a similar purpose: they acknowledged the real position of humans in relation to their

Anna spent her days praying and fasting in the temple courts.

The Baker Illustrated Guide to Everyday Life in Bible Times

Creator. This included admitting their failure to live up to the Creator's high demands, recognizing their general vulnerability to the consequences of sin, and developing a proper and heartfelt humility. Fasting led the Israelites to negate their focus on themselves and their abilities in order to better see and acknowledge God's presence and power.[5]

During the typical dawn-to-dusk fast, not even things as insignificant as dates were eaten.

Given the powerful role that fasting might play in developing this perspective, the biblical authors are roundly critical of those who abuse it. Typically, the presentation of fasting is surrounded by positive connotations, as when Luke mentions the widow Anna, who spent her days at the temple praying and fasting (Luke 2:36–37). But those who presumed that the mere act of fasting was sufficient in and of itself as leverage with which to force the Almighty into recognizing them and doing their bidding faced censure. "Yet on the day of your fasting, you do as you please and exploit all your workers. Your fasting ends in quarreling and strife, and in striking each other with wicked fists. You cannot fast as you do today and expect your voice to be heard on high" (Isa. 58:3–4; see also Zech. 7:4–5).

Jesus confronted another form of abuse that was associated with fasting, criticizing those who used the fast to solicit the attention of others. The hunger pangs that attended fasting might show up in their facial expression, but those fasting did the ritual a grave disservice if they intentionally played up the discomfort in their facial expressions and posture. "When you fast, do not look somber as the hypocrites do, for they disfigure their faces to show others they are fasting" (Matt. 6:16). Jesus was equally critical of those who took the next step and publicly announced their fasting schedule. "I fast twice a week and give a tenth of all I get" (Luke 18:12). Of course, Jesus was not opposed to fasting; he simply observed that there was a proper time and a proper way to do it (Matt. 9:14–15). Fasting that was done improperly—either in a self-congratulatory way or as a means of leveraging divine submission—was better left undone.

Upon the death of a loved one, the family's grief was expressed by their visiting the tomb and abstaining from food.

FIRSTBORN SON

The biblical authors paid a great deal of attention to birth order. If twins were born, they immediately identified the firstborn as the babies left the womb (Gen. 38:28). Genealogies vigilantly noted which son in the list was first to be born (for example, Gen. 10:15; 22:21; 25:13; 35:23). This was in part because the firstborn son was considered to be a sign of his father's strength (Gen. 49:3), but even more important were the social responsibilities and economic advantages that attended being the firstborn.

As the father aged, a time came when the family formally transferred those responsibilities and advantages to the firstborn—a time marked by the aging leader of the family placing his hand on the heir apparent and pronouncing a blessing (Gen. 27:1–40; 48:9–20). From that moment on, the transition to the new family leader was underway as the firstborn son began to assume the responsibility of leading and superintending the well-being of the extended family.[6]

A loving couple gazes at their son. Firstborn sons had many distinct and important roles to play in the culture of God's Old Testament people.

Ancient inheritance laws helped provide the resources to meet those responsibilities because the oldest son received a double share of the estate. This was the case even if the actual firstborn was the son of a less-favored wife (Deut. 21:15–17). Within royal families, the eldest son enjoyed yet another privilege: he became the heir apparent to the royal throne (2 Chron. 21:3).

Within the culture of God's Old Testament people, the firstborn son of every Israelite woman had to be redeemed. There is a subtle but important difference to note here since many men at that time had more than one wife: the requirement applied not just to the firstborn of the father but also to the firstborn of each woman (Exod. 13:12; 34:19; Num. 18:15). The Lord claimed these sons as his own to serve in the tent of meeting as mediators between him and the entire nation. But the Lord called for the firstborn sons to be redeemed from that special service and replaced by members of the tribe of

Levi. All Levite males became substitutes for all the firstborn males of Israel in performing the service the Lord required in the sanctuary (Num. 3:11–13, 40–51; 8:18). The formal redemption took place when the firstborn son was one month old and it required payment of five shekels of silver (Num. 18:15–16; see also the dedication of Jesus in Luke 2:22–24).[7]

The rationale for the Lord's claim on every firstborn Israelite son builds on the exodus event. The tenth and most striking of the plagues the Lord used to break down the resistance of the Egyptian pharaoh was the death of every firstborn son in Egypt, "from the firstborn son of the Pharaoh, who sits on the throne, to the firstborn son of the female slave, who is at her hand mill" (Exod. 11:5). The Lord graciously spared the Israelites from this devastating plague and so laid a claim on each of the firstborn sons among his people, setting apart those sons for himself (Num. 3:13; 8:17). The ritual redemption of firstborn sons not only honored the Lord's claim but also reanimated the memory of the event lest it ever be forgotten (Exod. 13:14–15).

With all this social and religious attention given to firstborn sons that enhanced their prominence in Israelite culture, we appropriately pay closer attention to sons who played the role of firstborns even though they were not. This list includes Isaac, Jacob, Joseph, Ephraim, David, and Solomon. None of them were firstborn sons, but in each case their lives were flush with responsibilities and advantages normally associated with the firstborn. The

This massive gate marks the entry to Solomon's city of Gezer. Like his father, David, Solomon defied expectation in rising to the throne as a son who was not the firstborn.

firstborn's importance also makes it appropriately shocking when we read about the execution of firstborn sons. Within the culture of the ancient world, this was not just a personal tragedy but an event that created a social tidal wave that overturned normal life. That was the Lord's intention in targeting the firstborn sons in Egypt during the tenth plague (Exod. 11:5; 12:12, 29), and it was the consequence of the curse pronounced on anyone who attempted to rebuild Jericho (Josh. 6:26; 1 Kings 16:34). The importance of the firstborn also added to the horror of people sacrificing their firstborn sons in an attempt to manipulate divine favor (2 Kings 3:27; Mic. 6:7).

The prominent role the firstborn played in society provides the energy behind the metaphorical designation of someone as firstborn. This honorary title was given to Israel as a way of distinguishing that nation as the Lord's own special people whom he would not disown even when they abandoned him (Exod. 4:22; Jer. 31:9). Although Jesus was literally the firstborn son of Mary (Luke 2:7), this descriptor is also used as a way of magnifying Jesus's status in other settings. He is called "the firstborn over all creation" (Col. 1:15). And he is also called the "firstborn from the dead" (Rev. 1:5) because not only was he the first one to be raised from the dead never to die again but he also is the most important of all who will ever rise from the dead (see Rom. 8:29). Finally, the biblical authors also refer to Christians with this honorary designation (Heb. 12:23).

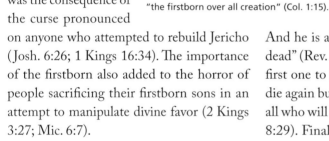

Jesus was not just the firstborn son of Mary but also "the firstborn over all creation" (Col. 1:15).

FISH

Illustration of the cast net in use.

*F*ish are a wonderful source of protein; and as early as Genesis 9, the Lord affirmed that these creatures could be caught and consumed by humans (vv. 2–3). Later the dietary laws given to the Israelites clarified the matter by limiting the aquatic portion of their diet to the creatures that have both fins and scales (Lev. 11:9–12). So it is that we find fish as food in many biblical stories, whether they be Israelites during their time of slavery in Egypt (Num. 11:5) or a wide-eyed, young boy with two small fish who offered his lunch to feed thousands (John 6:9). Fishing harbors lined the Sea of Galilee to service the commercial fishing operations conducted on that body of water, and there was a fish market in Jerusalem located just inside the city's Fish Gate (2 Chron. 33:14; Neh. 12:39; 13:16).[8]

The biblical authors refer to fish from the Nile River, the Mediterranean Sea, and the Sea of Galilee. Because the Israelites spent most of their time far from Egypt, and because they hardly ever had control of the coastal plain during their history, fishing in the Nile and Mediterranean are mentioned only in passing (Num. 11:5; Neh. 13:16; Isa. 19:8). The most frequent mention of commercial fishing operations is linked to the Sea of Galilee, where more than eighteen species of fish could be found. And because so much of Jesus's earthly ministry occurred along the shores of this lake, it is fishing associated with this body of water

A model of a trammel boat used for fishing on the Sea of Galilee during the first century.

that is mentioned most often by the biblical authors.[9]

The Bible speaks of four methods used for catching fish. First is the simple *hook and line* used with or without a pole (Job 41:1; Isa. 19:8; Amos 4:2). This is the way Jesus directed Peter to catch the fish that held the coin necessary to pay the temple tax they owed (Matt. 17:27). The second tool used for fishing is the *cast net*. This is a round net with a diameter of eighteen to twenty-five feet with weights fastened around its perimeter. The fisherman twirls this net over his head to open it to its full size before throwing it over shallow water where it sinks and traps fish beneath it. This is the kind of net Peter and Andrew were using when Jesus called them to become his disciples (Matt. 4:18; Mark 1:16; see also Ezek. 32:3). Another type of net used along the shoreline is the *drag net*. This rectangular net hangs vertically in the water like a twelve-foot curtain. Floats positioned along the top of the net keep it floating, and weights on the lower line keep it vertically oriented. At one thousand feet in length, it is deployed using a boat and land crew. The men in the boat take one end of the net and pull it into the water perpendicular to the shoreline while the land crew holds the other end on shore. Once the net is fully extended, the boat turns and travels parallel to the shoreline while the land crew walks up the shoreline driving fish as they go. Eventually the boat circles back to

Illustration of the drag net in use.

the shore, corralling the fish, which are then pulled up and onto the shore (Ezek. 26:5, 14; 47:10; Hab. 1:15; Matt. 13:47–48). Finally, there is the *trammel net*, which is deployed in deeper water. The trammel net is also designed to stand vertically in the water through the use of floats and weights. It is composed of several curtains of netting and is deployed by boats to form a circular, aquatic corral around a school of fish. The fishermen create a disturbance within the corral in order to panic the fish, causing them to flee in the direction of the net. They pass easily through the first layer of the net only to bump into the finer mesh of the inner curtain. When they attempt to turn, they are entangled in the outer curtain. This type of fishing was typically done at night so that it was more difficult for the fish to see the net (Luke 5:1–11; John 21:1–14).[10]

Saint Peter's fish, harvested from the Sea of Galilee.

The rhetorical mention of fishing and fishing nets varies dramatically between the Old and New Testaments. The Old Testament tells the story of Jonah, who became the prey devoured by a huge fish (Jon. 1:17; 2:1), and of victims of metaphorical nets and fishhooks. These can be the cruel nets of unexpected misfortune (Eccles. 9:12) or symbolic nets of captivity deployed by the empires of Assyria and Babylon (Jer. 16:16; Amos 4:2; Hab. 1:14–15).

In contrast, the New Testament uses fishing and fishing nets to create very positive images of the church. At least one-third of Jesus's disciples were professional fishermen who were called to a new role of fishing for people (Matt. 4:19; Mark 1:17; Luke 5:10). Jesus described increasing the kingdom of God with fishing imagery (Matt. 13:47–50); and when Peter appeared to be leading his fellow disciples back into a life of ordinary fishing following the resurrection of Jesus, it was Jesus who performed a miracle that paralleled the one at their first calling in order to redirect their focus (Luke 5:1–11; John 21:1–14). When we combine and interpret this fishing imagery, three things become clear: (1) There were many people to catch in this net of the gospel. (2) The disciples were to focus on gathering rather than sorting. (3) True success lay in following Jesus's direction rather than their own experience or intuition.

The Sea of Galilee (below) continues to produce fish for local consumption, as it did in Jesus's day.

FLOG
(WHIP, SCOURGE)

*F*logging was a form of punishment that employed a variety of devices to lash the exposed flesh of the victim. The biblical authors describe this grisly business with a variety of Greek and Hebrew terms, each of which has been translated in our English versions in more than one way. That makes this phenomenon a bit more difficult to trace through the pages of our Bible. But we will get the basics by tracing the terms *flogging*, *whipping*, and *scourging*.

In the Jewish culture, flogging employed either an oxtail whip or a strap of leather cowhide that was folded multiple times and attached to a wooden handle.[11] Old Testament law limited the number of strokes to no more than forty (Deut. 25:2–3), though that apparently was reduced to thirty-nine as a hedge against violation of this command (2 Cor. 11:24).[12] The Jewish traditional writings offer even more details about the administration of this punishment. People who

The biblical authors liken heartache to the painful blows of a whip.

were flogged were tied in a slightly bent over position with their hands on each side of a pillar. The administrator of the punishment would then tear off their clothing to expose the region of the body to be beaten. Then one-third of the determined number of blows were struck on the front of the body and two-thirds on the back of the body.[13] While this beating caused physical pain and embarrassment, the Bible is clear that the person flogged should never be degraded to the point of public ostracism (Deut. 25:3). Its purpose was to correct errant behavior and attitude (Prov. 19:25). Jesus warned his disciples that as they spoke about him and his message, they could expect that the synagogue leaders would use flogging in an effort to punish them and discredit their message (Matt. 10:17; 23:34; Mark 13:9). And this is exactly what the apostles experienced shortly after Jesus's ascension (Acts 5:40).

The Romans appear to have had at least two types of whips for flogging. The more serious of the two, the *flagellum*, consisted of a handle with leather straps attached to it. Knots were tied into the straps with bone or sharp metal bits tied onto them.[14] This was the device used prior to crucifixion to brutalize those condemned so severely that they would be incapable of effective resistance. There was no limit to the number of blows that could be

The Baker Illustrated Guide to Everyday Life in Bible Times

struck, and the beating often continued until the flesh hung down in bloody strips. This is the kind of punishment Jesus anticipated when he spoke to the disciples about their final trip to Jerusalem, and it is what he received prior to his crucifixion (Matt. 20:19; 27:26; Mark 10:34; 15:15; John 19:1).

The Roman flagellum was used to beat the condemned and so reduce their resistance when being crucified.

The other types of Roman whips, the *scutica* and the *virga*, lacked the metal and bone fragments and consisted only of a handle with thongs made of twisted parchment or leather. These devices were deployed when the goal was to get better information during an interrogation or punish a crime that was not serious enough to merit crucifixion. Paul was about to receive such a flogging in Jerusalem in connection with an interrogation over an uproar that had occurred in the temple complex. But just before it was administered, Paul used his Roman citizenship to stop the process (Acts 22:24–29).

The Bible also contains examples of flogging that are figurative or symbolic. In several places in Proverbs we read of a spirit that has been flogged (NIV "crushed"). Heartache can be unbearable; it can beat down one's spirit like a whip on the bare back, robbing us of joy and leaving us physically exhausted (Prov. 15:13; 17:22; 18:14). Sometimes that heartache is caused by those who speak maliciously about us. That is why the tongue itself is likened to

In northern Israel (below), residents who sought relief from Solomon's son Rehoboam were told that they would be scourged with scorpions (1 Kings 12:14).

the whip that delivers a flogging (Job 5:21).

David was given an array of wonderful promises (see 2 Samuel 7), including the promise that his rule would pass to his sons, thus forming a royal dynasty. The Lord warned, however, that when any of David's descendants traveled on godless paths, it would lead to that person being flogged. "I will punish him with a rod wielded by men, with floggings inflicted by human hands" (2 Sam. 7:14; see also Pss. 39:10; 89:32).

A satirical scene from Egypt that depicts a disobedient boy being punished by a cat and a mouse.

David's grandson Rehoboam deployed the whip rhetorically as his kingdom teetered on the brink of division. He could try to hold together his fracturing kingdom with kindness or coercion; in the end he chose the latter. Subjects from the northern part of his kingdom asked Rehoboam to lighten the burdens they had carried under his father. Rehoboam's response precipitated the shattering of his kingdom: "My father scourged you with whips; I will scourge you with scorpions" (1 Kings 12:14).[15]

Even Jesus made a whip out of cords and used it to clear the temple of animal sellers and money changers (John 2:15). This was clearly a literal act, and the flailing whip helped Jesus create the intended disruption. But given what we know of Jewish flogging, we see important symbolism attached to his use of a whip. This was the tool used by Jewish leaders to embarrass and hurt Jews who had gone astray. Thus his use of a whip became a metaphorical flogging of the temple leadership who ran the temple market in a way that was disruptive to the intended spirit of worship there.

Paul was nearly beaten at the Antonia Fortress (right) by Roman soldiers before being exempted from the treatment because of his Roman citizenship.

The Baker Illustrated Guide to Everyday Life in Bible Times

FLY

Though the fundamental principles of flight were largely understood by the Middle Ages, sustained, controlled flight was not possible until the Wright brothers accomplished it in 1903.[16] Today three of every four Americans will take at least one airline flight in their life, and many will fly and even build their own personal aircraft. This guarantees that the perception of flight and the connotations associated with flight in the ancient world differ markedly from those of the modern reader.

While no human mentioned in the Bible flew, we do read about animals, objects, and spirits that did. On the literal side, we read that the Lord gave a variety of birds and insects the ability to fly (Gen. 1:20; 8:7; Lev. 11:20; Deut. 14:19; Nah. 3:16). And clouds float peacefully in the sky while under them certain weapons, such as arrows and javelins, are designed to take flight en route to their targets (Ps. 91:5; Isa. 60:8; Hab. 3:11). As God created birds with the ability to fly, so he has given his heavenly spiritual servants both wings and flying skills (Isa. 6:2, 6; Rev. 4:7–8). Finally, God himself is pictured in flight. The Spirit of God hovered above the formless surface of the world as it took shape, the Lord mounted the cherubim and soared on the wings of the wind, and Jesus rose above the disciples at his ascension (Gen. 1:2; 2 Sam. 22:11; Ps. 18:10; Acts 1:9).

Figurative flyers included ships, riches, and wealth. From a distance, ships with unfurled sails riding on the sea looked like clouds floating through the sky (Isa. 60:8–9). Flight was also used as a metaphor for the phenomena of rapid disappearance of riches and glory: "Cast but a glance at riches, and they are gone, for they will surely sprout wings and fly off to the sky like an eagle" (Prov. 23:5; see also Nah. 3:16). And the prophet Hosea warned that "Ephraim's glory will fly away like a bird" (Hosea 9:11).

In order to fully connect to the connotations the biblical authors linked to flight and so appreciate their rhetorical use in the Bible,

Even the most common birds of Jerusalem such as this jackdaw become exceptional creatures when they take flight.

we must look at life from a nonflying perspective. Prior to the Middle Ages people did not fully grasp the principles that made flight possible, much less fly themselves. "The way of an eagle in the sky" is still "too amazing" to fully grasp in the modern era (Prov. 30:18–19); how much more so in the past. Flying was truly a mysterious and otherworldly phenomenon. For this reason, those living in ancient times frequently depicted their otherworldly deities with wings or with the ability to hover in flight.[17] No surprise then that the inspired authors of the Bible who wished to capture the otherworldly uniqueness of God did so by picturing him in flight.

The flight habits of birds can communicate the connotation of peaceful security. The eagle and vulture are very striking because they do not constantly beat their wings in a frenzied effort to stay aloft; instead, with a few deft strokes they seek out thermals so they can set their wings in a fixed position and soar. They make flying look easy and peaceful. Thus those who hope in the Lord are said to "soar on wings like eagles" (Isa. 40:31) with hardly a wing beat to disturb the serenity of the moment. This is also the

The terrain of Edom (below) seemed to offer security, but Obadiah said that though they soared like the eagle, from the heights the people of Edom would be brought low (1:4).

The Baker Illustrated Guide to Everyday Life in Bible Times

Mythical creatures are often distinguished by their wings and their ability to fly.

image that informs the language of Exodus 19:4, in which the Lord reminds Israel how he carried them out of Egypt on eagles' wings. The Edomites presumed they too enjoyed this secure mode of flight, but God had a different picture for them: "Though you soar like the eagle and make your nest among the stars, from there I will bring you down" (Obad. 1:4). The soothing connotation of security is also communicated by the flight image of hovering. Here God becomes the wary parent who hovers like a watchful eagle above the nest of its young: "Like birds hovering overhead, the LORD Almighty will shield Jerusalem; he will shield it and deliver it, he will 'pass over' it and will rescue it" (Isa. 31:5; see also Deut. 32:11). For many birds it is not the ability to soar for extended periods of time that gives them security but rather their ability to burst quickly into flight, leaving predators behind. This is the security that David sought in poetic verse, asking the Lord to deliver him from the conspiracy that threatened to take away his throne and his life: "Oh, that I had the wings of a dove! I would fly away and be at rest" (Ps. 55:6; see also Rev. 12:14).

Yet another connotation associated with flight is the sudden harm it can bring. What comes into focus here are the raptors and their tactic of diving on unsuspecting prey from above at speeds that can exceed seventy-five miles per hour. In David's lament for Saul and Jonathan, he celebrated their military skills by likening them to swift eagles that swoop down on their prey (2 Sam. 1:23). The leaders of powerful non-Israelite nations are also pictured with this same threatening image (Deut. 28:49; Isa. 11:14; Jer. 48:40; 49:22; Lam. 4:19; Hab. 1:8).

Finally, it is also the remarkable diving speed of the raptors that likely informs the connection between flight and the rapid passage of life. "Our days may come to seventy years, or eighty, if our strength endures; yet the best of them are but trouble and sorrow, for they quickly pass, and we fly away" (Ps. 90:10; see also Job 9:25–26).

A Jerusalem dove. "Oh, that I had the wings of a dove! I would fly away and be at rest" (Ps. 55:6).

FOOT
(TO PLACE ON)

*B*ecause people of Bible times walked long distances over difficult terrain, they developed strong muscles in their legs and feet.[18] The link between feet and strength was so forged that putting one's foot on a piece of property came to symbolize ownership while placing one's foot on a person indicated dominance or control over him or her.

Placing one's foot on a piece of property to confirm ownership is alluded to in Ruth 4:7, which mentions the transfer of a sandal from one person to another as an indication that land ownership had been transferred. When an owner wanted to transfer property rights, it appears that he walked the boundary line of the parcel of land in a pair of sandals and then gave one sandal to the new owner to symbolize that the property had changed ownership.[19] When the Lord was ready to transfer ownership of the Promised Land into the hands of Abraham and his descendants, he did not mention the sandal, but he did speak of putting the feet of the new owners on the land. God told Abram, "Go, walk through the length and breadth of the land, for I am giving it to you" (Gen. 13:17). Caleb was told that in return for his faithful service he would receive a special piece of property, "the land he set his feet on" (Deut. 1:36; see the promise fulfilled in Josh. 14:9). And God promised the Israelites in general that if they were faithful to the covenant, "Every place where you set your foot will be yours" (Deut. 11:24). But this property ownership did not extend into the territory the Lord had determined to give Edom. The Israelites were not to provoke them because "I will not give you any of their land, not even enough to put your foot on" (Deut. 2:5). Note that years later when Moses sought transit through the Edomites' land, he asked that they be allowed to "pass through on foot—nothing else" (Num. 20:19). Note that *on foot* is clearly distinguished from putting one's *foot on* the land.

Placing one's powerful foot on a person carried the connotation that he

Victorious generals often placed their feet on the defeated as a sign of their absolute dominance over them.

or she had been fully humiliated and defeated. This is a symbol that we find in the literature and art of many ancient Near Eastern cultures.[20] Following the successful effort of Joshua in defeating the five-king alliance in a battle that began near Gibeon, he forced those proud rulers to lie on the ground so that his victorious commanders could each place their foot on the necks of the conquered leaders (Josh. 10:24). Like Joshua, King David also was very successful in defeating the local kings who opposed the expansion of his kingdom. Recalling those victories, David described how he "crushed them completely, and they could not rise; they fell beneath my feet" (2 Sam. 22:39; see also Ps. 18:38). Solomon echoed the idea and image in 1 Kings 5:3. And the psalmist celebrated in song God's role in all the victories from the time of Joshua through the time of David: "He subdued nations under us, peoples under our feet" (Ps. 47:3).

There are cases when a person fell at the feet of a leader as a voluntary act to show willing submission rather than the humiliating subjugation of a conquered foe. Abigail bowed before David, begging forgiveness for the foolish acts of her husband and thus saving her household from bloodshed (1 Sam. 25:23–24). And Esther fell at the feet of King Xerxes, pleading for an edict that would save the lives of the Jews (Esther 8:3).

The biblical authors also describe the Lord as putting persons or places under his feet.

Despite the challenges offered by this terrain, the people of Bible times traveled from one place to another on foot.

Humans were assigned a prominent place in the hierarchy of the created world; everything was under their feet (Ps. 8:6). That grant could be given only by the Creator, who had made heaven his throne and earth his footstool (Isa. 66:1). But since the fall into sin, not everything in creation remains a willing subject of the Lord; rebellious enemies abound. While we may receive battle scars as a consequence of this ongoing fight, the ultimate defeat of the opposition is never in doubt. We are promised that a special seed of the woman will put his foot on the leader of this revolt (Gen. 3:15). This messianic king is invited by his father to "sit at my right hand until I make your enemies a footstool for your feet" (Ps. 110:1; see its echo in Luke 20:41–44; Acts 2:34–35; Heb. 1:13; 10:13). The battle will rage on into the last days, but the outcome is fully assured; everything will be put under his feet, including the one leading the rebellion (Ps. 45:5; Eph. 1:22; Heb. 2:8). The divine promise is crystal clear: "The God of peace will soon crush Satan under your feet" (Rom. 16:20).

If we see the foot as a symbol of strength, we will gain new insight into several other passages where the biblical authors mention feet. As Jacob's life was coming to a close, he gave special instructions to his sons and then "drew his feet up into the bed" (Gen. 49:33). Strong legs

A Hittite ruler with his throne and footstool. "The LORD says to my lord: 'Sit at my right hand until I make your enemies a footstool for your feet'" (Ps. 110:1).

that had once walked the Promised Land were now weakened by age, signaling that the end of his life was near. Similarly, we can make better sense of an event from the life of Balaam (Numbers 22). This man was hired by Balak, the son of the king of Moab, to put a curse on God's people. Though the Lord allowed Balaam to start his journey, it was punctuated by a reminder that it was the Lord and not Balaam who was in control. Even before his donkey talked, it crushed Balaam's foot against a wall as a way of symbolizing the real weakness of the man who claimed to have power (Num. 22:25).

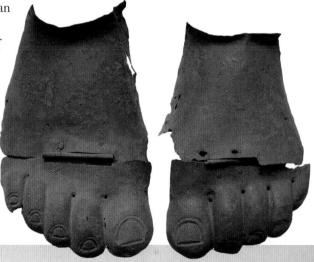

A pair of bronze foot guards.

FORTIFY

Children love to build forts, whether in their playroom or nearby woods. This play fort-building stands in stark contrast to the deadly serious business of fortifying a city in Bible times. When either local neighbors or distant empires turned a covetous eye toward a city's food supply, natural resources, or trade revenues, the residents had the option of exiting their city and fighting their attackers or seeking shelter within the city. At times it was more prudent to flee behind the multiple barriers that shaped the defenses of a fortified city. Those barriers were designed to slow down the attackers and create such a cost in lives and resources that they would move on to another target—one with a softer outer core of protection.

The types and numbers of barriers that comprised a fortified city varied with era and location. Here we summarize the full complement of components that might have comprised a fortified city, presenting them in the order that an attacker would meet them.[21] The first was a *dry moat* that was dug around all the other defenses of the city. Its depth created an exposed killing zone, removing any form of cover from fire for the attacker. On the side of the moat facing the city, the residents constructed a *revetment wall* that was a lower wall line outside the perimeter of the main wall. Between this revetment wall and the main wall was a *rampart* or *glacis*. This artificially pitched slope of thirty to forty degrees was often coated with clay or plaster. The severe slope and the slippery surface discouraged those who made it past the moat and revetment wall from proceeding any farther. The dry moat, revetment wall, and rampart all guarded access to the *main wall* that itself bristled with towers that allowed the defenders to strike

The defensibility of Arad's fortress (below) was improved greatly by locating it at the top of rising terrain.

their exposed attackers from above. Access to the fortified city through this main wall was via a *gatehouse* rather than just through a simple gate. This gatehouse extended beyond the wall line to allow withering attack to be directed from above on any who tried to attack the main entry. Within the gatehouse there were multiple rooms on each side of the path into the city from which soldiers attacked those who made it past the first gate.

The biblical authors mentioned fortified cities or their components for a number of reasons. Sometimes this information was shared because it helped define the challenge ahead that summoned Israel to trust the Lord. Fortified city-states built by Canaanites awaited any Israelites who attempted to cross into the Promised Land. Moses sent a team to explore the land, asking them to specifically report on whether the urban areas were "unwalled or fortified" (Num. 13:19). The exaggerated report of fortified cities terrified the people and eradicated their passion for an invasion (Num. 13:28)—a lack of faith that stands in stark contrast to the faith that allowed for the successful destruction of other cities (Deut. 3:5–6; Josh. 14:12).

When the biblical authors wished to showcase the success of Israelite kings, they could do so by describing the cities they had fortified or border fortresses they had built (1 Kings 12:25; 15:17; 22:39; 2 Chron. 8:5; 11:5–11; 14:6; 26:9).[22] But accompanying these compliments was the warning about trusting in fortified cities at the expense of trust in the Lord as their supreme defense (Isa. 17:10; Jer. 5:17). Failure to trust God met with a necessary correction: "They will lay siege to all the cities throughout your land until the high fortified walls in which you trust fall down" (Deut. 28:52). It is sad that this correction occurred not just once but many times at the hands of the Assyrians, Egyptians, and Babylonians (2 Kings 18:13; 2 Chron. 12:2–4; 32:1; Isa. 17:3; 36:1; Jer. 34:7; Hab. 1:6, 10). "Israel has forgotten their Maker and built palaces; Judah has fortified many towns. But I will send fire on their cities that will consume their fortresses" (Hosea 8:14).

The notion of fortification occurs in figures of speech as well. The fortified city became a symbol of urban living just as the agricultural watchtower symbolized rural life. Thus the merism "from watchtower to fortified city" was employed to describe the sum total of all lands, both urban and rural (2 Kings 17:9; 18:8).

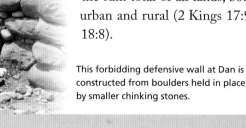

This forbidding defensive wall at Dan is constructed from boulders held in place by smaller chinking stones.

Access to the city of Laish was through this gate, which dates to the time of Abraham.

The fortified city brings to mind two connotations that appear in metaphors. The first is that a fortified city is a safe haven, a place that ensures future survival. Thus wealth can be perceived as a fortified city: "The wealth of the rich is their fortified city; they imagine it a wall too high to scale" (Prov. 18:11; see also 10:15). In reality, only the Lord offers such security (Prov. 18:10). "Truly my soul finds rest in God; my salvation comes from him. Truly he is my rock and my salvation; he is my fortress, I will never be shaken" (Ps. 62:1–2).

The second set of metaphors likens people to the absolutely unyielding fortified city. The wise poet warns, "A brother wronged is more unyielding than a fortified city" (Prov. 18:19). And the unyielding character of Jeremiah was described with similar language. "Today I have made you a fortified city, an iron pillar and a bronze wall to stand against the whole land—against the kings of Judah, its officials, its priests and the people of the land" (Jer. 1:18; see also 15:20). This description is so fitting given that Jeremiah had to confront the leaders of God's people and their subjects, who had built fortified cities without a complementary faith in the Lord (Jer. 4:5).

FOUNDATION
(TO LAY)

*A*s the lifestyle of the ancient Israelites evolved from living in tents to living in villages and cities, they also realized the need for developing effective techniques for laying a foundation to support their homes, public buildings, and defensive walls. The purpose of these foundations was to create a sturdy link between the structure above and the earth below. A well-laid foundation was capable of carrying the load-bearing weight of the wall above without shifting, sinking, or collapsing.

The best way to achieve this goal was to lay a structure's foundation on stable bedrock. But when that was not possible, an alternative strategy was put into practice. The process began by digging a trench deep enough to reach a more stable layer of the subsoil. The wall builders

then lined the bottom of the trench with a layer of sand that would allow groundwater to drain away from the base of the foundation rather than collect against it. Then either naturally shaped fieldstones or artificially shaped blocks of cut stone (called *ashlars*) were interlaced with one another to establish the foundation proper on which the wall was built. If the subsoil at the bottom of the trench had the proper qualities, then the builders could lay a foundation that was the same width as the wall that would rise above it. If not, the stones that composed the foundation were laid in steps—wider at the bottom and narrowing to the width of the wall at the top of the trench—in order to spread the load more evenly on the less stable subsoil.[23] Although the process and product were not particularly glamorous and the end product remained largely out of sight, everyone knew about its importance. Jesus's parable of the wise and foolish builders who constructed homes on very different foundations gathers its power from this reality (Matt. 7:24–27; Luke 6:46–49).

Furthermore, the laying of a foundation carries two important connotations. The first is related to ownership. The one who lays the foundation is recognized as the owner of the building or wall that rises

The ideal foundation for any wall was bedrock.

above it. The second is the assumption that when one lays a foundation, the completion of the structure is virtually ensured. It was a mark of great shame to lay a foundation and fail to finish the building project (Luke 14:29–30).

This explains why the laying of the temple's foundation in Jerusalem received so much attention from the biblical authors. The temple itself was clearly an important structure that lent a sense of permanence to the divine presence in the Promised Land. Consequently, the laying of the foundation of the first and second temples was noted, celebrated, and deplored in ways that naturally follow (1 Kings 6:37; 2 Chron. 8:16; Ezra 3:6, 10–13; 4:4–5, 12; 5:16). Every expectation was that the laying of its foundation was the first step in its completion. That is why a halt in the construction of the temple after its foundation was laid was so shocking and animated Haggai to speak out as he did (Hag. 1:2–11).

The command of God regarding laying the foundation of Jericho and the violation of that command also got the attention of the biblical authors. Jericho was the first city the Lord directed Israel to defeat once they had crossed the Jordan River. The reasons it had to fall were the same reasons we would have expected the Israelites to rebuild it. This city lay directly opposite an important travel artery that descended from the Transjordan and connected travelers with a natural ford of the Jordan River. Just to the west of Jericho were a variety of important travel arteries leading into the Promised Land.[24] It was unthinkable for the Israelites not to maintain a fortification there, but that is exactly what the Lord commanded, putting a curse on anyone who attempted to rebuild it (Josh. 6:26–27). Instead, Israel was to trust the Lord to be the

More recent structures in Jerusalem (below) are frequently built on foundations that date to Bible times.

guardian of their eastern gate. The violation of this command during the days of Ahab says a lot about where his trust was placed (1 Kings 16:34).

The biblical authors also speak of the earth as having a foundation that was laid by the Lord. "By wisdom the LORD laid the earth's foundations" (Prov. 3:19). This characterization of God not only points out his wisdom but also imbues him with a powerful otherness referred to in biblical poetry (Job 38:4; Pss. 102:25; 104:5; Isa. 48:13; 51:13, 16; Zech. 12:1). And because the one who lays the foundation is regarded as the owner not only of the foundation but also of the structure that rises above it, this description of the Lord certifies him as the owner of this created world (Ps. 89:11).

The concept of a foundation is used figuratively to describe the basic ideas or activities on which the Christian life is based (Matt. 7:24–27; 2 Tim. 2:19). For example, repentance is regarded as the first step toward faith. The writer to the Hebrews calls it the foundation of the Christian experience but laments those who fail to build on it (Heb. 6:1). Paul calls the teaching of the apostles and prophets the foundation that is laid beneath and that unites all believers, with Jesus as chief cornerstone (Eph. 2:20). The image changes slightly when he writes to the Corinthians: "By the grace God has given me, I laid a foundation as a wise builder, and someone else is building on it. But each one should build with care. For no one can lay any foundation other than the one already laid, which is Jesus Christ" (1 Cor. 3:10–11).

A copper foundation figurine.

Brick walls were often laid on top of fieldstone foundations.

GLEAN

The Hebrew verb *lqṭ* can signify the general gathering of stones, firewood, and even flowers (Gen. 31:46; Jer. 7:18; Song of Sol. 6:2), but most often it is used as the technical term for *glean* (translated variously in the NIV as "gather" or "glean" (Num. 11:8; 2 Kings 4:39; Ruth 2:7–8). Gleaning was part of the social contract among God's people that allowed the less fortunate in the Promised Land to gather food for personal consumption from land they did not own.[1]

The concept of private land ownership was well established among the Israelites, yet it was always conditioned by God's directives. Each tribe, clan, and family received a portion of the Promised Land that they could use to plant and harvest basic foods like grapes, olives, and grain (Joshua 13–19).[2] At the same time that the Lord saw to the distribution of this land for private use, however, he also retained the right to impose restrictions on the use of that land. That is why we encounter divine laws that required fallowing of the land every seven years, restrictions that governed the type of seed that could be planted in a field, as well as laws that required that a portion of the agricultural produce be left in the field (Exod. 23:10–11; Lev. 19:19).

Not everyone who lived in the Promised Land had direct access to farmland, due to

A grain field. By design, God wanted every family to have access to grain, whether through land ownership or gleaning rights.

changing personal circumstances, such as widows and orphans, or due to their national heritage, like the Moabite Ruth. It is for this reason that the Lord put specific regulations in place that included the right to glean in the fields. Consequently, the very edges of the grain field and fallen grain kernels were not to be collected by the landowner but instead were left for the poor and foreigners. Something similar applied to the vineyards as well. The landowner was not to go over the vines a second time or pick up individual grapes that had fallen to the ground (Lev. 19:9–10; 23:22).

This process was further defined within the traditional teachings of the Mishnah, particularly in *Peah*. There the gleanings are defined as the produce that falls to the ground as part of the harvesting process, not produce that is dropped accidentally. This tractate further states that those hired by a landowner were not permitted to glean in that field even if they were poor because they might be tempted to be less cautious in the harvesting process. And those harvesting in the vineyard

In order to provide fruit for those gleaning, vineyard owners were not to go over their vines a second time or collect grapes that had been dropped.

were cautioned to avoid putting a basket beneath the vine as they harvested to catch falling grapes, since that was regarded as stealing from the poor (Mishnah, *Peah* 7:3).[3]

When the idea of gleaning is formally mentioned by the biblical authors, whether figurative or real, it highlights the great misfortune of someone in those verses. The desperate circumstances created by a famine forced thousands to migrate to Egypt in search of food. As head of the grain supply effort, Joseph gleaned (NIV "collected") all the money to be found in Egypt and Canaan, ironically gleaning from those who had nowhere to glean at home (Gen. 47:14). King Adoni-Bezek boasted that seventy Canaanite kings were forced to glean under his table (Judg. 1:7; NIV "picked up scraps"). At the time of Elisha, another famine so parched the land of food that people gleaned not in agricultural fields but in the pastures, seeking wild herbs and vines (2 Kings 4:39; NIV "gather"). The prophet Micah bewailed his troubled state by saying, "I am like one who gathers summer fruit at the gleaning of the vineyard" (Mic. 7:1). Real gleaning in grain fields also suggests desperate circumstances—something we see particularly in the book of Ruth. In the second chapter of this book, gleaning is formally mentioned twelve times in twenty-two consecutive verses to highlight the circumstances in which Ruth and Naomi found themselves even though there was not a famine gripping the land (Ruth 2:2–3, 7–8, 15–19, 23).

The mention of gleaning can also be used rhetorically to emphasize dependence on the Lord and his gracious provision during desperate times. While the Israelites wandered in the wilderness, the planting and harvesting of grain was out of the question. Consequently, the Lord promised and provided a special food called *manna*. In Exodus 16 the process of gathering manna is repeatedly described by the Hebrew verb for gleaning (*lqt*, Exod. 16:4–5, 16–18, 21–22, 26–27; NIV "gather"). Though this gleaning is far from what we have come to know as the traditional gleaning of the poor, repetition of this verb nine times within twenty-four verses highlights Israel's dependence and God's gracious provision.

The idea of gleanings can also be used figuratively to describe the paucity of something left behind that is not grain or grapes.

The fading glory of Ephraim is likened to the gleanings left in a grain field (Isa. 17:5). The devastation of the earth during the last days will leave little behind. "So will it be on the earth and among the nations, as when an olive tree is beaten, or as when gleanings are left after the grape harvest" (Isa. 24:13). And the judgment speeches against Edom found in both Jeremiah and Obadiah ask the rhetorical question that suggests there will be very little left of that nation after the Lord allows Babylon to do its worst—less left over than one would expect after the grape harvest. "If grape pickers came to you, would they not leave a few grapes?" (Jer. 49:9; see also Obad. 1:5).

Harvesters left behind any grain they dropped for those who would glean in the field behind them.

GREET

International visitors are often caught off guard by the greeting rituals displayed in the country they are visiting. Those rituals may appear peculiar to the visitor because of their length and content and even by the nonverbal elements associated with them such as kissing, hugging, or bowing. Here our focus will be on the verbal dimension of in-person greetings rather than the greetings found in correspondence or physical gestures associated with ancient greetings.[4]

Greetings in the ancient world differed markedly from those in the modern West in terms of their breadth and length. We do not expect that our casual, "How are you doing?" will precipitate a lengthy conversation. But that is exactly the norm in the Middle East to this day. What is more, the corporate (versus individualistic) worldview virtually guarantees that the reply will take into account all of the family members, friends, and circumstances that impact the well-being of the person who has been greeted. For instance, Joseph's inquiry into the well-being of his brothers was linked to an inquiry concerning the well-being of his father (Gen. 43:27). And Moses's father-in-law's inquiry into his well-being quickly led into a recitation of the history of the Israelites over the preceding years (Exod. 18:7–8). A typical greeting formula recorded in 1 Samuel 25:6 illustrates how such a conversation was initiated: "Long life to you! Good health to you and your household! And good health to all that is yours!"

Certain phrases became part of the greeting, including the Hebrew *shalōm*. This word communicates much more than a sense of peace; it presses beyond that into an inquiry about the broader well-being of the person and all that impacts that person's life (for example, Gen. 43:27–28; Exod.

The Church of All Nations (left) is the traditional location of the most heinous greeting of all time, where Judas kissed Jesus while betraying him in the Garden of Gethsemane.

18:7; 2 Sam. 18:28). The greeting exchanged between Boaz and his workers illustrates another set of phrases employed in greeting: "The LORD be with you!" "The LORD bless you!" (Ruth 2:4). These formulas speak of the idealized life of the believer described in Psalm 1. And in the New Testament, we encounter the shortest of the greeting formulas, on par with our quick "hi" or "hey there." It is translated in the NIV as "greetings" and in the NASB as "hail" (Matt. 26:49; 28:9).

Western visitors are often taken aback not only by the smells and sounds of modern Jerusalem (above) but also by the public greeting customs.

Whether the greeting was exchanged between family, friends, or state representatives, the connotations of acceptance and harmony lingered around the meeting. So it follows that when Jesus sent out the twelve disciples, he told them to be sure to exchange greetings with those in whose homes they stayed (Matt. 10:12). The greeting between state representatives could carry with it the additional connotation of national alliance (2 Kings 10:15–17).

Most greeting exchanges that occurred in connection with Bible events are unreported, which makes those that are recorded worthy of our notice. Some are particularly noteworthy because the greeting was unreturned, taught a lesson, or was misused. When a greeting was given and not reciprocated, it was an indication that there was a problem. Saul's unauthorized sacrifice was quickly followed by the appearance of Samuel. Saul attempted to diffuse the situation with a greeting, but Samuel abandoned the expected response and instead asked a question: "What have you done?" (1 Sam. 13:11). When David's men delivered a greeting to Nabal, they waited for a response but received only an insult in reply (1 Sam. 25:5–6, 9–11, 14). And the priests at the temple in Jerusalem greeted the arriving Nicanor but received an insult from the Roman general in response (1 Macc. 7:33–34). Such unreciprocated greetings were a sign of trouble.

In the New Testament, unusual greetings occasionally became part of the lesson. For the young girl Mary, an unusual messenger joined with an unusual greeting to help mark the special conception: "The angel went to her and said, 'Greetings, you who are highly favored! The Lord is with you.' Mary was greatly troubled at his words and wondered what kind of greeting this might be" (Luke 1:28–29). The special nature of Mary's child was again emphasized when she greeted her cousin Elizabeth and both Elizabeth and her unborn child responded in a unique way to Mary's greeting (Luke 1:40–41, 44). Much later, Mary's son Jesus called for his followers to adopt new greeting customs that exceeded cultural norms to illustrate the uniqueness of the kingdom of God. "And if you greet only your own people, what are you doing more than others? Do not even pagans do that?" (Matt. 5:47). Jesus also taught how important the mission of the disciples was in spreading the gospel when he directed them to avoid the lengthy greetings that could otherwise impede their travel and give primary attention to their mission (Luke 10:4; for an Old Testament precedent, see 2 Kings 4:29).

Finally, the Bible contains examples of greetings that were misused. Jesus put the Pharisees and the teachers of the law under strict censure for the way they basked in the greetings of the general public. Those religious leaders were greeted in the marketplace in a special, distinctive way. Whether

A wood carving of the Annunciation. "Greetings, you who are highly favored! The Lord is with you" (Luke 1:28).

that had to do with being the first to receive a greeting or the use of special language for the greeting, these men were feeding their egos in unhealthy ways from the practice.

Because the disciples would find themselves faced with a similar situation, Jesus forewarned them of this temptation (Matt. 23:7; Mark 12:38; Luke 11:43; 20:46). But the most heinous greeting mentioned in the Bible is the one offered by Judas. Greetings were well-wishes; but when Judas approached Jesus in the Garden of Gethsemane, he had anything but Jesus's well-being in mind. The words, "Greetings, Rabbi!" only thinly veiled the intended betrayal (Matt. 26:49).

Jesus criticized the Jewish leaders who basked in the greetings they received in the marketplace.

GRIND

Most of the things that require grinding today can be purchased in ground form, like coffee or herbs. But in the households of the ancient Near East, items that required grinding had to be ground at home. While the Bible mentions the need to grind the ingredients to make the incense for the tabernacle (Exod. 30:36), the majority of the literal grinding mentioned in the Bible is the grinding of grain. Bread was a fundamental, daily food, and in order to make the bread, it was necessary for each household to grind grain on a daily basis (Isa. 28:28).[5] That is why there was a law that prohibited taking grinding tools as security on a debt because that would be the equivalent of removing food from the mouths of a family (Deut. 24:6).

A variety of tools were developed and evolved over time to accomplish the task of grinding grain. In all cases, the grinding was accomplished by rubbing the grain between two coarse stone surfaces. Typically, the tools were composed of two elements— one that was stationary and one that moved against its mate. The *mortar and pestle* were used to grind the incense

mentioned in Exodus 30:36, but they were also used to grind manna and grain (Num. 11:8; Prov. 27:22). The pestle was simply an oblong stone that could be held in the hand and used to pound or grind the substance in a stationary mortar; the mortar was a portable container or a recess worn into a natural stone surface. The *saddle quern* was a second device used in the Old Testament for grinding grain. The saddle was the stationary part of the tool and was approximately thirty inches long by eighteen inches wide. The quern was an oblong stone ten to fifteen inches in length. The person doing the grinding knelt in front of the saddle, spread grain on it, and then using both hands ground the grain by rubbing

A mortar and pestle (right) ground the incense used in the Israelite sanctuary.

the quern back and forth on the saddle.[6] Another type of mill involved grinding with rotation.[7] The *rotary hand mill* consisted of two circular stones, eighteen to twenty-four inches in diameter, with one resting on top of the other. Each stone had a hole in the center so that a wooden axle could be used to maintain the stones' orientation as the top stone rotated over the stationary lower stone. The operators placed grain between the two halves of the mill and then two individuals sat facing each other and applied force to the single wooden handle attached to the upper stone, rotating it to create the milling action (Matt. 24:41). Finally, we have the *donkey mill*—the largest of the mills, standing as tall as three feet. The lower, stationary stone rose to form a cone shape over which the rotating, hourglass-shaped stone was placed. Grain was poured into the top of the hollow upper stone. As a donkey turned this heavy upper millstone, the flour trickled out the bottom.

Grinding grain for the baking of daily bread was a normal activity in Bible times.

No matter which type of mill was used to grind the grain, two important connotations are linked to the process: First, the sound of grinding was heard every morning and became a symbol for life in its normal rhythm. Thus on the Lord's return, "two women will be grinding with a hand mill" (Matt. 24:41). The inspired poet likened his daily study of the law to the daily grinding of grain (Ps. 119:20; NIV "consumed with"). In describing the aging process, another poet noted that when one's hearing goes (poetically depicted as closing the door to the street), then the normal sounds of daily life, "the sound of grinding," fade (Eccles. 12:4). Judgment speeches also used this connotation of grinding to indicate that

The donkey mill typically employed an animal to turn the heavy upper stone around the mill's base.

themselves above such a task are pictured as grinding grain (Samson, Judg. 16:21; "queen city of the Babylonians," Isa. 47:1–2; young men, Lam. 5:13).

Figurative grinding is also found in the Bible. The two stones of the saddle quern in Job 31:10 stand for a man and woman having sexual intercourse. Job declared that if he had been unfaithful to his wife, "then may my wife grind another man's grain."[8] A fool and his folly are so intertwined that even grinding such a person would not separate him from his ungodliness. "Though you grind a fool in a mortar, grinding them like grain with a pestle, you will not remove their folly from them" (Prov. 27:22). And finally, grinding becomes a metaphor for the violence that can be done to another person. The Lord asks, "What do you mean by crushing my people and grinding the faces of the poor?" (Isa. 3:15).

life as normal would end; that is, the "sound of millstones" would be banished (Jer. 25:10; see also Rev. 18:22).

The image of grinding was also employed by the biblical authors to describe the hardship that had come on the free male members of a community. Grinding was most often done by slaves, servants, or women. But when difficult days arose, society was turned upside down, and those who had formerly considered

A woman crushing grain with a saddle quern.

HAND
(TO RAISE OR STRETCH OUT)

As students, we learned to raise our hand in the classroom to gain recognition to speak. The en masse raising of hands at a sporting event signals celebration. Neither of these forms of hand raising are apparent in the art and literature of the ancient Near East, but we do find both mortals and gods depicted with uplifted hands in a variety of scenarios.

Mortals are pictured as raising a hand when taking an oath, offering a blessing, attacking an opponent, or praying.[1] Abram refused to accept the plunder he had rightfully won in combat, saying instead to the king of Sodom, "With raised hand I have sworn an oath to the LORD, God Most High, Creator of heaven and earth, that I will accept nothing belonging to you" (Gen. 14:22–23; see also Rev. 10:5). Uplifted hands accompanied not only an oath but the blessing given by Aaron on all Israel (Lev. 9:22).

Ironically, the raised hand is also associated with bringing harm. Weapons used in

A raised hand carried the connotation of violence, as it does in this relief depicting the Hittite storm god.

hand-to-hand combat were often raised so that the arm functioned as a lever that added force to the downward blow. Although Saul saw David as a competitor for the throne, he would not personally "raise a hand against him." Instead Saul arranged for David to be put in harm's way, hoping that the Philistines would end his life (1 Sam. 18:17; see also 22:17).

Frequently, raised hands are connected with worship, perhaps a gesture that began naturally as the supplicant reached in the direction of heaven for assistance (1 Kings 8:22, 38, 54; Ezra 9:5–6; and especially Pss. 28:2; 63:4; 134:2; Lam. 2:19). "May my prayer be set before you like incense; may the lifting up of my hands be like the evening sacrifice" (Ps. 141:2).

Apart from these examples of literally raising hands, we also find biblical examples of this action in two related figures of speech. The mutinous revolt against established authority is described as raising one's hand against a sitting ruler. Shortly after David survived the coup attempt of Absalom, Sheba initiated a revolt against David (2 Sam. 20:1). Joab characterized this act of aggression by stating that Sheba had "lifted up his hand against the king" (2 Sam. 20:21; see also 18:28; Ezra 6:12). The violence behind this figure of speech is also present in the figurative raising of the hand against the less fortunate—in other words, mistreating them in some fashion. In defending his innocence, Job said, "If I have raised my hand against the fatherless, knowing that I had influence in court, then let my arm fall from the shoulder, let it be broken off at the joint" (Job 31:21–22).

As a spirit, God himself does not literally have hands to raise, but he figuratively raises his hands when he is described as taking an oath or commencing aggressive acts against opposition. In addition, he often is pictured with an upraised hand when the promise of the land is in view. Given the power that resided in Egypt, the slave-class Israelites appeared to have no hope of ever returning to the

The Promised Land. "I will bring you to the land I swore with uplifted hand to give to Abraham, to Isaac and to Jacob" (Exod. 6:8).

Aaron lifted his hands when blessing God's people. The priestly benediction of Numbers 6:24–26 is contained on this late seventh century BC scroll discovered at Ketef Hinnom in Jerusalem.

Promised Land. But God emphatically assured them, "I will bring you to the land I swore with uplifted hand to give to Abraham, to Isaac and to Jacob" (Exod. 6:8; see also Neh. 9:15). Following the exodus and the Israelites' refusal to enter the land as God directed, a near parallel statement with the same powerful image bars access to a rebellious generation: "Not one of you will enter the land I swore with uplifted hand to make your home" (Num. 14:30; see also Ps. 106:26). As mortals put weapons in their hands to harm one another, so the gods of the ancient Near East were stylized with weapons in a raised hand poised to strike.[2] In the Bible,

God is pictured in this pose when he is ready to strike those who rebel against him or to fight in defense of the helpless (Pss. 10:12; 118:13–16; Isa. 5:25; 10:4; 19:16).

The book of Exodus is particularly rich in this imagery, perhaps because the rulers of Egypt were associated with this posture to demonstrate their power.[3] Thus the powerful plagues directed against Egypt were often linked to the Lord's upraised arm, which often became the surrogate hand of either Aaron or Moses. This was the gesture that initiated many of the plagues as well as the gesture that opened the Red Sea before the fleeing Israelites (Exod. 3:20; 7:5, 19; 8:6, 17; 9:15, 22; 10:12, 21; 14:16).[4] The raised hands of Moses, at times supported by Aaron and Hur, marked the divine presence in the battle against the Amalekites as well (Exod. 17:11–16).

Finally, the uplifted hand of the Lord is also employed in two refrains—one speaks of the escalating judgments the Lord's raised hand will bring down on the Israelites (Isa. 9:12, 17, 21), while the other characterizes a series of oaths the Lord made to Israel (Ezek. 20:5, 15, 23, 42).

Raised hands sometimes carried the connotation of deep grief.

HARVEST
(REAP)

Growing food was a necessity for most people living in Bible times. Virtually everyone was intimately connected with the family grain and fruit production that provided ancient households with their food. Consequently, the harvest was a familiar, annual event that became part of the regular rhythm of life (Jer. 40:9–10). When the grapes and dates reached maturity or the grain plants dried sufficiently to allow for easier separation of the grain kernel from the stalk, the harvest began. It may be more accurate to characterize harvest in the plural because various commodities were harvested during different months of the year. Even the harvest of a particular crop could vary with the elevation at which it was grown and the climate of that particular year, but the following generally remained true.[5] The barley harvest commenced in the middle of April with the wheat harvest following just a few weeks later. All grain harvesting was done by hand, either using a sickle or pulling the plants up by the roots.[6] Figs, dates, pomegranates, and grapes were handpicked at the end of the summer

Moisture-rich pomegranates are harvested in the summer.

months. And the olives were knocked from the trees with long sticks starting about mid-September (Isa. 24:13). This harvesting cycle was so well known that it became one way to reference the time of year or observe the passage of time (Josh. 3:15; Judg. 15:1; 1 Sam. 6:13; 12:17; 2 Sam. 21:9–10; Jer. 8:20).

The Bible's authors looked beyond technique and science for the cause of a successful grain or fruit harvest; they consistently linked it to the Lord (Pss. 67:6; 85:12; 107:37–38; Jer. 5:24). Consequently, three religious festivals were collocated on the calendar with harvest events: Passover during the barley harvest, the Feast of Weeks (Pentecost) with the wheat harvest, and the Feast of Tabernacles (Booths) with the summer fruit harvest (Exod. 23:14–17). Obedience to the law required that no harvesting be done on certain days or in certain years, trusting that the Lord would provide even when the fields were idle (Exod. 23:10; 34:21; Lev. 25:5, 11, 20–22). And in response to the leading of the law, the prophets drew a connection between covenant obedience and a successful harvest (Lev. 26:5, 10; Deut. 28:38; Jer. 5:17; 8:13; 12:13; Amos 9:13; Mic. 6:15; Hag. 1:6). Thus harvesting in Bible times was intimately linked to the religious worldview and was not merely a secular enterprise.

By the time the harvest began, it was apparent that the food supply for the year ahead had been secured, making the harvest season a time that was imbued with hope and joy, particularly if the expected grain harvest of ten to fifteen times the amount planted grew to one-hundred-fold (Gen. 26:12; Matt. 13:8). Such joy filled the harvest season even if it had been preceded by a time of grief. "Those who sow with tears will reap with songs of joy" (Ps. 126:5). In the book of Ruth, the harvest provided an important backdrop to Naomi's changing circumstances. She returned from Moab at the celebrative season of the barley harvest, but she was so undone by her life's circumstances that even this joyous season could not lift her spirits (Ruth 1:20–22). It was not long, however, before hope and joy overcame her bitter pain throughout the remaining grain harvest season as the romance of Ruth and Boaz unfolded in the grain fields outside Bethlehem (Ruth 2–4).

The figurative uses of the harvest are all linked to natural expectations associated with it. First, the harvest was a time-sensitive

Darnel weeds. Certain immature grain plants and weeds look very similar, just as believers and unbelievers can. Jesus urged the disciples to allow "wheat" and "weeds" to grow together until the final harvest (Matt. 13:30).

operation that had to be accomplished in a timely way. Thus the harvest became a metaphor for seizing the opportune moment (Prov. 6:6–8; 10:5). This is the premise that underlies Jesus's depiction of society as a ripe grain field awaiting the disciples. "Don't you have a saying, 'It's still four months until harvest'? I tell you, open your eyes and look at the fields! They are ripe for harvest" (John 4:35; see also Matt. 9:37–38; Rom. 1:13).

At the human level, there was a general expectation that when the appropriate preparation and care were given to an agricultural field or vineyard, a good harvest would result (Isa. 5:1–4). Conversely, poor planning or maintenance resulted in a poor harvest. This led to the axiom, "A man reaps what he sows" (Gal. 6:7), evidenced not just in the agricultural fields but in the moral arena as well. Those who live their lives according to God's design will generally enjoy better outcomes in their daily living than those who choose to live otherwise. "A wicked person earns deceptive wages,

The harvest of these date palms occurs just before the fall plowing season begins.

but the one who sows righteousness reaps a sure reward" (Prov. 11:18; see also 22:8; Hosea 8:7; 10:12–13). "Let us not become weary in doing good, for at the proper time we will reap a harvest if we do not give up" (Gal. 6:9).

Finally, because the harvest marked the end of a long process that started with plowing months earlier, it became a metaphor for judgment. This could be a judgment that would occur during the course of this world's history or at its close: "Also for you, Judah, a harvest is appointed" (Hosea 6:11; see also Isa. 17:5; 18:4–5). By contrast, Jesus told his disciples that they were not to spend their time separating the "wheat" from the "weeds" but to allow both to "grow together until the harvest" at the end of time (Matt. 13:30, 39; see also Joel 3:13; Rev. 14:15–16).

This shelter was built by a Jewish family in celebration of the Feast of Tabernacles, the ancient religious festival that occurs at the time of the summer fruit harvest.

HUNT

Permission to hunt wild animals was given immediately after Noah and his family stepped off the ark (Gen. 9:2–3). And by the time the Israelites arrived at Mount Sinai, it is presumed that a culture of hunting existed and was tacitly approved in the dietary laws that mentioned the need to properly field dress animals by draining their blood (Lev. 17:10–14). From this point on we find hunting mentioned either directly or by reference to various devices or weapons used by hunters.

People hunted for a variety of reasons and used a variety of devices in the process. Ritually clean animals such as partridges, deer, gazelles, and ibex were hunted as food. Bears and lions were hunted when they became threats to the livestock (1 Sam. 17:34–36). And evidence drawn from Egyptian and Assyrian reliefs

suggests that the royals engaged in hunting as a sport.

Each of these hunted animals was designed by God with special skills that assisted in their survival. For some it was the ability to fly or to flee with lightning-fast bursts of speed. For others it was their sheer strength that enabled them to prevail in a fight. Successful hunters developed methods that countered these defensive skills in a number of ways.[7] Fine mesh bird nets with weights tied around the perimeter were carefully hung in tree branches with a tripping mechanism attached. The hunter then baited the area beneath the branch and

This relief depicts an Assyrian deer hunt that employed nets.

waited for the prey to be in the right position before triggering the collapse of the net over it (Ps. 124:7; Prov. 1:17; Jer. 5:26). Nets were also used to capture swift deer and gazelle. In this case, the hunter looked for a place where the natural features of the land created a narrowing corridor into which fleeing animals could be funneled. At the end of the corridor a camouflaged, vertical net was hung in place. The goal of the hunter was to panic the animals into fleeing toward the restricted space, where they would become entangled in the net (Ps. 141:10; Isa. 51:20). Another method of hunting animals was using a pit trap. As the name suggests, the hunter dug a pit and then covered it with camouflage to make it look like the surrounding space. When the animals were driven or lured to the trap, their weight collapsed the apparently solid cover and held them in a confined space from which they could not escape (2 Sam. 23:20). Hand thrown or operated weapons were also used either in conjunction with or independently of these traps. These weapons included the throwing stick used to knock birds from the air,[8] the javelin, and the bow and arrow (Gen. 27:3).

An Egyptian hunting birds from a boat in the Nile marsh.

As the story of God's love advanced in the Promised Land, that real estate became increasingly settled. As the land was converted from its natural state into farm fields and pastures, it became less hospitable for wild game at the same time that there was less time to devote to hunting.[9] While the practice and imagery of hunting were not extinguished from the common vocabulary, they grew less common. Thus the connotation of specialness became attached to the hunter and grew into a way for the biblical authors to define someone as special. We see this with hunters like Nimrod and Esau (Gen. 10:9; 27:3, 5, 27, 30, 33). And because lions were considered the ultimate hunters (Job 10:16; 38:39), those who overcame them were marked for special mention—such as Samson, David, and Benaiah (Judg. 14:5–6; 1 Sam. 17:34–36; 2 Sam. 23:20).

The same vocabulary that is used of humans hunting animals can be used figuratively for mortals or God himself hunting down people. David used his prowess as a hunter of large predators in his attempt to convince Saul that he was worthy of entering the fight against Goliath. But later it was David who became the prey as Saul ruthlessly pursued him "as one hunts a partridge in the mountains" (1 Sam. 26:20; see also 24:11). The poetry of the prophets and psalms also used images of hunting to describe the way in which the wicked sought to harm the righteous. Like hunters, they figuratively set traps, dug pits, spread out nets, and lay snares to bring harm to those who were vulnerable (Pss. 31:4; 35:7–8; 140:5; 141:9; 142:3). The adulteress hunted down her next target to prey upon (Prov. 6:26). Micah described the bloodlust violence around him by saying, "They hunt each other with nets" (Mic. 7:2). And Jeremiah lamented, "Among my people are the wicked who lie in wait like men who snare birds and like those who set traps to catch people" (Jer. 5:26).

Finally, God or his empire agents were also likened to hunters. Job decried the fact that the Lord was stalking him like a lion (Job 10:16). Isaiah prophesied that the Lord would eventually target Babylon, pursuing them like a gazelle (Isa. 13:14)—but not before the Babylonians punished the Israelites for their covenant violations. The prophets repeatedly painted Babylon as a relentless hunter who hunted "them down on every mountain and hill and from the crevices of the rocks" (Jer. 16:16). The Lord said, "I will spread my net

Those who maliciously seek to harm others are depicted as hunters who lay traps and snares, as shown here.

for him [the king], and he will be caught in my snare. I will bring him to Babylon and execute judgment on him" (Ezek. 17:20; see also 12:13). The Babylonians stalked God's people on every street (Lam. 4:18), leading one victim to state, "Those who were my enemies without cause hunted me like a bird. They tried to end my life in a pit and threw stones at me" (Lam. 3:52–53).

Those who kill lions are called out for special notice, such as Samson, who killed a lion in the Sorek Valley (below).

The Baker Illustrated Guide to Everyday Life in Bible Times

INHERIT

The Bible speaks to all of life's issues, including the realities of death and the need to pass personal property to one's heirs. This process that was guided by ancient custom as well as law is mentioned in both literal and figurative settings.

Ideally, when a father died, his home and personal property transferred quickly and easily to his heirs (Prov. 13:22; 19:14). That process is addressed in the narratives and laws of the Bible, largely reflecting the culture described in other ancient Near Eastern law codes.[1] The sons were the direct heirs of the estate, and each of them received an equal share, with the exception of the oldest brother, who was given a double share (Deut. 21:15–17). Daughters did not formally receive a share in the inheritance even if there were no sons (Gen. 31:14; but see the exception in Job 42:15). This practice may have been motivated by the reality that the daughters of a household received their share of the inheritance in the form of a dowry.[2] A widow was not eligible to receive a share in the estate but was cared for by her oldest son, who had received the double share. If the husband died without a son and his wife was still of childbearing age, then a brother of the deceased man had the responsibility to marry the widow and father a son, who would then inherit the estate of the deceased man (Deut. 25:5–6).

A number of special cases are also mentioned in the Bible. If a man died childless, his inheritance moved to his brothers or his uncles, or failing that to his nearest relative (Num. 27:9–11). This might mean Abram was using hyperbole when he said that his inheritance would likely pass to a trusted servant (Gen. 15:2). The sons of servant wives were not automatically counted among the heirs unless they were formally adopted. This appears to be the case in Jacob's family, in which the sons of both wives and servant wives were treated equally (Gen. 35:23–26; 49:1–28). And this was what Sarah tried to avoid by banishing

Inheritance law governed all personal property, even the clay vessels that were employed in the home.

Hagar and Ishmael from the family compound (Gen. 21:10). If a family was only blessed with daughters, the daughters could become heirs of the estate thanks to the legislation put in place to meet the needs of Zelophehad's daughters (Num. 27:1–11); the only restriction was that they had to marry within the family clan (Numbers 36).

Over against these expectations, the Bible mentions unfortunate and ungodly circumstances in which property of the deceased did not move in the expected fashion but rather was confiscated by the king (1 Kings 21:15–16) or sought by scoundrels who murdered potential heirs (Matt. 21:38). Micah deplored the social injustices he observed, which included defrauding heirs (Mic. 2:2), and the inspired poet of Lamentations mourned when his inheritance passed to foreigners who had invaded the land (Lam. 5:2).

Biblical references to inheriting occur most often in figures of speech—in cases in which what was inherited was not concrete, the grantor of the inheritance had not died, or both of these conditions applied. Though the Bible characterizes the land owned by non-Jewish nations as their inheritance received from the Lord (Deut. 32:8), the most frequent mention of land as an inheritance from the Lord is connected with the nation of Israel. It was a promise issued to Abraham and recalled by Moses (Lev. 20:24) that became the focused mission of Joshua and the reason that the conquest of Canaan was successful (Josh. 1:6; and more than fifty times throughout the Bible). "So Joshua took the entire land, just as the LORD had directed Moses, and he gave it as an inheritance to Israel according to their tribal divisions" (Josh. 11:23).

An inheritance was a deeply cherished possession, and that is the sense that most clearly informs the figure of speech. The Bible acknowledges that God created and cares for the people of all nations, but there was something very special about the people of Israel. Thus this striking term of

Inheritance law directed not just the transfer of land but also the houses that were built on the land.

endearment was used when speaking of the people of Israel—the Lord's own inheritance (Exod. 34:9; Deut. 9:26, 29; 32:9; 1 Kings 8:51, 53; Pss. 28:9; 33:12; Jer. 10:16). Reciprocally, the Levites, who did not receive land for their tribe, were reminded that the Lord was their inheritance (Num. 18:20).

Because law and custom combined to create a clear path for inheritance proceedings to follow, the notion of inheriting also became linked to the sense of destiny. "The wise inherit honor, but fools get only shame" (Prov. 3:35). "The simple inherit folly, but the prudent are crowned with knowledge" (Prov. 14:18). Perhaps this is what lies behind Elisha's request that he "inherit a double portion of [Elijah's] spirit" in carrying forward the ministry of Elijah (2 Kings 2:9).

The Lord reminds us through John that we are regarded and will be treated as God's children, who are destined to receive the promised inheritance (Rev. 21:7). When the New Testament writers speak of what that inheritance is, they most often speak about it as the kingdom of God or eternal life (Matt. 25:34; Mark 10:17; 1 Cor. 6:9–10; 15:50; Gal. 5:21; Eph. 5:5). Jesus contrasts what we will receive with what we may have given up: "And everyone who has left houses or brothers or sisters or father or mother or wife or children or fields for my sake will receive a hundred times as much and will inherit eternal life" (Matt. 19:29). The kingdom we inherit will be much more wonderful and enduring than any inheritance we may obtain on earth, "an inheritance that can never perish, spoil or fade. This inheritance is kept in heaven for you" (1 Pet. 1:4).

The family animals were among the most valued of possessions and so were included among the items inherited upon the death of the owner.

KISS

oday a wave, handshake, hug, and kiss can mark varying degrees of intimacy in a relationship. In the ancient Near East the meaning of a kiss could overlap with many of these. Its message was determined by a number of variables, including whether the kiss was given on the hand, mouth, or cheek or if the person kissed the ground (Song of Sol. 1:2; Sir. 29:5),[1] as well as the length of the kiss, the gestures associated with the kiss, the social relationship of the ones exchanging the kiss, and whether the setting for the kiss was public or private.

In general we can speak of four categories of kissing: (1) the greeting kiss, (2) the departure kiss, (3) the kiss of respect, and (4) the erotic kiss. Friends and family members were often described as greeting one another with a kiss (Gen. 29:11–13; Exod. 4:27). Note that this kiss might have been accompanied by a respectful bow when someone of lower social status was acknowledging his or her position before a superior (Gen. 33:3–4; Exod. 18:7). The greeting kiss delivered the connotation of acceptance, so it was mentioned particularly in contexts where relational tension had been resolved and was often connected with a heartfelt embrace (Gen. 33:4; 45:14–15; 48:10; Luke 15:20).

The antithesis to the greeting kiss is the departure kiss (Gen. 31:55; 2 Sam. 19:39; 1 Kings 19:20; see also Gen. 31:28). This kiss connoted the connection that endured even when the two were separated by distance or death. This is the kiss that Joseph gave to the cooling body of Jacob as death separated father and son; the kiss that Naomi gave to her daughters-in-law as she planned to leave them, but which Ruth could not bring herself to give in return; the kiss that David and Jonathan exchanged when it became clear that the realities

A subject could show deference to a king whose authority he recognized by kissing his feet.

of life would keep them apart; and the kiss that the Ephesian Christians gave Paul, knowing that they would not see him again (Gen. 50:1; Ruth 1:9, 14; 1 Sam. 20:41; Acts 20:37).

The kiss was also a way of showing respect to someone who was socially superior. It was customary in the ancient Near East to kiss the ground before a king.[2] After anointing Saul as Israel's king, Samuel may have delivered this kind of kiss in front of Saul (1 Sam. 10:1), and it is also the kiss the psalmist called for the kings of all nations to render to God's Son (Ps. 2:12). And it was customary for students of a rabbi to kiss their teacher in respect.[3] In an ironic twist, it was the sign Judas used to betray his teacher, kissing him to indicate the one the mob should arrest (Matt. 26:48–49). Though this kiss was not typically delivered to the feet of the rabbi, the sinful woman mentioned by Luke repeatedly kissed Jesus's feet as he reclined at dinner. When objections were raised, Jesus pointed out that she was the only one who had recognized him in this way. In fact, the host of the meal had not even greeted him with the traditional greeting kiss when he arrived (Luke 7:38, 45). In contrast, the kiss of respect

A greeting becomes a betrayal when Judas kisses Jesus in the Garden of Gethsemane.

delivered to the feet of or on the ground before an idol was a pagan worship practice from which the biblical authors recoiled (1 Kings 19:18; Job 31:26–27; Hosea 13:2).

Finally, there is the erotic kiss on the lips as foreplay to more intimate acts to follow. The adulteress used this private kiss in the open streets in an effort to lure her next paramour into bed with her (Prov. 7:13). This was the kiss that the lover longed to share privately with her beloved, but she found herself prevented from having even the most innocent kiss with him in public. "Let him kiss me with the kisses of his mouth—for your love is more delightful than wine" (Song of Sol. 1:2; but see 8:1).

Special mention is deserved for three other types of kisses reported in the Bible: the kiss that was deceptive in nature, the holy kiss between believers in the early church, and the figurative kiss. The first reference to the deceptive kiss was when Jacob kissed his father pretending to be his brother in a bid to steal his brother's birthright (Gen. 27:26–27). Later, Absalom had been welcomed back into the good graces of his father with a greeting

An Assyrian soldier subdues his enemy. In similar fashion, Joab grabbed Amasa's beard and drew him closer to give him a greeting kiss, deflecting Amasa's attention away from the dagger in Joab's other hand (2 Sam. 20:9–10).

kiss (2 Sam. 14:33), but shortly afterward he used a kiss to foster a revolt against his father. "Whenever anyone approached him to bow down before him, Absalom would reach out his hand, take hold of him and kiss him" (2 Sam. 15:5). And Amasa thought that Joab was delivering a friendly greeting kiss, but it was only meant to distract his attention from the knife in Joab's other hand (2 Sam. 20:9–10).

The encouragement to "greet one another with a holy kiss" is mentioned frequently in the closing of New Testament letters (Rom. 16:16; 1 Cor. 16:20; 2 Cor. 13:12; 1 Thess. 5:26; and perhaps 1 Pet. 5:14). This kiss was used by the early Christian community to show their connection to one another through Christ.

This leaves the figurative kiss, which is used in three ways: (1) The ideal world is described as one in which "righteousness and peace kiss each other" (Ps. 85:10). (2) An honest answer is as desirable as an erotic kiss on the lips (Prov. 24:26). (3) The truism that criticism from friends can hurt but is more helpful than the compliments of enemies is captured in this metaphor: "Wounds from a friend can be trusted, but an enemy multiplies kisses" (Prov. 27:6).

The erotic kiss is part of the Bible in the Song of Solomon.

LAMP
(TO LIGHT A)

For the ancients, the lighting of an oil lamp was akin to flipping on a light switch in our home today. The act was so ordinary that it easily got lost in the many details of the day (Jer. 25:10). But when we put lamp lighting in the context of the larger biblical presentation of light and darkness, we find this ordinary act filled with new and deeper meaning mentioned in both literal and figurative contexts.

God created some of his creatures with strong night adaptation skills, but humans were not among them. It takes upward of thirty minutes for our eyes to fully adjust to a dark environment. Even when fully adjusted to night, our vision is a poor semblance of what it is in daylight, lacking in sharpness, color resolution, and depth perception. So we know what it means to grope around in the dark (Job 12:25). And we can understand the need for people in a world before electricity to work while it is day, for the night is coming when no one can work (John 9:4).

The earliest lamps were open bowls with a pinched notch that held the wick.

In response, the Lord created one of the great mysteries of this world: light (Gen. 1:3–5; Job 38:19). Because light is the fundamental building block of all life on our planet, the Lord's first act in transitioning the amorphous raw materials of the created world into the working whole we enjoy was the creation of light (Gen. 1:3–4; Ps. 136:7–9). He also provided the raw materials and creative skills that led to the development of lamps that allowed people to extend their effective working time into the night. The first ancient lamp was an open clay bowl, about the size of a cereal bowl, that had from one to four V-shaped notches pinched around the rim.[1] The bowl was filled with olive oil and a flax wick was draped through one or more of the notches. The wick drew the fuel to its tip where the oil was ignited to produce a low-power but efficient source of light. These simple lamps changed shape throughout Bible times,[2] but they always faced the same limitations: the oil had to be replenished and the wick had to be pulled out or trimmed as it was consumed (Prov. 31:18; Matt. 25:1–4, 7). When this was done, the oil lamp provided artificial illumination in the home at night, for searching dark corners during daylight hours, and for walking outside in the dark (Matt. 5:15; 25:1; Luke 15:8).

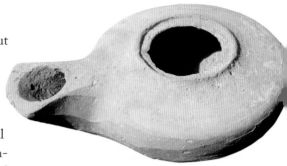

During the New Testament era, a lamp was an enclosed basin with a hollow spout for the wick.

In addition to natural and artificial light, we also read of a special divine light. By definition, God is intimately linked to light. "The LORD wraps himself in light," and he resides "in unapproachable light" (Ps. 104:2; 1 Tim. 6:16; see also Isa. 60:1–2; Matt. 4:16; John 12:46; Rev. 21:23). This reality is illustrated in the Old Testament worship facilities of Israel. Within the enclosed Holy Place of the tabernacle and the temple was a special lamp. At one time God filled the room with his divine light directly (Exod. 40:34–35). But as an ongoing reminder of the Lord's presence, there was a seven-branched candlestick that constantly provided light in this enclosed space (Exod. 25:31–37; 1 Kings 7:49). This was in addition to other oil lamps in the Holy Place that were lit when the sun set (Exod. 30:8; 2 Chron. 13:11). Thus the ever-burning menorah was more than a mere source of light in this room (Lev. 24:2); it was a reminder of the Lord's presence in this place—the one true God who exudes light as part of his very essence.

The seven-branched candlestick provided light for the sanctuary and was a constant reminder of the Lord's presence there among his people.

Consequently, darkness became a problem that required solving not just in the physical world but in the spiritual realm as well. "This is the message we have heard from him and declare to you: God is light; in him there is no darkness at all. If we claim to have fellowship with him yet walk in the darkness, we lie and do not live by the truth" (1 John 1:5–6; see also Rom. 13:12; Col. 1:13).

Used as a metaphor for God, his Word, and the life of the Christian, the lighted lamp combats this darkness. The Lord is not just divine light; he becomes the vehicle that conveys that divine light: "You, LORD, are my lamp; the LORD turns my darkness into light" (2 Sam. 22:29; see also Job 29:3). But even more frequently the lighted lamp was used as a metaphor for the Word of God that he shares with us: "Your word is a lamp for my feet, a light on my path" (Ps. 119:105). "For God, who said, 'Let light shine out of darkness,' made his light shine in our hearts to give us the light of the knowledge of God's glory displayed in the face of Christ" (2 Cor. 4:6). "For this command is a lamp, this teaching is a light" (Prov. 6:23).

Jesus also mentioned the lighting of a lamp on several occasions when speaking about the lives of the disciples. He urged the disciples to let their new life in him glow in their works: "Neither do people light a lamp and put it under a bowl. Instead they put it on its stand, and it gives light to everyone in the house. In the same way, let your light shine before others" (Matt. 5:15–16). The disciples were to let their message glow for others to see because "no one lights a lamp and hides it in a clay jar or puts it under a bed" (Luke 8:16). And as the disciples let the light of this lamp flow outward, Jesus also encouraged them to let it flow inward in order to change them to the very core of their being (Luke 11:34–36).

An Old Testament lamp. "Your word is a lamp for my feet, a light on my path" (Ps. 119:105).

LAY ON HANDS

When we gently lay a hand on the head of our child or on the shoulder of our spouse, this gesture communicates love and affection through touch. That same gesture carried a variety of connotations in the biblical world, depending on the social setting and the participants involved.

In the religious world, this gesture was most often associated with ritual animal sacrifice. When God's people brought a bull or another animal from the flock to offer in connection with the burnt, sin, or fellowship offerings, the worshipers placed their hands on the head of the animal before its life was taken (Exod. 29:10, 15; Lev. 1:4; 3:2, 8, 13; 4:4, 15, 24, 29, 33; 8:14, 18, 22). This highly personal gesture built a bridge between the worshiper and the sacrifice, marking the animal as belonging to the worshiper or as the substitute for the one who laid the hand on the animal.[3] In a similar way, the Levites were separated from the people as religious leaders when the Israelites laid their hands on them (Num. 8:10). While the Levites were not slaughtered in connection with a ritual sacrifice as the animals were, they became substitutes commissioned for divine service in place of the firstborn male child of every Israelite woman (Num. 8:16–18). There was only one instance when this gesture was formally linked to the transfer of sin guilt; that occurred on the Day of Atonement. Two goats were selected and one was sacrificed as a sin offering in the usual way. But the other, the scapegoat, was designated to carry the sins of the people away into the desert (Lev. 16:10). Before this goat was led away, the sins of the people were symbolically transferred to the animal as the high priest laid his hands on

When Peter and John placed their hands on the people living in Samaria (below), the people received the Holy Spirit (Acts 8:17).

The Baker Illustrated Guide to Everyday Life in Bible Times

the head of the scapegoat and confessed the sins of the people (Lev. 16:20–22).

The biblical authors also mentioned this gesture in connection with the designation of leaders. Moses was directed to lay his hands on Joshua and commission him as his successor (Num. 27:18, 23; Deut. 34:9). In the early Christian church, the apostles laid their hands on new leaders in the church such as Stephen, Barnabas, Paul, and Timothy (Acts 6:5–6; 13:2–3; 1 Tim. 4:14; 5:22).

The same gesture used in connection with sacrifice and commissioning was also employed during miraculous healings, whether physical or spiritual. Naaman, the Gentile general, expected Elisha to come out of his house and wave his hand over the spot where he had leprosy (2 Kings 5:11). A similar gesture accompanied magical healing in Hellenistic religions.[4] But when Jesus put his hands on those who were sick, disabled, or unable to hear or see, it was the touch of God himself, and the power of God flowed into their lives and made them whole again (Mark 5:23; 6:5; 7:32; 8:23–25; Luke 4:40; 13:13). This gesture was also linked to the imparting of the Holy Spirit, marking the spiritual healing that had come into their lives (Acts 8:17–19; 19:6; 2 Tim. 1:6).

Ironically, this gesture that had such positive connotations was also deployed as a symbol of violent acts against a person. This connotation may stem, in part, from its association with the execution of a blasphemer. The penalty for blasphemy was death by stoning. All those who heard the individual commit the crime had to "lay their hands on his head," and the entire assembly participated in the execution (Lev. 24:14). This gesture also symbolized other violent actions as one person harmed

Israelites built a bridge between themselves and the sacrificial animal they were offering by placing their hands on the animal's head.

another (Gen. 22:12; Josh. 2:19; Job 30:24; Luke 22:53; John 7:30, 44). Less frequently but just as powerfully, this symbolic language was used to describe the manner in which the Lord would bring judgment on a nation that opposed the advance of his kingdom plan (Exod. 7:4; Ezek. 39:21).

The book of 1 Samuel makes interesting and noteworthy use of this image; it becomes another tool used by the biblical author to advance the case for David's accession to the throne of Israel in place of Saul. Jonathan, the son of Saul, introduced the image by offering David this reassuring encouragement: "'Don't be afraid,' he said. 'My father Saul will not lay a hand on you'" (1 Sam. 23:17). Nothing could be further from the truth. Saul relentlessly pursued David, doing all he could to violently lay his hands on the one perceived to be the competitor for his throne. Ironically, it was David who frequently had the chance to harm Saul; yet over and over again David refused to "lay a hand on" the divinely anointed king (1 Sam. 24:6, 10; 26:9, 11, 23).

Saul is diminished in the reader's eyes as he repeatedly attempted to lay hands on David in a violent manner, contrary to the expectation expressed by Jonathan. And David is elevated in our eyes as he repeatedly passed up the opportunity to lay his hands on Saul, even when it appeared to be the way in which the Lord had offered a clear path to assuming leadership of God's people.[5]

Jesus frequently laid his hands on those he was healing.

LOTS
(TO CAST)

Important decisions call for divine input. Today that means we add prayer and the counsel of godly friends to the process of rationally weighing our options. The Bible mentions a device called the *lot* that was often used to solicit God's direction regarding an important decision: "The lot is cast into the lap, but its every decision is from the Lord" (Prov. 16:33).

When we combine the biblical descriptions of this mechanism with the archaeological evidence, it appears that the word *lot* refers to a category of devices that could take a variety of forms and could be manipulated in a variety of ways. The lot always consisted of more than one piece. Some lots, like Urim and Thummim, consisted of two pieces—one designed to give a *yes* answer and another to provide a *no* answer (Exod. 28:30; Lev. 8:8). The Bible also speaks of the casting of lots where up to seven pieces appeared sequentially one after the other (Josh. 18:11; 19:1, 10, 17, 24, 32, 40). Archaeologists have discovered a variety of physical items that they have identified as ancient lots. These include pebbles, pieces of wood and bone, as well as potsherds

The casting of lots is mentioned frequently during the final division of the land among the Israelites at Shiloh (below).

on which there is writing.[6] These devices produced an answer to a question that was posed just before they were manipulated. That manipulation is variously described as causing to fall, coming out, throwing, going up, pulling out, and sending.[7]

The term *lot* may designate a category of devices that include dice.

With the evidence we have, it appears that lots delivered their message in one of three ways; in each case a particular person, group, or option was assigned to an individual lot or portion of a lot. (1) Without looking, an individual extracted one of the lots from a pouch to determine the will of God.[8] (2) If the lot was a multisided die with identifying inscriptions on each side, the die was thrown and divine will was determined by which side of the die was up.[9] (3) Multiple pieces of the lot could be placed into a bowl or vase that was vigorously shaken up and down and side to side until one of the components fell out.[10]

The Bible speaks of lots being cast to make decisions in a wide variety of settings. In three cases, the casting of the lot was performed by pagans. (1) The sailors on Jonah's escape vessel attempted to determine who was responsible for their plight (Jon. 1:7). (2) Ill-intentioned Haman selected a day for the extermination of the Jews in the Persian Empire (Esther 3:7; 9:24). (3) The Roman soldiers at the foot of Jesus's cross heaped yet another indignity on him by casting lots to determine which of them would get his clothing (Matt. 27:35; Mark 15:24; Luke 23:34; John 19:24; see also Ps. 22:18).

But more often than not, the Bible speaks of God's people casting lots to determine his will. On the Day of Atonement, the high priest cast lots to determine which goat would die as a sin offering and which would be driven into the wilderness (Lev. 16:8–10). The lot was also used to determine where individuals lived, which clergy would be given the privilege of serving in the temple, and who would be a leader in the early church (Neh. 11:1; Luke 1:9; Acts 1:26). "Casting the lot settles disputes and keeps strong opponents apart" (Prov. 18:18).

One particular topic is intimately connected with the casting of lots: the division of the Promised Land among the Israelite tribes. Either because the distribution of the land was such an important part of God's plan or because the process of fairly distributing the land proved to be contentious, or both, the Lord carefully laid out the manner in which

Broken pieces of clay vessels were easily written on and so could be used as lots.

this was to be done long before the actual distribution took place. First, a census was taken to determine the relative size of each tribe, and then the land was surveyed to determine the relative value and productivity of the various parcels. But in each case, we are reminded that the process for actual land distribution was not just directed by such pragmatics as tribal size and land quality; it also employed the casting of lots to determine which particular tribe received which parcel of land (Num. 26:55–56; Josh. 18:4–6). Then as the reality of distribution drew closer and during its execution, the casting of the lot rings like a refrain throughout the verses that describe the land distribution (Num. 33:54; 34:13; 36:2–3; Josh. 14:2; 16:1; 18:6, 8, 10–11; 19:1, 10, 17, 24, 32, 40, 51; 21:4–6, 8, 10).

The literal casting of the lots is joined by other instances in which the biblical authors employ the casting of lots as a figure of speech. For instance, the parcel of land received by the casting of a lot was referred to as the "lot" or, better, "allotment" of that tribe (Josh. 15:1; 17:1, 14, 17). The other metaphorical use leans on the connection between the casting of lots and future events. It is a short step for the lot to become the figurative equivalent of one's destiny. "Lord, you have assigned me my portion and my cup; you have made my lot secure" (Ps. 16:5 TNIV; see also Prov. 1:14; Isa. 17:14; 57:6; Jer. 13:25).

One of the ways in which lots were cast was by loading them into a vase. The vase was then shaken vigorously until one of the components popped out.

MEASURE

Body parts helped define length and width measurements such as the handbreadth and cubit.

We use measurements when we purchase a gallon of milk, prepare to hang new window treatments, or glance at our odometer. Measuring and measurements were just as much a part of the biblical world. Commodities like flour, grain, and wine were all measured through the use of containers, and the names of those containers often became the names of the units for measuring wet and dry volume, such as the *ephah*, *omer*, *bath*, and *hin*.[1] By contrast, the measurement of length was often done in units associated with parts of the body. For example, the *cubit* was the distance between the tip of the elbow and the tip of the middle finger, and the *handbreadth* was the width of the hand.[2] When linear measurements were taken, it could be done by using a rope, line, rod, or reed (Isa. 44:13; Zech. 2:1; Rev. 11:1; 21:15).

We make an assumption about measuring today that was not assumed in the past. We expect the measuring cup in our kitchen and the tape measure in our workshop to produce the same results as similar tools in our neighbor's home. This was not the case even in Egypt, where one-cubit measuring rods were subdivided into segments as small as one millimeter. When we compare Egyptian measuring tools that all claim to reflect a one-cubit standard, we find them to be of slightly different lengths. Perhaps each tool was linked to a particular building project, providing the standard for measuring at that building location.[3] Ropes that were utilized to measure larger distances had some stretch in them, thus providing different results, depending on how hard one pulled them. And given the handmade nature of ceramic containers, these too varied in size from one to another. As long as these differences were not exploited (Amos 8:5; Mic. 6:10–11), everyone seems to have accepted these linear and volume variations as the norm.

Instances of literal measuring in real time are rare in the Bible, which challenges us to find some interpretive value in those cases that refer to measurements being taken. Sometimes people measured because it was necessary to accomplish a divine directive such as providing pastureland for the clergy on the outskirts of their towns or measuring the distance between a murder victim and the town that lay closest to the murder scene (Num. 35:5; Deut. 21:1–3). Measuring could also mark an act of mercy, even though to us it does not seem to be one at first blush. For example, David made the defeated soldiers lie down in a straight line on the ground and then measured them using a length of cord. "Every two lengths of them were put to death, and the third length was allowed to live" (2 Sam. 8:2). Given the fact that most enemy soldiers were executed or mutilated and then enslaved, this grisly measuring actually became an act of mercy.

Real-time examples of measuring are very infrequent compared to the measuring that occurs in visions. Ezekiel 40–43 takes the prize for the most sustained description of measuring. With Solomon's temple in ruins, Ezekiel was given a vision of a man with a linen cord and a measuring rod in hand (Ezek. 40:3). He was then given a tour of a new temple as this man went about measuring the place component by component. Interpretations of this act vary, but we can say two things for sure: (1) Because all the measurements are provided in cubits, we are able to compare the structure

The Lord directed the Israelites to measure three thousand feet outward from the heart of a Levitical city such as Gibeon (below). This territory was removed from tribal ownership and reserved as pastureland for the clergy living in that city.

in his vision with other structures of Ezekiel's day, including Solomon's temple. (2) There is a striking symmetry between various components of the temple. Zechariah also had a vision, though it is reported much more succinctly. In his vision, a man with a measuring line was on his way to measure Jerusalem to determine how wide and long it was (Zech. 2:1–2). Given the importance of relocating a temple on its former foundation, this may well have been an effort to precisely determine the former location of Solomon's temple in advance of building the second temple.[4] A third vision also included measuring. This time John was given a reed to measure the temple and altar in his vision (Rev. 11:1–2). At the close of Revelation, John saw an angel who measured the city with a gold rod, which illustrated that the New Jerusalem will be perfectly symmetrical, just like the Holy of Holies, where the Lord made his presence known.[5]

Measuring also has a figurative dimension in the Bible. The special, even spectacular nature of something can be emphasized by how immeasurable it is. For example, Isaiah asked, "Who has measured the waters in the hollow of his hand, or with the breadth of his hand marked off the heavens?" (Isa. 40:12; see also Job 11:9; 38:4–5; Jer. 31:37). Jesus urged caution in establishing the standards we use to judge others, for "with the measure you use, it will be measured to you" (Matt. 7:2; Luke 6:38). Finally, Paul cautioned his detractors about the standards they were using to measure themselves: "When they measure themselves by themselves and compare themselves with themselves, they are not wise" (2 Cor. 10:12).

In Egypt, surviving one-cubit rods vary somewhat in length from one another, suggesting that each measuring rod was associated with a specific building project, such as the Sakkara Pyramid (below).

The Baker Illustrated Guide to Everyday Life in Bible Times

MELT

Solids become liquids when sufficient heat is sustained over an adequate amount of time. As the temperature reaches the melting point, the molecules within the solid begin to move so quickly and chaotically that they are no longer able to sustain their grasp on each other and so they begin to flow away from each other, changing what once was a solid into a liquid. This phenomenon of melting was both observed and instigated by the ancients.

Though people in Bible times did not fully understand the physics behind the process of melting, they did observe it happening in many situations. For example, the higher elevations in the Promised Land received snowfall during the winter months. As the seasons changed and temperatures moderated, that snow melted (Job 6:16; see also Ps. 147:18). A more common example was the intentional melting of beeswax (Pss. 22:14; 68:2; 97:5; Mic. 1:4). The equivalent of today's signature was executed in the ancient world by making an impression in a softened substance with a signet ring or stamp seal that was unique

Wax was prepared to receive the unique impression of a signet ring (above) when it was heated to the melting point.

to the owner. That impression was most frequently made in clay, but it could also be made by pressing the seal into wax.[6] Beeswax was also melted during the lost-wax casting process. The artisan began by shaping a positive model out of wax of the object being produced. Then clay or sand was packed around the wax model in order to create a mold. Careful application of heat hardened the mold into the shape of the wax model while at the same time melting the wax from the mold. A molten metal such as silver, copper, iron, lead, or tin that had been heated in a crucible or furnace was then poured into the mold and hardened to produce a religious object, tool, or weapon (Ezek. 22:20–22).

The average person's knowledge of and experience with melting meant that this process could be used as a metaphor by the biblical authors. While melting had positive and utilitarian roles in the ancient world, the Bible almost always presents figures of melting with a negative connotation. People's hearts melted when difficulties in life came. This image is used to describe a loss of resolve, confidence, or courage in the one who had undergone that change in state. Personal challenges in life such as illness or a storm-tossed sea could also cause such melting (Ps. 107:26; Isa. 10:18; NIV "wastes away"). "My heart has turned to wax; it has melted away within me" (Ps. 22:14). People's hearts also melted metaphorically in the face of divine judgment that was precipitated by sin at the personal or national level (Isa. 13:7; 14:31; 19:1; Ezek. 22:20–22; Nah. 2:10).

The Bible also speaks of the mountains and the earth melting. Psalm 97 introduces this phenomenon together with lightning as the way in which the Creator of this world demonstrates his existence and power: "His lightning lights up the world; the earth sees and trembles. The mountains melt like wax before the LORD, before the Lord of all the earth" (Ps. 97:4–5). The hard limestone mountains of the Promised Land erode at a rate of about one centimeter every one thousand years. But should he wish to do so, the Creator who shaped the mountains could melt them down in an instant and reform them afresh. This will literally take place during the formation of the new heaven and the new earth (2 Pet. 3:12–13).

The melting of the earth or mountains is also a symbol of divine judgment: "Nations are in uproar, kingdoms fall; he lifts his voice, the earth melts" (Ps. 46:6). Because mountains were often symbols of religious or political power in the ancient world, they became representatives of those forces that opposed the advance of God's kingdom that would be metaphorically melted down by divine judgment (Mic. 1:4; Nah. 1:5).[7]

Phrases that contain the term *melting* are strewn across the books of Exodus through Joshua and into 1 Samuel in a literary string that invites our attention. Consider the implications of whose hearts should have been melting and whose hearts actually melted in the following settings. The song of Moses

A storm-tossed sea is among the experiences in life that can cause one's heart to melt.

The Baker Illustrated Guide to Everyday Life in Bible Times

introduces this image shortly after the Red Sea crossing: "The chiefs of Edom will be terrified, the leaders of Moab will be seized with trembling, the people of Canaan will melt away" (Exod. 15:15). But when it came time to enter the Promised Land, a discouraging report caused not Canaanite but Israelite hearts to melt in fear (Deut. 1:28; Josh. 14:8). Hope was again revived by the assessment of Rahab given to the two spies who penetrated Jericho. She told them that "all who live in this country are melting in fear because of you"—saying it not once but twice (Josh. 2:9, 11). The spies repeated that image in their report to Joshua, and it was confirmed later when the Israelites crossed the Jordan River (Josh. 2:24; 5:1).

The great miracles that had ushered the Israelites into the Promised Land disabled the resistance. There was nothing to stop their aggressive advance through the country

Metal was melted during the process of casting jewelry.

except for reservations or disobedience in the hearts of God's people. Although God had forbidden them to take spoils of holy war as their own, Achan was not able to resist. As a result, when the Israelites went to war against a more modest force at Ai, the Lord allowed disaster to strike. Achan's sin precipitated a surprising and horrible defeat. "At this the hearts of the people melted in fear and became like water" (Josh. 7:4–5).

Throughout the period of the judges, there is no mention of nations whose hearts melted at the sight of God's people. The next time we see this metaphor used is when Saul's son Jonathan made a daring raid on a Philistine outpost. The Lord shook the ground and sent a panic through the Philistine ranks. "Saul's lookouts at Gibeah in Benjamin saw the army melting away in all directions" (1 Sam. 14:16).

MILK
(TO DRINK)

From mother's milk to goat's milk, dairy products were fundamental to the Israelites' well-being. The people of the past drank milk as we do to obtain the calcium, proteins, and vitamins that their bodies demanded. The milk of cows, sheep, and goats was available to meet these nutritional needs in Bible times (Deut. 32:14), but it was the goat that was best suited to the task. The cow offered good quality milk in significant quantity, but cows did not do as well on the steep hillsides of the central mountains or the wilderness pastures that were of poorer quality. Both sheep and goats could handle steep terrain, and they produced milk when pastures were less than lush, but goats generated milk at twice the rate of sheep. In addition, the milk goats produced was superior in nutritional quality to the milk produced by the sheep.[8] Thus when the Bible speaks of milk and dairy products derived from it, most often it refers to goat's milk.

Without refrigeration, fresh milk soon spoiled, so it was processed into a variety of dairy products, most of which involved the churn. The churn of Bible times was typically a goat skin that had been sewn closed and was suspended so it could be swung. After the milk soured, it was agitated in the churn in order to produce products like yogurt, butter, and cheese that had a much longer shelf life than raw milk.[9]

When the biblical authors formally mention milk, it is most often in a phrase used to characterize the Promised Land as "a land

Goats (below) surpass sheep in both the quantity and the quality of the milk they produce.

flowing with milk and honey" (Exod. 3:8, 17; 13:5; 33:3; Lev. 20:24; Num. 13:27; 14:8; 16:13–14; Deut. 6:3; 11:9; 26:9, 15; 27:3; 31:20; Josh. 5:6; Jer. 11:5; 32:22; Ezek. 20:6; 20:15). This description calls attention to two commodities of the Promised Land—bees' honey and goats' milk—that capture the pastoral nature of this land when contrasted to agricultural Egypt.[10] The Israelites would find the Promised Land to be very different from Egypt and extraordinarily different from the dry wilderness they inhabited prior to entering the Promised Land. This expression appears most often in Exodus, Numbers, and Deuteronomy as the Lord whetted the appetite of his people for what was to come. But Deuteronomy in particular links the obedience of the Israelites to their covenant obligations; the land will flow with milk and honey only when God's people live the unique life God called for them to live. We see how quickly this perspective was lost as the rebellious Israelites complained that Moses had led them out of a land flowing with milk and honey—Egypt —and had not led them into a new land flowing with milk and honey as promised (Num. 16:13–14).

Another curious reference to milk is found in Exodus 23:19: "Do not cook a young goat in its mother's milk" (see also Exod. 34:26; Deut. 14:21). Based on an ancient text from Ugarit archives, many have reported that this was a Canaanite religious ritual that the Israelites were not to replicate, though this perspective has been challenged.[11] What we can say for sure at the moment is that God commanded the Israelites to distinguish themselves from the other cultures around them by not using milk in their diet in this way.

The biblical authors also mention milk being offered to arriving guests. For example, Abraham brought out food, including curds and milk, when three visitors arrived in his camp compound (Gen. 18:2, 8). This offer of hospitality plays a more significant role in the narrative that describes the death of the Canaanite general, Sisera. Exhausted after fleeing from the battle his army had lost to the Israelites, Sisera sought refuge in the company of a perceived ally and within the tent of Jael. Her intentions were to execute him, but as part of the ruse that put him at ease, she met his request for a drink of water with a bowl filled with milk (Judg. 4:18–19; 5:25).

Because milk was such an important element of the ancient diet, the biblical authors employ the

Because milk is the first food consumed by infants such as the one depicted here, it is also used as a metaphor for the fundamentals of faith.

consumption of milk as a metaphor for abundant physical blessings. Isaiah pictures the future glory of Zion by telling God's people, "You will drink the milk of nations and be nursed at royal breasts" (Isa. 60:16). Joel similarly images abundance with milk in these encouraging words: "In that day the mountains will drip new wine, and the hills will flow with milk" (Joel 3:18).

While cows produce good-quality milk in great quantity, they require better pastures and less aggressive terrain than is offered by much of the Promised Land.

In the New Testament, the consumption of milk is linked to engagement with God's Word. Given the life-giving quality of this amazing liquid, milk became an apt symbol for the message that fundamentally changes our spiritual health. "Like newborn babies, crave pure spiritual milk, so that by it you may grow up in your salvation, now that you have tasted that the Lord is good" (1 Pet. 2:2–3). In two other locations, however, milk is used as a metaphor for the most basic elements of theology that Christians learn at the beginning of their faith experience. Easily digestible milk is the place to start, but mature people move on to eat solid food. "Though by this time you ought to be teachers, you need someone to teach you the elementary truths of God's word all over again. You need milk, not solid food! Anyone who lives on milk, being still an infant, is not acquainted with the teaching about righteousness" (Heb. 5:12–13; see also 1 Cor. 3:2).

The southern portions of the Promised Land (below) favor pastoralism over agriculture. This may be the land of milk (from goats) indicated in the phrase "the land of milk and honey."

MOUNTAIN
(TO MOVE)

A visit to the mountains can change us like few other experiences in life. Their stunning size and beauty inspire awe of the Creator. Their inaccessibility highlights our mortal limitations. And their seemingly unchanging appearance becomes an apt metaphor for eternity and a reminder that the sum total of our days is but a small fraction of time.

Given what mountains represent, it is no wonder that mountains and worship are often linked. The first call to climb and worship on a mountain came to Abraham when the Lord directed his steps to the region of Moriah, where he was to sacrifice his only son on a mountain to which God would direct him (Gen. 22:2). But later Mount Moriah gave way to the dramatic massif of Mount Sinai, where God summoned Moses and the liberated Israelites to this rising terrain in order to organize their lives around their divine mission (Exod. 3:1; 19 NLT). Centuries later God selected and invited his chosen people to worship at yet another mountain—Mount Zion—that would become the home of their king and his temple (Pss. 2:6; 78:68; Isa. 24:23).

Mountains are fitting places to worship God, but as metaphors they become particularly effective theology instructors when moved or disturbed at God's direction. As the Lord's unlimited presence took up residence on Mount Sinai, the mountain trembled, smoked, and blazed as a way of showing how unique and powerful God's presence was

Mountains on any continent inspire mortals' awe of their Creator.

(Exod. 19:16–19). This event was recalled centuries later when the poet spoke of the Lord as the one "who touches the mountains, and they smoke" (Ps. 104:32; see also 144:5). The mountains of the Promised Land are made of very durable limestone that shows virtually no change in appearance over thousands of years, but when God wants to change them, he can. "The mountains melt like wax before the Lord, before the Lord of all the earth" (Ps. 97:5; see also Mic. 1:4). And this is only the start of references in the Bible to mountains trembling, skipping, swaying, and quaking in the presence of the Lord (Job 9:5–6; Ps. 114:4, 6; Isa. 54:10; Nah. 1:5).

The beauty of the mountains can lose its luster for travelers who are forced to either lengthen their trip by circumnavigating them or accept the bone-wearying challenge of climbing their steep ridges. At times ancient travelers chose the latter, but while shortening the distance to be covered, this decision left them gasping for breath as they trudged and scrambled up steep slopes into thinner and thinner air. It is this literal travel experience that makes the image of mountains being made level so very inviting. This recasting of the landscape is mentioned by the biblical authors as a way of facilitating the mission of Cyrus, the return of the exiles, and the arrival of the Messiah (Isa. 40:4; 45:2; 49:11; Zech. 4:7; Luke 3:5).

Not all mountains are created equal. Though Mount Zion received many accolades, it was not the highest mountain in the world, the highest mountain in the Promised Land, or even the highest mountain in the greater Jerusalem area. The fact of the matter is that the shrines of other deities were located on rising terrain that was often considerably higher in elevation than Mount Zion (Ezek. 6:13; 18:11; Hosea 4:13; John 4:20). For example, Mount Zaphon, home to a Canaanite sanctuary, is over twice the elevation of Mount Zion (Ps. 48:2). No pagan deity deserved a mountain shrine higher than the Lord's, which means something has to be fixed in the days to come.

The Lord established his sanctuary on Mount Zion, or Jerusalem (below).

The Lord summoned the Israelites to Mount Sinai (above) in order to further define their lives and their mission.

"In the last days the mountain of the LORD's temple will be established as the highest of the mountains; it will be exalted above the hills" (Isa. 2:2; see also Mic. 4:1).

Finally, there is a remarkable example of engineering that moved a mountain and a more remarkable call to faith that can allow that same mountain to be moved again. Herod the Great identified a building site on the fringes of the Judean wilderness for which he had big plans. He wanted to build a remarkable palace complex that would offer him a place for personal repose with breathtaking views just right for entertaining his guests. This same palace was to serve as a lookout station to watch for invaders from the east. And most importantly, this palace was to become the eternal resting place for Herod's remains—a mortuary monument that could be seen from Jerusalem.[12] Because no single mountain was considered high enough to accomplish all these purposes, Herod directed his architects to move the material from one of two adjacent

mountains and pile it on the other. The completed palace built on this moved mountain was called the Herodium.

During the last week of Jesus's life on earth, as he was crossing the crest of the Mount of Olives with his disciples, this building came into view. While his disciples were marveling at how quickly the cursed fig tree had withered, Jesus pointed them in the direction of the Herodium. "I tell you, if anyone says to this mountain, 'Go, throw yourself into the sea,' and does not doubt in their heart but believes that what they say will happen, it will be done for them" (Mark 11:23). For those interested in building the kingdom of God, the excesses and political abuses of the Herodium represented everything the kingdom of God sought to replace in people's hearts. Withering a fig tree was nothing. Jesus told his disciples their mission in life would be to move a mountain. Through their faith-filled work, they would take all that the Herodium represented and cast it into the sea. Our understanding of this metaphor becomes complete when we see the proximity of the Herodium to the Dead Sea and understand that traditional Jewish thought regarded that sea as the appropriate place for any item or implement associated with the pagan world to be thrown.[13]

For those who traveled from place to place by walking, mountains were obstacles. Thus the leveling of mountains became an image associated with the dawn of a better day.

MOURN
(TO GRIEVE)

Mourning encompasses both what people feel inside when they experience a great loss and what they do on the outside to show what they are feeling in those horrible moments in life. The inspired poet observed, "It is better to go to a house of mourning than to go to a house of feasting" (Eccles. 7:2); that is because mourning can teach us so much. While loss and mourning offer great life lessons, the learning experience does not feel good, and it does not feel the same for everyone. Each of us mourns in our own way, but we know enough to sympathize with those who have suffered a devastating loss. We know about the emptiness, loss of appetite, bouts of weeping, and tired sadness that are the polar opposite of how we want to feel (Lam. 5:15; Amos 8:10; Matt. 11:17).

Because those in mourning do not feel normal, they naturally seek out ways to express externally their internal grief. When the Bible mentions rituals associated with mourning, we should not presume that a particular ritual was performed in every era or that every individual participated in them all, particularly since some of the rituals mentioned are contradictory. Deep grief could lead to tearing open one's clothing (Gen. 37:29, 34–35; 2 Sam. 1:11; 3:31), wearing itchy sackcloth next to one's skin,[14] or going without jewelry or footwear (Exod. 33:4; 2 Sam. 15:30; Ezek. 24:16–17). Those in mourning might cover the lower portion of their face and put ashes on their head (Esther 4:3) or leave their hair unkempt or shave their head altogether (Lev. 10:6; Jer. 16:6; 47:5; Mic. 1:16). The practice of both fasting and eating special meals is mentioned (Ezra 10:6; Jer.

The Dominus Flevit chapel marks the traditional site at which Jesus wept over the apostasy of Jerusalem.

16:5; Hosea 9:4) as well as unnatural wailing and intense weeping (Lam. 1:2; Amos 5:16). Others grieved by writing down their tribute to the one lost in elegant poetry (2 Sam. 1:17–27; 3:33–34; 2 Chron. 35:25).[15] Because life does not return to normal very quickly after a significant loss, formal mourning periods lasted from thirty to seventy days (Gen. 50:3–4; Num. 20:29; Deut. 34:8).

Mourning rituals are associated with life events of various kinds. Perhaps the baseline for all mourning is the death of a beloved spouse, child, or friend (Gen. 23:2; 2 Sam. 19:1; 1 Chron. 7:22; John 11:31, 35). Personal calamities that do not involve the death of a loved one can also animate mourning—such as the loss of freedom, an unrelenting illness, unanswered prayer, personal attacks, or disruption of family life (Deut. 21:13; 2 Sam. 13:37; Job 14:22; Pss. 35:13–14; 38:5–6; 42:9; 43:2).

The members of a nation might grieve as one when a national tragedy crosses family and political borders. When the Israelites failed to honor God's promises with their enduring trust, their nation often met penalties that caused them to mourn as a nation. National mourning could be precipitated by punishment that took the form of famine, withdrawal of a privilege, or death of a national leader who had violated God's directions (Exod. 33:3–4; Num. 14:35–39; 1 Sam. 6:19; Jer. 14:1–2; Joel 1:9). The most serious judgment Israel faced was foreign invasion of the Promised Land, often accompanied by the destruction of their cities and personal exile to distant lands. Nehemiah wept over ruined defensive walls and gates even as the gates of Jerusalem metaphorically wept over the city's destruction and the roads mourned that they were no longer traveled by people going to festivals in Zion (Neh. 1:3–4; Isa. 3:26; 29:1–2; 32:13; Lam. 1:4). The nation also mourned when a devoted leader was called from this world by death. All Israel mourned at the death of Aaron, Moses, Samuel, and good king Josiah (Num. 20:29; Deut. 34:8; 1 Sam. 25:1; 2 Chron. 35:24). But after Saul was rejected by the Lord as king and Samuel began to mourn for him as though he had died, the Lord instructed Samuel to cease mourning and be about the business of anointing Israel's next king (1 Sam. 15:35; 16:1).

For those who deeply love the Lord, there is yet another occasion that produces mourning; that is the presence of sin in our lives or in the lives of others around us. When Ezra saw the returning exiles going back to patterns of behavior that had precipitated their exit from the Promised Land, he went into mourning (Ezra 10:6). They had forgotten the urgent words of Jeremiah, who had exhorted

An Egyptian mourning statue. Mourning entails both what one feels on the inside and what one does on the outside to express grief.

Mourning is expressed in the gestures of the captives depicted in this Assyrian relief.

laughter to mourning and your joy to gloom" (James 4:9).

In the end, the Bible's perspective is that seasons of mourning and grief will continue to be a regular but unnatural part of the believer's life on this earth (Eccles. 3:4; Matt. 5:4). But the insights offered in God's Word allow us to grieve without crossing over into the devastating grief of those who have no hope (1 Thess. 4:13). We look forward to a new living space scrubbed clean of grief. Within the New Jerusalem, "There will be no more death or mourning or crying or pain, for the old order of things has passed away" (Rev. 21:4).

them to see sin for what it is and add mourning to their words of repentance: "Put on sackcloth, my people, and roll in ashes; mourn with bitter wailing as for an only son" (Jer. 6:26; see also Joel 2:12). Those who properly regard their sin for what it is will respond in a similar way. "Grieve, mourn and wail. Change your

King Josiah's death in a battle near Megiddo (below) brought his subjects to their knees in mourning.

The Baker Illustrated Guide to Everyday Life in Bible Times

NAKED

When the Bible says a person is naked, it can mean being either fully unclothed or partially unclothed, and the context is usually the only clue as to which of the two is meant. To understand the cultural connotations associated with nakedness, we need to begin where it all started—in the Garden of Eden. The very last thing we are told about Adam and Eve before the temptation is that they were fully naked and yet felt no shame (Gen. 2:25). This vividly indicates just how different their living circumstances were from our own. Once the fall occurred, their nakedness became the reason for hiding from God and the starting point for divine interrogation (Gen. 3:7, 10–11). Eventually the puny efforts of these humans to solve their problem with fig leaves was addressed more adequately by God, who provided them with clothing (Gen. 3:21). From this point on, wearing clothing in public became the norm and imposed nakedness became a mark of shame and an indicator of troubled times (2 Sam. 10:4–5).

Being naked does not take one back to a prefall world of innocence but firmly places one in the sin-filled world where nakedness connotes trouble. It is linked with those who abuse alcohol, beginning with Noah (Gen. 9:20–23; Hab. 2:15–16). The art of the ancient Near East as well as the descriptions in the Bible pictured those captured in war being marched into captivity without clothing as a way of further humiliating them.[1] "So the king of Assyria will lead away stripped and barefoot the Egyptian captives and Cushite exiles, young and old, with buttocks bared— to Egypt's shame" (Isa. 20:4; see also 2 Chron. 28:15; Amos 2:16). The poor are often described as unclothed or underclothed (Job 22:6; 24:7, 10; Rev. 3:17). Thus one attribute of godly believers is that they provide clothing for the naked (Isa. 58:7; Matt. 25:44–45). Paul included being underdressed in a list of challenges he had faced, but he

In ancient art, prisoners and exiles are often distinguished from free people by being depicted without clothing.

trumpeted the fact that not even poverty and its associated nakedness would be able to separate him or any other believer from the love of Christ (Rom. 8:35; see also 2 Cor. 11:27).

In the ancient Near East the image of a naked man could have positive connotations, but an image of a naked woman was often of a sexualized woman in trouble.[2] This is also the case in the Bible when the women who were stripped naked were either prostitutes or wives who had been unfaithful to their husbands (Isa. 47:2–3; Hosea 2:3; Nah. 3:5).[3] Pagan fertility worship involved naked figurines, thus linking nudity with the worship of false gods. For this and other reasons, great care was taken to make sure Israel's clergy covered themselves with undergarments when ascending the steps to the altar (Exod. 20:26; 28:42–43). And to these we can add many more examples of individuals in the Bible whose lack of clothing indicated a more troubled time, such as the partially naked King Saul or

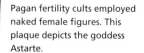

Pagan fertility cults employed naked female figures. This plaque depicts the goddess Astarte.

Two naked athletes competing in the pankration, a mixture of wrestling and boxing.

the prophet Micah, the demon-possessed man who had gone without clothing for some time, and the young man who "fled naked, leaving his garment behind" as Judas led an armed crowd to arrest Jesus (1 Sam. 19:24; Mic. 1:8; Mark 14:51–52; Luke 8:27).

The negative connotations of nakedness can be used rhetorically as a form of criticism. On the day the ark of the covenant was carried back to Jerusalem, King David set aside his royal garments and joined the crowd in celebrating the special day (2 Sam. 6:14). By contrast, his wife Michal, the daughter of Saul, criticized David for "going around half-naked in full view of the slave girls of his servants as any vulgar fellow would!" (2 Sam. 6:20). The prophetic books use the image of nakedness in a more sustained way to criticize the sin of God's people. As early as the book of Deuteronomy, the Lord warned Israel that one of the penalties for covenant unfaithfulness would be the humiliating nakedness imposed by those who led them into exile (Deut. 28:48). The prophets seized on the image of Israel as God's straying bride stripped naked to emphasize the penalty for her covenant violation and as a call for this wayward woman to repent (Isa. 57:8; Lam. 1:8; Hosea 2:3, 9). This image appears repeatedly in the verses of Ezekiel. Israel is the young, naked child over whom the Lord unfurls his garment to cover her nakedness. But she quickly unleashes her sexuality in the presence of other men, even becoming a prostitute who uses her nakedness to entice lovers into her bed. Consequently, she will be punished and treated as a wayward wife or prostitute rather than honored as a bride (Ezek. 16:7–8, 22, 35–39; 23:10, 18, 29).

Two other figurative uses of nakedness merit special mention. First, fortified cities of the ancient world were carefully designed to protect those within, but they never could be designed without potential points of weakness. Joseph accused his brothers of coming as spies to inquire into the nakedness of his land (Gen. 42:9, 12; NIV "see where our land is unprotected"). The Edomites called for the foundations of Jerusalem to be made naked (Ps. 137:7; NIV "tear it down"; see also Isa. 23:13). Second, we have the image of the naked newborn who participates in delivering the message that humans never truly own anything they can carry with them into eternity. Job succinctly sums up the situation by bracketing his life with nakedness: "Naked I came from my mother's womb, and naked I will depart" (Job 1:21; see also Eccles. 5:15).

The efforts of Adam and Eve to cover their nakedness with fig leaves did nothing to solve the larger problem of sin that had entered their lives.

NAME
(TO GIVE A)

*R*egions, cities, altars, and wells all received names in the Bible; but here we consider the process of naming or renaming a person. When we give names to our children, we want them to sound just right with the proper blend of vowels, consonants, and cadence. We also want them to be unusual, but not so unusual that they become a social burden. Similar concerns and passions filled parents in Bible times as well.

The process of giving a name to a child appears to have been a role that father and mother shared; one or both were given credit for assigning the child's name (Gen. 4:25; 5:3; see also Gen. 16:13, 15). The most detailed

description of the process comes to us from the life of Zechariah and Elizabeth when they named their son (Luke 1:59–63). According to the custom of that time, the day of John's circumcision was the day on which he received his name. The family was ready to name the child Zechariah after his father, but Elizabeth quickly objected, insisting that his name be John. The extended family protested because no one in their family had that name. In the end they turned to the temporarily mute Zechariah, who wrote, "His name is John."

Two different connotations have been attached to the process of name-giving in the Bible. The first flows somewhat naturally from the renaming of Israelite kings by their empire overlords. For example, the Egyptian pharaoh gave the new name Jehoiakim to Eliakim and the Babylonian king gave the new name Zedekiah to Mattaniah (2 Kings 23:34; 24:17). In such cases, the suzerain was expressing his authority over the vassal in this process of renaming. While some have suggested that this is the primary connotation behind the process of naming that should be extended to circumstances like Adam naming the livestock, birds, and wild animals as well as Eve (Gen.

This simple altar marks the traditional spot where Mary learned that the name of her son would be Jesus.

2:20; 3:20), this supposition has been challenged.[4] The study of name-giving in ancient Egypt suggests that the connotation of *essential relationship* may lie behind the giving of a name. This seems to be a better explanation for most instances in which a name is given in Scripture.[5]

The general rationale behind this process is the one that is operative today: it is a short and easy way to make reference to a person. It would be entirely possible to call a young child to come home with a longer phrase like, "The child with the brown hair next to the dark goat, it is time for dinner." But this is a highly inefficient way for us to communicate in everyday life, and it would have made the genealogical lists carefully recorded in the Bible all but impossible to produce.[6] Thus it was natural to give personal names to children.

The names given in Bible times were typically issued in the language that was spoken in the home and often communicate an idea or image that is not apparent in translation. A personal name could be a reference to a type of plant or animal. For example, Jonah means "dove." A name could also be composed of a noun and verb or noun and adjective that created a phrase or sentence, such as the name Abraham, which means "father of many." While being cautious in using the etymology to interpret a text unless that lead is provided by the biblical author, we do find that lead offered on more than one occasion. This is particularly the case in the early books of the Bible where

In the region of Caesarea Philippi (below), Jesus gave Simon the new, meaning-filled name of Peter.

a name might reflect life's circumstances at the time of the child's birth. For example, Eve named her third son Seth, Hebrew for "put in place." She explained her name choice by saying, "God has granted me another child in place of Abel" (Gen. 4:25). Far removed from the Promised Land, Moses named his first son Gershom, Hebrew for "stranger there," saying, "I have become a foreigner in a foreign land" (Exod. 2:22). The most sustained list of names given an etymological rationale can be found in Genesis 29:31–30:24, which tells of the birth of each of Jacob's sons.

Names can also be a way of assimilating someone into a new culture. A number of instances of renaming appear to have had this motivation. The Egyptian pharaoh gave Joseph the name Zaphenath-Paneah. In Babylon Daniel, Hananiah, Mishael, and Azariah were not just given an assimilating education but also assimilating Babylonian names: Belteshazzar, Shadrach, Meshach, and Abednego (Gen. 41:45; Dan. 1:6–7; see also the Judean kings of 2 Kings 23:34 and 24:17).

The most noteworthy examples of naming or renaming, however, are those in which the name of a person was formally linked to his or her life mission or destiny. This started with Eve, whose name so very appropriately means "the mother of all the living" (Gen. 3:20), and it continued with Abram/Abraham, Sarai/Sarah, Jacob/Israel, Simon/Peter, and Saul/Paul, all of whom received new names that charted a new course in

Adam gave his wife the name Eve, for she would become the mother of all the living.

This name-filled tablet preserves the genealogy of Hammurabi.

life for them (Gen. 17:5, 15; 32:28; Mark 3:16; Acts 13:9). And then there is our Savior from sin who received a cascade of powerful names (Isa. 9:6), but none more powerful than the name *Jesus*, which formally links him to the mission of saving people from their sins (Matt. 1:21). Jesus knew all that his name entailed because he prayed, "Holy Father, protect them by the power of your name, the name you gave me, so that they may be one as we are one. While I was with them, I protected them and kept them safe by that name you gave me" (John 17:11–12).

ORPHAN
(FATHERLESS)

In the Bible an orphan was a boy or girl, Israelite or non-Israelite, who was unmarried and had lost one or both parents. The circumstances of such children are best understood when compared to the perceived ideal family living situation in Israel. The ideal was a father, mother, and their sons and daughters who owned farmland inherited from the father's family. The land allowed them to grow their food and graze their animals with the support of and under the protection of the extended family. If the father of this family unit died, it not only generated emotional trauma associated with his passing but also diminished the surviving family's economic and physical security. Older children could become the heir of the family property and so continue to use it for their support and the support of their widowed

A Greek marble statue of a young girl who had been separated from her parents. The Bible aggressively calls for the protection of those who have lost their parents.

mother (Num. 27:7–11; Deut. 21:15–17). A widow with younger children could inherit the property, but the Bible generally paints her circumstances as particularly grim (2 Kings 4:1–2). The situation became more ambiguous and therefore more tenuous when a younger child lost both parents. We presume the child fell under the care and protection of the extended family, but the orphan's presence might not always have been welcomed, and the disposition of the parents' land might have been left in limbo. Even worse was the case of the non-Israelite, who did not hold property rights at all in the Promised Land; the foreigner's destiny was truly precarious. While some level of inference is required to draw this diminishing picture of personal security, we can say for sure that the more tenuous their hold on property rights and the more uncharitable the extended family became, the more difficult life was for orphaned children, who were at increased risk of going without the basics of food, clothing, and social protection.

Given that reality, the Lord addressed the plight of orphans in the laws given to the Israelites. God's people were to set aside a tenth of their field produce and animals born in their herds as a gift given at the sanctuary. Every third year, however, this tithe was to remain in storage at the local level so the disadvantaged of society, including orphans, would have access to it (Deut. 14:22–29; 26:12–13). In addition, Israelites were to refrain from gathering a portion of their grain, olive, and grape harvest so that orphans and other disadvantaged people could gather food from land they did not own (Deut. 24:19–21). Finally, the Lord also addressed the general treatment of orphans. Though they might lack the protection offered by a larger clan, they were to be

A painting of Jesus's birth. The family most likely to prosper in Bible times consisted of both parents and children.

treated with respect and to receive fair and impartial treatment (Deut. 24:17).[1]

Where the biblical authors formally mention orphans, they often are used as emblematic of the most disadvantaged members of society. This becomes evident in the merisms that cast orphans on the less-privileged side of the social spectrum. God wanted all Israelites from all social strata to be present for the festivals at the sanctuary. The invitation was valid from top to bottom in society, from royals to orphans (Deut. 16:11, 14). Similarly, when the judgment of God fell on Israel, the consequences were felt from one end of the social

Orphans often lived without access to agricultural land that they owned. This fact alone threatened their very survival.

The Baker Illustrated Guide to Everyday Life in Bible Times

spectrum to the other, from elders to orphans (Isa. 9:14–17).

Something similar can be said for mention of the fatherless outside of these merisms; again the orphan may stand rhetorically as the representative of all who are socially disadvantaged. Surveying the ruin of people and land, the inspired poet of Lamentations called himself nothing more than an orphan (Lam. 5:3). And when Jesus was preparing his disciples for his departure, he assured them that he would not leave them "as orphans" (John 14:18).

As the biblical authors address the ethics of political leaders and believers in general, they state that it is the treatment of the most disadvantaged members of society—the orphans—that is to distinguish them as God's people. The Lord paved the way of this moral high road by identifying himself as the one who is the provider of food and clothing for the fatherless (Deut. 10:18). He is the helper, defender, and father of the orphan (Pss. 10:14, 18; 68:5;

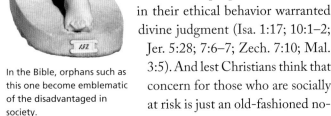

In the Bible, orphans such as this one become emblematic of the disadvantaged in society.

146:9). Furthermore, the Lord demanded that his public representatives sustain a similar demeanor and criticized them roundly when they failed (Ps. 82:3; Isa. 1:23; Jer. 22:3; Ezek. 22:7).[2]

No one was to take advantage of the fatherless in any way (Exod. 22:22–24; Deut. 27:19; Prov. 23:10). Job picked up this ethical thread and used it to defend his innocence before those who wished to prove his misfortunes in life were the product of his immoral lifestyle. He separated himself from those who cast lots for orphans, drove their donkeys away, or snatched them from their mother's breast as debt slaves (Job 6:27; 24:3, 9). Instead Job asserted that he had rescued orphans, provided food for them, and defended their legal rights (Job 29:12; 31:17, 21). The prophets warned God's people that this failure in their ethical behavior warranted divine judgment (Isa. 1:17; 10:1–2; Jer. 5:28; 7:6–7; Zech. 7:10; Mal. 3:5). And lest Christians think that concern for those who are socially at risk is just an old-fashioned notion, James issued this challenge: "Religion that God our Father accepts as pure and faultless is this: to look after orphans and widows in their distress" (James 1:27).

PHARISEE

The Pharisees became a recognizable group on the landscape of Jewish culture in the second century BC, making their presence felt throughout the New Testament era.[1] The Pharisees were a highly identifiable group during the time of Jesus given their distinguished leaders, distinctive habits of living, and regular meetings. A person became a Pharisee not by family heritage as did the clergy of Israel or by being born into a wealthy, aristocratic family like the Sadducees but by pledging to lead a pure life that conformed to the many rules of the group. Pharisees attended regular meetings during which they were provided additional opportunities to learn as well as to encourage and police the all-important lifestyle choices required of their members. Leadership

and education were provided by the scribes (or teachers of the law), who were considered the best Scripture scholars of the day.[2] In addition to attending the meetings, the Pharisees took the lead in the community as rabbis or authorized teachers in the synagogues. A general rule that assured that orthodoxy would be maintained was that only those whom the scribes had authorized to teach were perceived as worthy interpreters of Scripture.[3]

Three components of the theology of the Pharisees are important to understand in observing their interaction with Jesus and their influence on other New Testament writings. (1) Their source of theology was not limited to the written Scriptures but was also based on the traditional interpretation and extensions of the written Scriptures that were passed down orally by authorized teachers within Judaism. (2) Moral uprightness received prominence in their teaching, given their goal to create a righteous community that might properly receive the coming Messiah. In particular, we see this in their careful monitoring of behavior on the Sabbath. (3) The Pharisees paid particular attention to the topic of the spirit world and life after

The authorized teaching chair in the synagogue, called the seat of Moses, was typically occupied by a Pharisee (Matt. 23:1–3).

death, identifying the roles of angels and demons, championing the immortality of the soul, and advocating for a bodily resurrection.

This temple warning inscription blocked Gentile access to certain segments of the temple complex. In the same way, the Pharisees resisted the notion that Gentiles would be part of the kingdom of God.

Clearly there were those among the Pharisees who came to know Jesus as their Savior, including prominent figures like Nicodemus and Saul (John 3:1; Acts 23:6). But in almost all other instances, we meet the Pharisees as people who found Jesus's lifestyle and teachings to be problematic. At base they saw Jesus functioning as an authorized teacher without having the approval of one of their authorized teachers (Matt. 21:23; Mark 1:21–22; 2:6–10). The Pharisees also saw Jesus's free association and welcoming demeanor with public sinners to be at cross-purposes with their group's agenda of lifting the morality of the Israelites (Matt. 9:11; Luke 7:36–39; 15:1–2).

For these and other reasons, we frequently find the Pharisees trying to reduce Jesus's influence. They explained away his miracles as enabled by fallen spirits (Matt. 9:34; 12:24). They sought to manipulate his itinerary with threats (Luke 13:31). They approached him with seemingly innocent questions in an attempt to entrap him (Matt. 19:3; 22:15; Luke 11:53; John 8:3–6). They threatened his supporters with excommunication from the local synagogue, trying to silence their testimony (John 9:22; 12:42). And when all that failed to end this man's growing influence on the people whom they hoped to influence, the Pharisees joined in the efforts to have him arrested and executed (Matt. 21:46; John 11:45–50).

A first-century synagogue foundation from Gamla. In the days of Jesus, the Pharisees exercised their influence over Jewish society as leaders in the synagogues.

Pharisee

The Gospels also record Jesus's response to the Pharisees. In two instances he honored them: First, playing on the high moral standards set by the Pharisees, Jesus observed that unless one's righteousness surpassed that of the Pharisees and teachers of the law, one could not enter the kingdom (Matt. 5:20). Second, unwilling to destabilize the synagogue system as a teaching place, he urged his listeners to respect their teachers when they taught the written law of God but cautioned them not to emulate the Pharisees' lifestyle when it did not match their rhetoric (Matt. 23:1–3).

But of all the groups with whom Jesus shared space in the New Testament, it was the Pharisees whom he most often publicly criticized, perhaps because their popularity and influence most threatened Jesus's message. He took them to task for elevating their traditions, placing them on a par with the written Word. Again and again Jesus sidestepped criticism that he had failed to observe the law when, in fact, he had only failed to honor their human traditions (Matt. 12:2–8; 15:1–8; Luke 11:39–42; 14:1–3). He also lambasted the Pharisees for loading down the common people with legal burdens that no one could carry (Luke 11:46). In addition to his concern about their emphasis on authorized tradition, Jesus also warned against the so-called yeast of the Pharisees—their uncharitable view toward Gentiles (Mark 8:14–21). But most of all, we find Jesus taking the Pharisees to task on their character—the very things the Pharisees believed distinguished them from the ordinary people of the land. Through ostentatious displays of dress and worship, by always seeking the places of highest honor in social settings, by being self-absorbed, and by being filled with the love of money, they had become walking, talking hypocrites, "whitewashed tombs" (Matt. 23:1–36; Luke 11:37–50). Perhaps no words are more insightful and troubling than those of the Pharisee in Jesus's parable of the Pharisee and the tax collector in which the Pharisee prayed, "God, I thank you that I am not like other people—robbers, evildoers, adulterers—or even like this tax collector" (Luke 18:11).

Nicodemus was among the Pharisees who came to know and love Jesus as his Savior.

PLANT/SOW

With few exceptions, everyone in the biblical world knew the feel and smell of broken soil because everyone got their hands dirty planting their farm fields, vineyards, trees, and gardens. This critical process began the life cycle of the plants that provided them with food. It was not mortals, however, but their Creator who first planted in the Bible when he established a garden in Eden (Gen. 2:8). This divine sowing imbued the action of planting with very positive connotations. In much of the biblical writing that follows, planting continued to have positive connotations, linked to a peaceful normalcy that was part of the regular rhythm of life (Gen. 8:22; 9:20; Prov. 31:16; Jer. 29:5, 28)—so normal that it is one of the routine activities in which people will be engaged at the time of Jesus's return (Luke 17:26, 28). In Bible times, the life lived under divine blessing was one in which the family would eat what they had planted and even eat what others had planted—when God's people received ownership of the Promised Land (Deut. 6:11; Josh. 24:13; Isa. 65:21–22).

But with the fall into sin, the process of growing food also became connected with negative connotations (Gen. 3:17). In fact, the curses for covenant disloyalty included this shocking possibility: "You will plant seed in vain, because your enemies will eat it" (Lev. 26:16; see also Deut. 28:30, 39). So when Israel planted but failed to harvest, the Lord expected them to inspect their lifestyle for signs of trouble (Judg. 6:3–4; Mic. 6:15; Zeph. 1:13; Hag. 1:6). Even planting that led to harvesting could have a negative connotation if the

Planting and growing grain became a symbol of peaceful normalcy in the culture of the biblical world.

one planting expected to find satisfaction in the process without taking account of God's presence in the process (Eccles. 2:4–5, 11).

The Bible mentions a wide variety of things that ordinary people planted, each of which helped provide the nutrients required for a healthy life. They planted vineyards, olive trees, date palms, pomegranate trees, fig trees, sycamore trees, wheat, barley, and vegetable gardens, to name the most popular. In the gardens they grew lentils, fava beans, chickpeas, cucumbers, watermelons, onions, leeks, and garlic.[4]

The time and manner of planting were affected by climate, culture, and divine law. There was a proper time to plant in the Promised Land (Eccles. 3:2) that generally corresponded with the arrival of the winter rains that softened the soil and provided the vital moisture that nurtured the sprouting plants. When this moisture combined with appropriate soil temperature, the seeds germinated and

One way grain was planted was by dribbling it from bags fastened to a donkey, which was walked back and forth through the plowed field.

the plants matured.[5] In the case of fruit trees and grapevines, the preference was always to plant a seedling rather than a seed—often a cutting from a successful plant. In the case of other commodities, the plants were grown from seeds. We have the most information from the Bible and associated archaeology from the ancient world on the process of planting grain. Once the early rains of October and November softened the soil for plowing, the farmer broke open the soil and then scattered seed over the plowed field. This scattering could be done with a sweep of the hand, by a donkey led back and forth across the plowed field dribbling seed from bags secured to its back, or by a plow that deposited seeds behind the plow point using a funnel-and-tube system called a *seed drill*.[6] No matter how the planting was done, it was also considered an act of worship responding to the divine law that limited the kinds of seed that could be planted in a field and the years the field was to be left unplanted (Lev. 19:19; 25:4, 20; Deut. 22:9).

Planting is also used as a figure of speech in the Bible in four different ways:

The Baker Illustrated Guide to Everyday Life in Bible Times

1. The image of planting is used to describe the way in which the Lord established his people in the Promised Land following their departure from Egypt (Exod. 15:17; 2 Sam. 7:10; Pss. 44:2; 80:8, 15; Isa. 5:2).

2. After Israel was torn up by its root from Canaan and sent into exile, the return from exile is pictured as replanting: "I will plant Israel in their own land, never again to be uprooted from the land I have given them" (Amos 9:15; see also Jer. 24:6; Hosea 2:23).

3. The Scriptures further speak of the believer's life with related imagery. The blessed man is "like a tree planted by streams of water, which yields its fruit in season and whose leaf does not wither" (Ps. 1:3; see also 92:12–13; Jer. 17:7–8).

4. Figurative planting is also used for the planting of God's Word in the hearts of his people. A number of Jesus's parables employ the image of sowing, including his parable of the sower, parable of the weeds, and parable of the mustard seed, all of which illustrate the ways in which the gospel arrives in people's lives and faith matures (Matt. 13:1–32). And when combating divisions in the church at Corinth, Paul used this same image for the one who evangelizes (1 Cor. 3:6–8).

Vineyards were planted with cuttings taken from successful vines.

Because the average person knew what it was to get their hands dirty when planting seeds in the soil, everyone shared a common perspective on the outcome. The kind and quality of seed planted had a direct impact on the resulting harvest. As a result, the relationship between people's actions and consequences in daily life was related to the familiar planting and harvesting cycle (2 Cor. 9:6; Gal. 6:7–8). If they lived life well, they could expect good things to follow (James 3:18). "The one who sows righteousness reaps a sure reward" (Prov. 11:18; Hosea 10:12). But those who lived carelessly could expect just the opposite outcome (Job 4:8; Hosea 8:7; 10:13). "Whoever sows injustice reaps calamity" (Prov. 22:8).

PLEDGED TO BE MARRIED
(BETROTHED/ENGAGED)

arriage and family were very important values to those living in the ancient Near East, and they were particularly important to the Israelites, who had received the charge to grow into a great nation. Thus it was normal for young men and women to announce their intentions to marry through an engagement or betrothal that the biblical authors frequently refer to as "pledged to be married."

Though there are a few exceptions (Gen. 26:34–35; Judg. 14:1–2), most marriages mentioned in the Bible were thoughtfully arranged for their children by the parents. When sons and daughters reached the appropriate age,[7] their parents surveyed the field of potential mates within their extended family and began to negotiate a marriage contract. The details of this contract included agreement on the sum of the bride-price (*mohar*) that would be paid by the groom to the bride's family in compensation for the loss of their daughter and agreement on the amount of the dowry that the bride would bring into her new home.[8] After the prospective groom had paid the bride-price, the betrothal was formally established when he either provided his fiancée with a garment or covered her with a corner of his own garment to publicly announce that the betrothal had begun (Ruth 3:9; Ezek. 16:8).

With the engagement publicly announced, a set of legal limitations and social expectations were established. From this point on, the young man and woman were regarded as legally married to one another with a formal declaration of divorce being the only way in which to reverse the relationship. But although they were

A father and son. In the ancient Near East, it was typical for parents to arrange the marriages of their children.

The Baker Illustrated Guide to Everyday Life in Bible Times

considered legally married during the time of their engagement, the couple was barred from enjoying sexual relations with one another until the formal marriage celebration commenced (Deut. 22:23–24; 28:30; Matt. 1:18–19). The assumption was that the betrothal would mature into a marriage within approximately one year of the time the bride-price was paid. It was considered a grave embarrassment to the groom if the formal marriage did not follow, as in the case of Jacob, Samson, and David (Gen. 29:21–27; Judg. 14:20; 1 Sam. 18:19). And according to the early law code of Hammurabi, the prospective groom who changed his mind and broke the marriage contract to pursue a different mate forfeited the bride-price he had paid.[9]

The betrothal of sons and daughters was part of the regular rhythm of life in biblical times; however, it typically went unmentioned by the biblical authors unless some importance was attached to it. Perhaps the most striking case is the betrothal of Mary and Joseph. Their pledge to be married is mentioned in the Gospel accounts of Matthew and Luke (Matt. 1:18; Luke 1:27; 2:5).

The parents of this young man and woman who lived in Nazareth had made a marriage contract on behalf of their son and daughter. The marriage contract assured Joseph that his bride had no previous sexual relations and that she was committed to enjoy that privilege only with him. This assurance was meant not only for Joseph but for us as well. It confirmed a theological detail that is very important: the virgin birth of Jesus. To be an effective Savior-substitute, he had to be born of a virgin. Her unique pregnancy may puzzle us; it certainly confounded the engaged couple. But it was the betrothal and marriage contract of Mary and Joseph that validated Mary's declaration of her virginity when confronted by her impending pregnancy: "How will this be . . . since I am a virgin?" (Luke 1:34). Furthermore, it was the engagement of this couple and Joseph's willingness to continue in the relationship that afforded Mary and her unborn child security in the face of those

According to the law code of Hammurabi, the prospective groom who broke the marriage contract to pursue a different mate forfeited the bride-price he had paid.

who might have wanted her punished for her apparent indiscretion. Thus the biblical authors do more than give the betrothal casual mention; it becomes a point of emphasis within the birth narrative.

In Old Testament times, betrothal was used as a metaphor in two prophetic declarations. In the first, Joel described a devastating invasion of locusts, which was wreaking havoc on the agriculture of the Promised Land. To adequately capture the horrific nature of the moment, the inspired poet directed his readers to the experience of a young engaged woman whose husband had died unexpectedly. He called for Israel to pour out their grief like this girl: "Mourn like a virgin in sackcloth grieving for the betrothed of her youth" (Joel 1:8).

In the second instance, Hosea conjured language to describe the wonderful new relationship that would exist between the Lord and his fiancée, Israel. In the extended metaphor, this girl had been unfaithful to her future husband. But despite her indiscretions, the bridegroom offered to make a new marriage contract with his bride: "I will betroth you to me forever; I will betroth you in righteousness and justice, in love and compassion. I will betroth you in faithfulness, and you will acknowledge the LORD" (Hosea 2:19–20). If we change the word translated *in* to the word *with* (something permitted by the Hebrew preposition), then it appears that the Lord was offering

a new marriage contract in which the bride-price would consist of righteousness, justice, love, compassion, and faithfulness. These are amazing benefits that would not go to her parents but to her forever.

A Greek wedding scene.

The Baker Illustrated Guide to Everyday Life in Bible Times

PLOW

The critical role that grain played in the overall diet of those living in Bible times assures that the practice of plowing those grain fields was prominent in the culture of the Promised Land. Only if you were of royal birth or independently wealthy could you expect to find reprieve from the handle of a plow (1 Sam. 8:12; Luke 17:7). This meant that everyone was also familiar with the realities and connotations linked to this process.[10]

Plowing was a time-critical activity that was synchronized with the seasonal rainfall cycle. After months without rain under an unrelenting sun, the farm fields of the Promised Land were baked into inhospitable seedbeds. But the early rains of late October and November softened the soil, allowing the scratch plow to do its job. The goal was never to turn the soil over completely as with a modern moldboard plow. Instead, as its name implies, the scratch plow was designed to scratch open a channel approximately four inches deep into which the seed could be placed. A second series of passes with the plow at a ninety-degree angle to the first passes covered the seeds with soil.[11]

The plow itself was designed to harness the brute strength of draft animals with the cognitive skills of a human operator. It was made mostly of a durable hardwood such as oak, with the exception of the metal plow point. The draft animal's yoke was attached to a horizontal pole that extended to the operator where a waist-high handle was attached. Just below that handle a shorter hardwood fixture, four inches in diameter and twenty inches in length, was attached to the longer pole and pitched slightly downward. The bronze or iron plow point was attached to this fixture, providing a long-wearing point for cutting open the soil. As the animals pulled the plow forward, the operator had to press and hold down the plow point so it would engage the soil and open a furrow of sufficient depth. This process required the operator to maintain a high level of focus on what he was doing lest the plow point run on top of rather than through the soil and lest the metal point strike and be damaged by a large rock. Jesus noted that a similar commitment to the task is required of anyone wishing to serve in the kingdom of God (Luke 9:62).

Plowing was so much a part of the regular rhythm of the year that it carried with it the connotation of normalcy. The biblical authors could characterize people's lives as mundane by observing that they were or would be plowing in the fields (Job

The scratch plow looks different and functions differently than the modern moldboard plow.

1:14; 1 Kings 19:19; Ezek. 36:9). When the season was right, that was what people did unless it happened to be the Sabbath day, when even the critical plowing was expressly prohibited (Exod. 34:21). Conversely, if the biblical authors wanted to emphasize that life had taken an unusual turn, they could point out the absence of plowing. When a horrific famine struck Canaan, it was marked by the fact that no one was bothering to plow (Gen. 45:6). And in the heart of the plowing season, the dramatic change in Elisha's life was marked by the fact that he stopped plowing to follow Elijah. To add emphatic flair and finality to the moment, Elisha slaughtered the draft animals and burned the wooden plow (1 Kings 19:21).

Plowing appears in a variety of metaphors that exploit both the reality of plowing and its connotations. We note that plowing involved intimate acquaintance with the draft animals

Effective plowing required an intimate acquaintance with the draft animals.

and a marked cooperation between the operator and those animals. Consequently, when Samson criticized the wedding attendants who had threatened his fiancée in order to extract the answer to his riddle, he said, "If you had not plowed with my heifer, you would not have solved my riddle" (Judg. 14:18).

An intimate knowledge of the draft animals and experience with them barely reduced the hard work associated with plowing. Given the effort required, it was unthinkable to plow in a place where it was impossible to plant. Amos used that image, noting that it was just as unthinkable for God's people to break their covenant with God as it was for them to plow the rocky crags or the sea (Amos 6:12). Those violations would result in an exile whose difficulties Hosea likened to pulling a plow like a draft animal (Hosea 10:11).

Plowing can also be viewed from the perspective of the soil and then characterized as a painful and destructive process: "Plowmen

Only those born into royal families or wealth could expect to avoid the task of plowing, depicted here.

have plowed my back and made their furrows long" (Ps. 129:3). A judgment speech directed at the national leaders announced that Zion would be plowed (Jer. 26:18; Mic. 3:12). And the plow's indecorous tossing of soil clumps this direction and that was used to describe the way in which the remains of the wicked would be scattered (Ps. 141:7).

Plowing was the first of the agricultural tasks needed for a successful harvest. The sluggard who failed to honor this premise would not find anything to eat at harvest (Prov. 20:4). Because the plowing had to come first, breaking up unplowed ground became a metaphor for the repentance that marked the first step in returning to the Lord (Jer. 4:3; Hosea 10:12). But while plowing was the first task in the agricultural year, it was not the last—the season of plowing would come to an end. In the same way, Isaiah observed that the season of divine judgment would give way to a season of divine favor (Isa. 28:24–26).

Metal plow points cut the soil more effectively and stood a better chance of surviving repeated encounters with rocks.

PLUNDER

From an early age we are taught to respect the belongings of others even if our size and strength make it possible to take them by force. In order to understand the actions of the people of the ancient Near East, we need to make a major adjustment in this thinking. Within the cultural construct of this world, the expectation was that those who were victorious in battle had the right to seize the personal property of those defeated and even enslave the owners of that property. This practice of plundering is mentioned repeatedly in the literature of the ancient world and illustrated in the art of the empires that rose to power during the Old Testament era.[12] Plunder is also mentioned frequently in the Bible; it became one of the first things people contemplated when their leaders advanced the possibility of going to war (Num. 14:3).

In Bible times, plundering was the legitimate and expected confiscation of personal property and enslaving of defeated people following a military victory. When the fighting ended, the victors gathered and inventoried the goods (2 Chron. 20:25). Items on the list included people, animals, household goods, food, clothing, and various forms of jewelry made from precious metals (Gen. 34:29; Num. 31:9–12, 50; Josh. 7:21; Judg. 5:30; 1 Sam. 14:30). Once those items were gathered and inventoried, the process of distribution began (Num. 31:25–54; 1 Sam. 30:21–25). From these and other ancient texts we learn that there were three groups of recipients, each given or shown plunder for a reason:[13]

1. Soldiers: Plunder was the only compensation most soldiers received for going into battle. They were not paid a regular wage but were remunerated by plundering the personal possessions of those they defeated. Ezekiel alluded to this practice when noting the imminent hostilities between the kings of Egypt

This ornately decorated Philistine pot would have made an excellent prize for an Israelite soldier.

and Babylon: "He [the king of Babylon] will loot and plunder the land as pay for his army" (Ezek. 29:19).

2. Deity: Plunder was delivered to the sanctuary of the deity who sponsored the victory to pay homage to that divine being.[14]

3. Home community: The extraction of plunder and parading of the spoils of war before those back home who had not witnessed the victory persuaded them that the magnitude of the victory was commensurate with the claims made by their leaders.

When the biblical authors formally mention the act of plundering and the plunder itself, they are exploiting expected connotations. For the victors, plunder was a source of pride, cause for celebration, and a symbol of the total victory that had been earned with their efforts (Prov. 16:19; Isa. 9:3). By contrast, for the losers the surrender of plunder symbolized their disgrace, humiliation, and total defeat (Pss. 44:10; 89:41). These connotations can be used to influence our reading of passages in Scripture that emphasize dominance and that threaten or report divine judgment. For example, the tribe of Benjamin is characterized with this language: "In the evening he divides the plunder" (Gen. 49:27)—language that anticipates the military successes of its members such as Ehud, Saul, and Jonathan. Note how this image came to life in the language of the Benjaminite Saul: "Saul said, 'Let us go down and pursue the Philistines by night and plunder them till dawn, and let us not leave one of them alive'" (1 Sam. 14:36). In a similar fashion, the success of David was marked by his ability to collect plunder from those whom he defeated (1 Sam. 17:52–53; 2 Sam. 12:30–31). Conversely, when the Lord

The victory that David initiated in the Elah Valley (below) ended with the Israelites plundering the Philistine camp.

threatened the coming of divine retribution for social injustices and covenant violation or when that divine judgment was carried out on his chosen people who were guilty of such sins, it was often linked to being plundered (Judg. 2:14; 2 Kings 17:20; Isa. 42:22, 24; Jer. 17:3; Hosea 13:15). "Your wealth and your treasures I will give as plunder, without charge, because of all your sins throughout your country" (Jer. 15:13). When we consider the highly personal way in which this plundering touched the lives of every single Israelite with the loss of personal possessions so dear to them, we will see it as the powerful call to repentance it was intended to be.

Plundering was also applied metaphorically to those who had never formally taken up arms in the fight. We see this in the case of the Israelites who had been merely observers as the Lord slowly deconstructed the resistance of their Egyptian overlords with plagues. When it was time for God's people to leave the land, he charged each Israelite woman to ask her Egyptian neighbor for silver and gold articles as well as clothing. "And so you will plunder the Egyptians" (Exod. 3:22; see also 12:36).

One way to improve the quality and quantity of a soldier's equipment such as this breastplate was to take it from those defeated in battle.

Plundering was also used as a metaphor for taking advantage of those who are socially disadvantaged. In this case, there was no formal declaration of war and no use of conventional weapons. Rather, it was the leaders of God's people who made laws and the wealthy Israelites who leveraged their money in ways that brought harm to the poor and social outcasts. The prophets of the Lord criticized them for putting the plunder of the poor in their houses (Isa. 3:14) and for turning widows into plunder and plundering the orphans (Isa. 10:2; NIV "making widows their prey and robbing the fatherless").

The plunder that Titus took from Jerusalem included the seven-branched candlestick from the temple.

The Baker Illustrated Guide to Everyday Life in Bible Times

POTTER
(POTTERY MANUFACTURE)

*I*n Bible times, the potter played an important role in providing the basic household storage containers and vessels for cooking used on a daily basis. Even when broken, the larger pottery pieces functioned as scoops and smaller pieces became the equivalent of scrap paper used for jotting down notes and for composing initial drafts of correspondence (Isa. 30:14). No other artifact is found more frequently in archaeological sites of the Promised Land than the potsherd (not surprising given the language of Lamentations 4:2).[15]

The potter's craft is art, science, and hard work all at the same time—something wonderfully captured in the language of an ancient poet: "So too is the potter sitting at his work and turning the wheel with his feet; he is always deeply concerned over his work, and all his output is by the number. He holds the clay with his arm and makes it pliable with his feet; he sets his heart to finish the glazing, and he is careful to clean the furnace."[16] Because the nature of clay varied according to its parent rock, the potter first had to identify a fitting type of clay for the pieces he planned to compose. He added water to this raw clay and literally walked moisture into its structure to achieve the right consistency (Isa. 41:25 "treads").

Three different methods were used to manufacture pottery from this clay.[17] The first method resembled some of the earliest efforts with clay by students in a pottery class today. The potter rolled the clay into long, rope-like cylinders that were then coiled to compose the base and sides of the vessel. The sides were then smoothed to eliminate the spaces between the coils with slip added to improve the bond between the coils. A second method was for the potter to press moist clay into a mold—a technique often used when making a figurine. The third and fastest way to make a round vessel employed a potter's wheel. Operated with a sweep of the hand or kick of the foot, this rotating table added centrifugal force to the equation, which allowed the potter to produce more elaborate yet symmetrical shapes.

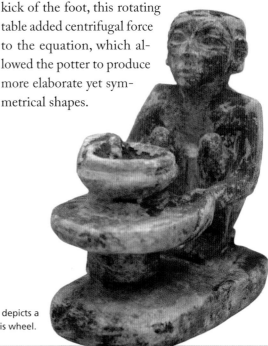

This statue depicts a potter at his wheel.

Once the vessel had been shaped, it was time to decorate and fire it. The overall color was established with slip—a creamy mixture of water, fine clay, and other minerals derived from quartz, sand, shells, or organic materials. Then the potter could paint or incise the pot with decorative elements to make it more appealing to the eye before firing it in the kiln. Careful design of the kiln and the right fuels allowed the temperature of the chamber to reach or exceed 1,000°F, hardening the soft clay into a very durable container or cooking pot.[18]

While we meet very few real potters in the Bible, the potter is frequently employed as a metaphor for the Lord.[19] Like a potter,

The use of color and design can reveal the source of a piece of pottery. This is part of a pot made by a Philistine potter.

the Lord is the one who fashions the physical world in which we live (Isa. 45:18; Amos 4:13). The same language is used to describe the origins of this world's human residents. "Yet you, Lord, are our Father. We are the clay, you are the potter; we are all the work of your hand" (Isa. 64:8; see also 27:11; 44:24). This hands-on shaping extends to the heart, the ears, the eyes, and even the spirit of humans (Pss. 33:15; 94:9; Zech. 12:1). This generates a highly personal image of the creating process and suggests an intimacy in the Lord's relationship with his creation. The

Careful design of a kiln such as this one allowed the potter to turn soft clay into very durable vessels.

The Baker Illustrated Guide to Everyday Life in Bible Times

election of the Israelites as God's chosen people is characterized with the same vocabulary; he is the one who carefully shapes Israel as a potter shapes his handiwork (Isa. 43:1; 44:2; Jer. 10:16; 51:19).

While such imagery conveys the intimacy between the Lord and his creation, it also defines the hierarchy in that relationship. As a potter, God is clearly sovereign. Only in a fully upside-down world would the clay criticize the potter; but that is the unlikely scenario presented by Isaiah when describing the behavior of the Israelites: "You turn things upside down, as if the potter were thought to be the clay! Shall what is formed say to the one who formed it, 'You did not make me'? Can the pot say to the potter, 'You know nothing'?" (Isa. 29:16). "Woe to those who quarrel with their Potter, those who are nothing but potsherds among the potsherds on the ground" (Isa. 45:9; NIV translates it "Maker" instead of "Potter"). Rather than diminish, this problem increased through the time of Jeremiah. So the

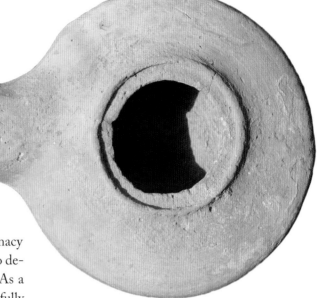

Potters made household items such as this first-century lamp.

Lord directed this prophet to go to a potter's house and observe the potter shaping a pot on a wheel, noting particularly the moment when the dissatisfied potter destroyed the imperfect piece on the wheel and reshaped the raw material into a better vessel (Jer. 18:1–4). "Then the word of the LORD came to me. He said, 'Can I not do with you, Israel, as this potter does?' declares the LORD. 'Like clay in the hand of the potter, so you are in my hand, Israel'" (Jer. 18:5–6).

PROSTITUTE

Within the larger ancient Near Eastern world, prostitution was legal and generally accepted by members of society, and there is evidence that some prostitutes in Mesopotamia gathered into professional associations linked to the goddess Ishtar.[20] The Hebrew of the Old Testament uses two different words when referring to those who functioned as prostitutes (*zônâ*, translated "prostitute" in Gen. 38:15; and *qĕdēšâ*, translated "shrine prostitute" in Gen. 38:21–22), which suggests that the prostitutes in Canaan were of two types: secular sex workers and prostitutes linked to pagan worship. Nevertheless, given the extent of the evidence we possess from the ancient world, we need to use caution in identifying the latter too closely with pagan worship rites that sought to increase the fertility of flocks, herds, and fields.[21]

No matter what the form, the biblical authors make it crystal clear that prostitution is a sin (Lev. 19:29; 21:9; Deut. 23:17–18); it is an activity pursued by the godless rather than the godly (Job 36:14; 1 Cor. 6:15–17). Consequently, it is not surprising to see such a woman characterized in very unflattering ways. We are told that she is not interested in sustaining a loving, marital relationship with her clients, "for a prostitute will bring you to poverty" (Prov. 6:26 NLT); she will be interested in you only long enough for you to squander all your money on her (Prov. 29:3; Luke 15:30). She walks about brazenly with a seared conscience devoid of shame or regret (Jer. 3:3; Ezek. 16:30). The Bible implies that a prostitute dresses in an identifiable way (Prov. 7:10), but ironically her attempts to solicit attention only create a life in which she is quickly forgotten (Isa. 23:16). This very negative assessment of the prostitute is

The Coliseum at Rome. In Revelation, not just the word *prostitute* but the phrase *great prostitute* is used to characterize the "great city that rules over the kings of the earth" (17:18), a city that many identified as Rome.

in no way improved by Tamar and Rahab (Gen. 38:15, 26; Josh. 2:1; 6:17, 22, 25; Heb. 11:31; James 2:25), even though the latter is mentioned in the genealogical record of Jesus (Matt. 1:5).

The formal mention of prostitutes in the Bible is often used to shape our impression of people with whom they were associated. Because the law of God was clear on this matter, the linking of a man with a prostitute, whether sexually or by birth, cast a dark cloud over his character. This included notables like Judah, Jephthah, and Samson (Gen. 38:15; Judg. 11:1; 16:1). When Joshua sent spies to Jericho, the population was so immoral that the one person of redeeming value found in the city was a prostitute (Josh. 2:1). And the image of Ahab was clearly tarnished by the fact that his bloody chariot was washed out at the place where the prostitutes bathed (1 Kings 22:38). By contrast, Israel's leaders who aggressively expelled shrine prostitutes from the Promised Land were celebrated for their efforts (1 Kings 15:11–12; 22:43–46; 2 Kings 23:3, 7). The Jewish leaders at the time of Jesus shunned prostitutes. But when they failed to recognize the authenticity of Jesus's claims to be the Messiah, those leaders found themselves facing a criticism they never thought they would hear: "Truly I tell you, the tax collectors and the prostitutes are entering the kingdom of God ahead of you" (Matt. 21:31).

The idea of the prostitute also appears in the Bible as a metaphor deployed in various ways. Simeon and Levi sought to defend their actions and tactics in harming the residents of Shechem by saying to their father, "Should he have treated our sister like a prostitute?" (Gen. 34:31). The "he" was the son of an influential resident of Shechem who had sexually violated the daughter of Jacob. He had used her sexually without providing a long-term commitment, paralleling the way a prostitute was used.

Not just the word *prostitute* but the phrase *great prostitute* was used to characterize the "great city that rules over the kings of the earth" (Rev. 17:1, 5, 16, 18; 19:2). For those living in John's day, this great city was known as Rome, but it was also symbolic of all great national capitals that opposed the coming of Christ's kingdom. The goal of the opponents of the Messiah was to make themselves and their

Samson grew up on this ridge, which had a Jewish orientation, but he is characterized in part by his use of a prostitute in the Philistine city of Gaza.

resistance to Christ stronger through financial dealings that were like those of the prostitute—financial gain without commitment to the well-being of the martial relationship.

Finally, the word *prostitute* was linked to God's own people, particularly as the prophets criticized their unwarranted political alliances and dabbling in the worship of pagan deities, both of which represented a breach in the marriage-like covenant they were to enjoy with the Lord (Deut. 31:16; Isa. 1:21; Jer. 2:20, 23–24; 3:1). Two extended metaphors in Ezekiel are worthy of note here. In Ezekiel 16, Jerusalem and its residents are likened to a female infant who was abandoned by her parents and was destined to be claimed by those who would raise her to be a prostitute.[22] The Lord rescued her from this life and made her his bride, only to have her choose a life of prostitution by engaging in pagan worship and alliances with nations that required pagan worship, such as Egypt, Assyria, and Babylon. "You adulterous wife! You prefer strangers to your own

Pagan fertility cults, which used naked female images, may also have employed prostitutes.

husband! All prostitutes receive gifts, but you give gifts to all your lovers, bribing them to come to you from everywhere for your illicit favors" (Ezek. 16:32–33). Just a few chapters later in Ezekiel 23:1–14, the extended metaphor that describes the two kingdoms of Israel and Judah as wayward sisters uses similar imagery.

The prostitute Rahab receives repeated mention in Joshua's account of the fall of Jericho (below).

The Baker Illustrated Guide to Everyday Life in Bible Times

QUARRY
(TO HEW)

The hard limestone of the Promised Land had many uses. It could be made to store water or the remains of loved ones. It could become a message board or a building that could endure both weathering and the withering assault of an enemy. But in order to obtain these and other products, the limestone had to be quarried or hewed from its parent rock.[1]

People quarried stone because of both the need to build chambers and the need to acquire stone used for constructing palaces, defensive walls, grinding mills, or stelae. Hewed stone chambers were used as the final resting place for loved ones, to capture and store surface water, or to collect the valuable juice from the grapes as they were stomped. Hand-hewed tombs, wine pressing floors, and cisterns or wells are formally mentioned in the Bible (Deut. 6:11; Isa. 5:2; 22:16; Jer. 2:13; Matt. 27:60). The virgin stone that quarrymen extracted from projects such as these, as well as from dedicated rock quarries, could become a tablet or stela on which to write a message (Exod. 34:1; Job 19:24), but the majority of quarried stone was trimmed into the large, square building stones called ashlars (1 Kings 6:7).

When we think about any form of quarrying, and in particular when we think about the hewing of ashlars, we need to understand the tremendous effort required to obtain the desired results. In Bible times there were no powerful machines that could hew on command and there were no explosives to drive rock from its longtime resting place. Instead stone was hewed by men whose muscles ached

Hewed stone chambers became the final resting place for loved ones who had died.

for the effort, aided only by pick, hammer, chisel, and lever. This was particularly true of the ashlar stones, which were cut so that they had six flat surfaces, each at a ninety-degree angle to its neighbor.[2] They were extracted from the quarry by first defining their outline by incising a long, narrow groove (5 to 10 centimeters deep by 30 centimeters long) around the perimeter of the stone or by drilling holes in a line that defined the intended shape of the stone. At times it was possible to crack the nascent ashlar from its parent rock by the use of chisels and levers. When this proved unproductive, wooden stakes were driven into the crack or drilled holes. Then water was poured on the stakes, causing them to expand and break the building stone from its resting place. The final symmetry of such stones was achieved by the deft blows of iron chisels, which produced stones that gave public buildings the sharp architectural lines desired. While their shape changed, their capacity to endure did not, eroding so slowly that stones excavated thousands of years ago can still be seen doing their job in ancient foundations excavated today.[3]

When the biblical authors mention quarrying like this or the stone that comes from quarries in real-life contexts, they are frequently leveraging one of two connotations: (1) the effort required of the excavators to free the stone, or (2) the enduring nature of the stone. As the Lord led the Israelites toward the Promised Land, he whetted their appetites for what was to come by telling them that they would be taking over water systems that other people had already excavated, thus avoiding the backbreaking labor excavating would otherwise have required (Deut. 6:11). After Moses broke the first set of tablets on which the law was written, the Lord directed him to hew out another set so the Lord could write them down a second time (Exod. 34:1; Deut. 10:1, 3). And repeatedly as the temple was rebuilt or refurbished, the biblical authors noted or alluded to the fact that it was composed of

Quarried stone could be fashioned into amazing shapes and structures, such as this Temple of Hercules in Amman.

quarried stone (1 Kings 5:15, 17–18; 7:9–11; 2 Kings 12:12; 1 Chron. 22:2, 15; 2 Chron. 2:2, 18). In contrast to other construction techniques, the use of quarried stone in shaping this building helped to define the structure as unique and able to endure. These same connotations are also tied to the quarried stone on which the Ten Commandments were written. The unique writing surface drew attention to the message while creating a surface on which the message would endure.

Quarrying also appears as a metaphor with various connotations associated with the quarrying of stone. We find the enduring nature of a quarried stone mentioned in Job. Through his pain, this man grasped at the only hope he could see: a living Redeemer who would allow him to live beyond death. This idea was so important to him that he longed for this message to be "engraved in rock forever" so that it would stand as an eternal monument (Job 19:24–27). The metaphor was also used by the prophets when they alluded to the amount of energy and force required to hew out stone when building a cistern or excavating rock from a quarry. Rather than enjoying what the Lord had offered them—"the spring of living water"—the Israelites immersed themselves in man-made religion, digging their own cisterns (Jer. 2:13). Hosea prophesied that unrepentant Israel would meet the hammer and pick blows of the prophets striking against the recalcitrant rock in the hard quarry of

An ashlar building block was being cut from this ancient Jerusalem quarry when quarrying operations ceased.

their hearts. God declared he would cut them in pieces with his prophets (Hosea 6:5). But to those who repented and looked for restoration, this invitation was offered: "Look to the rock from which you were cut and to the quarry from which you were hewn" (Isa. 51:1). In the same way that most qualities of the parent rock were transferred to the quarried ashlar, the promises made to Abraham, the rock from which they were cut, extended to his descendants as well.

Stone drills were used to define the edges of a stone block during the quarrying process.

27683

RIDE

When we travel overland for a long distance, we are most likely to do so by riding in a car, bus, or train. When we read about people riding in the Bible, we find they rode on donkeys, on camels, or in chariots.[1] But when average people moved from one place to the next, they walked. (Note the intended contrast between nobles and commoners in Judges 5:10.) This means that riding made one stand out in biblical times. For example, royal officials, appointees, and their family members rode (Gen. 41:43; 2 Sam. 18:9; Neh. 2:12; Jer. 17:25; 22:4). Soldiers rode everything from chariots to horses, donkeys, and camels (Isa. 21:7).[2] We also see Persian couriers riding carefully bred horses in order to speed royal announcements to the far-flung corners of their empire (Esther 8:10, 14).

While most people ride in our day, in Bible times only a select few are portrayed as riding. Consequently, riding carried connotations then that are different from those in our own age. The first is honor. The riders in the Bible did not board stretch limousines, but the honor they were given was as if they did. Once his status was elevated, Joseph was driven around in an Egyptian chariot (Gen. 41:43). The same is true of the judge Jair, whose thirty sons rode on thirty donkeys (Judg. 10:3–4; see also 12:14); of Solomon, who rode on his father's mule to the place of his coronation (1 Kings 1:33, 38); and of Elijah, who was carried into glory by a fiery chariot (2 Kings 2:11–12). Second, the connotation of urgency can be linked to riding. Sometimes people rode quickly in service to an urgent mission, like Balaam or Abigail on their donkeys, or Jehu, who drove his chariot like a madman (Num. 22:22; 1 Sam. 25:20; 2 Kings 9:16, 20). At other times people rode urgently to escape—for example, from a renegade son or an impending heavy rain (2 Sam. 16:2; 1 Kings 18:45). In addition to the connotations of honor and speed,

Camels were used to transport both goods and people in the ancient world, as they are today.

The Baker Illustrated Guide to Everyday Life in Bible Times

we can add a third connotation of terror when it was Israel's enemy who was riding. Before the time of King Solomon, the Israelites did not have horses and chariots for battle, so their presence on the battlefield filled the Israelite soldiers with dread (Exod. 14:9–10; Judg. 4:3; Ps. 66:12). And even after the Israelites had horses and chariots, the image of an advancing cavalry unit was still terrifying: "Look, an army is coming from the land of the north. . . . They sound like the roaring sea as they ride on their horses" (Jer. 6:22–23). But such a threat never exceeded the Lord's ability to intervene. "I will overturn royal thrones and shatter the power of the foreign kingdoms. I will overthrow chariots and their drivers; horses and their riders will fall" (Hag. 2:22; see also Jer. 51:21; Zech. 12:4).

Three forms of riding deserve special mention. First, God used this metaphor at the time of Moses and of Isaiah to speak of the way he blessed his people: "He made him [Israel] ride on the heights of the land and fed him with the fruit of the fields" (Deut. 32:13; see also Isa. 58:14). When people walked in the mountains of the Promised Land, they sought to minimize elevation changes. The best way to do that was to walk along "the heights of the land," that is along the ridgelines where elevation changes were at a minimum. This route saved travel time and preserved energy. The only way that route could get better was

Jesus's triumphal entry into Jerusalem is distinguished by his riding a donkey over the Mount of Olives (below) and into the holy city.

if you could avoid walking altogether and get a ride. To be able to walk on the heights was a blessing; to ride on the heights was even more of a blessing.

The second special instance of riding is related to the Lord riding. On a number of occasions the biblical authors picture the Lord riding on the clouds of heaven (Deut. 33:26; Pss. 68:4, 33; 104:3; Isa. 19:1). When the biblical authors say that the Lord alone is capable of doing this and so he alone is worthy of our praise, it can be read as a direct assault on the theology of Baal. Baal, the storm god, is often pictured in other ancient Near Eastern sources as riding on a storm cloud.[3] This near parallel language jettisons Baal from his riding position and puts the Lord in his proper place.

Finally, we have the special circumstances that surrounded Jesus riding a donkey for his triumphal entry into the city of Jerusalem. Jesus had entered Jerusalem on many other occasions, but this is the only time we

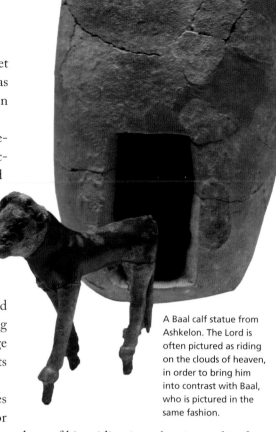

A Baal calf statue from Ashkelon. The Lord is often pictured as riding on the clouds of heaven, in order to bring him into contrast with Baal, who is pictured in the same fashion.

hear of him riding into the city; and in fact, it is the only time we hear about Jesus riding anywhere. When the crowds saw not just that he was riding into Jerusalem but that he was riding into Jerusalem on a donkey, their excited shouts filled the slopes of the Mount of Olives. Matthew helps us understand the cause of this celebration; this entry of Jesus into Jerusalem riding on a donkey fulfilled Old Testament prophecy (Zech. 9:9; Matt. 21:1–5).[4]

Those who rode in chariots were often being marked for special honor.

RUN

Walking was the most common way for people living in Bible times to get from one place to another on a daily basis. Given the fatigue that discourages sustained running, those who ran were either special people with unique vocations or ordinary people who were responding to unique situations. Those expected to run included athletes, couriers, and royal guards. The Greeks introduced the world to athletic contests that were the precursor to our Olympic games. The ancient games included running events of various distances in which athletes could compete against one another.[5] Couriers were also regular runners. Though there was no access to any form of electronic communication in Bible times, people still had important messages to deliver. One option was to use couriers like the unnamed Cushite who carried the news of Absalom's death to David (2 Sam. 18:21). The physical skills of couriers compare favorably to modern marathoners. Postal couriers from the Roman period were capable of maintaining a pace that put one hundred statute miles behind them by the time their day was done.[6] Members of the royal guard were also required to run while the leader they protected rode in a chariot (1 Sam. 8:11). Pretenders to the throne like Absalom and Adonijah duplicated this royal imagery as they tried to slip the throne from the hands of its rightful owner (2 Sam. 15:1; 1 Kings 1:5).

For individuals like these, running was normal; for everyone else, running was the

The rugged terrain of the Promised Land (below) made it difficult to walk anywhere, much less run. This informs the comforting words of Scripture, which declares we will run and not become weary (Isa. 40:31).

exception. Consequently, when the biblical authors tell us someone was running, we do well to pay close attention to what the excitement was all about. There are five special situations in which we most often find people running in the Bible.[7]

1. The excitement over a family event, whether a wedding or reunion, caused people to run for various reasons. Weddings were always an exciting time for families, and when a wedding was in the

Today most pilgrims walk quietly in the Church of the Resurrection (below), in contrast to the frenzied running of Peter and John, who were anxious to arrive at Jesus's tomb on Easter morning.

making, that excitement could manifest itself with an increase in people running (Gen. 24:17, 20, 28, 29; 29:12–13). The excitement that surrounded a family reunion could also cause people to leave behind their normal gait and break into a full-fledged run (Gen. 33:4; Luke 15:20).

2. Those carrying important news had trouble limiting their gait to a walk. This could be news of a pregnancy long thought to be impossible, the capture of the ark of the covenant, the death of a son, or the resurrection of Jesus (Judg. 13:10; 1 Sam. 4:12; 2 Sam. 18:19, 21–24, 26; 2 Kings 4:22, 26; Matt. 28:8; John 20:2).

3. Situations that demanded immediate action were marked by people running. Aaron ran into the midst of the Israelite assembly swinging his censor wildly to stop the spread of a plague that was streaming through the Israelite camp (Num. 16:47). Israelite soldiers ran to spring an ambush on the city of Ai (Josh. 8:19). And David ran directly at Goliath, shortening the time before the Philistine soldiers found themselves running from the valley in retreat (1 Sam. 17:48, 51).

4. In other situations an individual's running highlighted that person's commitment to duty. Samuel ran to Eli, David ran to check on the well-being of his brothers, and Elisha left behind his farm work to run after Elijah (1 Sam. 3:5; 17:17, 22; 1 Kings 19:20).

5. Finally, we read text after text that speak of people running to Jesus for help and assistance. Sometimes an entire crowd of people came running to him and at other times it was just an individual. Whether it was a person who was possessed by a demon or someone who had failed to find meaning in life despite his wealth (Mark 5:6; 9:15; 10:17), they ran trusting that Jesus could help. And this did not stop with his death because Peter and John ran to the tomb to see if the report of his resurrection was true (Luke 24:12; John 20:4).

The notion of running is also used in figures of speech that describe the spiritual life of a person. To run toward something suggests that you feel passionate about it. The wise poet of Proverbs warned his son about allowing sinners to set the pace for his life, "for their feet rush [run] into evil, they are swift to shed blood" (Prov. 1:16; see also Isa. 59:7; NIV "rush").

By contrast, the image of running can capture the passion for living a godly life: "I run in the path of your commands, for you have broadened my understanding" (Ps. 119:32). This kind of spiritual running has some striking advantages over real-world running: "When you run, you will not stumble" (Prov. 4:12). "They will run and not grow weary, they will walk and not be faint" (Isa. 40:31). The great number of believers who have run successfully over the centuries provides us encouragement to "run with perseverance the race marked out for us" (Heb. 12:1).

Because Paul so often wrote to those who were familiar with the Greek games and the running contests that were connected to them, he rather frequently described the Christian life as a race: "Do you not know that in a race all the runners run, but only one gets the prize? Run in such a way as to get the prize" (1 Cor. 9:24). Paul was not one to run—that is, live his life—aimlessly or in vain (1 Cor. 9:26; Gal. 2:2; Phil. 2:16). He called believers to keep running the good race, chiding the Galatians when it looked otherwise: "You were running a good race. Who cut in on you to keep you from obeying the truth?" (Gal. 5:7).

Greek athletes running in the Panathenaic Games.

SABBATH
(TO OBSERVE)

Many cultures have special days set aside for religious observance, but no other culture in the ancient world had a weekly day of rest like the Sabbath.[1] This twenty-four-hour period of quiet began as the sun set on Friday—a time eventually marked by the sounding of a ram's horn.[2] The Israelites were to keep this day holy (set apart) from all the other days of the week. They did so in various ways. For example, all the members of the Israelite household, including servants and working animals, discontinued the ordinary tasks that filled their week, resting as God rested on the seventh day of creation (Exod. 20:8–11; Deut. 5:12–15). In practice, this meant tasks such as the following were to cease: gathering food, preparing food, plowing, gathering wood, conducting commerce, treading grapes, carrying a load, or loading a donkey (Exod. 16:23, 25–26; 34:21; Num. 15:32–36; Neh. 10:31; 13:15–16; Jer. 17:21–22). Yet the Sabbath day was not to be a day of inactivity but rather a day of directed activity. The clergy continued to work at the sanctuary as the people brought that day's offerings (Lev. 24:8; Num. 28:9). And the people gathered before teachers and prophets on hillsides and eventually in synagogues to learn more of God's Word (Lev. 23:3; 2 Kings 4:23; Mark 6:2; Luke 4:15; Acts 15:21). This day off work was a day to reflect on the thoughts of God—a truly delightful day (Isa. 58:13).

The purpose behind the Sabbath was variously defined. It was a day to recall two important events on the calendar of this world's history: (1) the Lord's creation of the world, and (2) the exodus from Egypt (Exod. 20:11; 31:17; Deut. 5:15). The Sabbath was also defined as a "sign" and a "lasting covenant" between Israel and the Lord (Exod. 31:13, 16–18; Ezek. 20:12, 20), a reminder of their unique calling and privilege. And the Sabbath was the day to review and find peace in two powerful principles that grew from the events of creation and exodus: (1) God is in control, and (2) God has a plan (Psalm 92). No matter

The beginning of the Sabbath was marked by the sounding of a ram's horn.

what might be disturbing the people's lives, these two principles could calm the troubled waters.

Ironically, when the biblical authors formally mention the Sabbath day, it is frequently in connection with Israel's failure to honor this day. The directive was so important that Nehemiah used it as the exemplar for all the laws given by the Lord on Mount Sinai (Neh. 9:14). Disobedience was a capital crime (Exod. 35:2). Nevertheless, it was the rampant failure to observe this law that met prophetic criticism and that invited divine judgment (Exod. 16:27–29; Jer. 17:27; Ezek. 20:13–16, 23–24; Hosea 2:11). Even when the Sabbath was observed externally, there was the risk that the wrong attitude could compromise the effort. Lackluster convocations did not get it done (Isa. 1:12–13), particularly when accompanied by whining: "When will the New Moon be over that we may sell grain, and the Sabbath be ended that we may market wheat?" (Amos 8:5).

After the destruction of the first temple in Jerusalem and the exile of God's people from the land, Israelites with a passion to get it right gave increasing attention to purifying their Sabbath observance.[3] We see that passion in Jewish soldiers who allowed themselves to be slaughtered rather than pick up their weapons to fight on the Sabbath.[4] And the rabbis sought to define more sharply what it meant to rest; their efforts culminated in the very detailed directives of the Mishnah, in which an entire section

Carrying goods from one place to another was a necessary part of life but, like other daily tasks, was restricted on the Sabbath.

is directed to the definition of Sabbath. In it there is a list of thirty-nine categories of labor that are prohibited, such as baking, sewing two stitches, or writing two letters.[5] These are parsed even further in the Mishnaic discussions that follow.

It is no wonder that the religious leaders had so many problems with Jesus, who on a somewhat regular basis fell afoul of these extensions to the divine law. Jesus's disciples were criticized for scraping grain from ripe stalks on the Sabbath (Matt. 12:1–2; Mark 2:23–24; Luke 6:1–2). A disabled man Jesus healed was criticized for carrying his mat on the Sabbath (John 5:8–11). And Jesus himself was called to

Writing, particularly of religious texts, was very important to the Jewish culture, as illustrated in this Hebrew text from Qumran. But rabbis said that the writing of more than two letters constituted work, which was forbidden on the Sabbath.

task numerous times for healing people on the Sabbath (Matt. 12:9–14; Mark 3:1–6; Luke 13:10–17; 14:1–6; John 9:13–16). While obeying the biblical commands, Jesus responded to this criticism by reminding his detractors that "the Sabbath was made for man, not man for the Sabbath" (Mark 2:27); their criticism was unfounded given the kindness they extended to animals in need on the Sabbath (Matt. 12:11; Luke 13:15; 14:5). What is more, Jesus was the Lord of the Sabbath (Mark 2:28), much greater than David, whom they did not censure for his apparent violation of the law (Matt. 12:3–6).

Jesus invited people to come to him for true rest (Matt. 11:28), a "Sabbath-rest" the gospel offers that will last into eternity. "There remains, then, a Sabbath-rest for the people of God; for anyone who enters God's rest also rests from their works, just as God did from

his. Let us, therefore, make every effort to enter that rest" (Heb. 4:9–11). One generation of believers heard about and lived that rest when they went to the synagogue on the Sabbath. Later generations of believers learned of this rest directly from Jesus and from Paul just as we hear of it today from God's Word (Luke 4:14–21; Acts 13:14–15, 42–44; 17:2; 18:4). Ironically, this day of rest became a point of unrest as some insisted that it be observed under the new covenant as it was under the old. Paul put this matter to rest when he observed that no one was to be judged any longer by the old way of observing the Sabbath (Col. 2:16).

SACRED STONE
(TO SET UP OR TO DESTROY)

When contemporary hikers traveling the backcountry encounter places where the well-worn path gives way to solid rock, they often find cairns to guide their footsteps on an otherwise invisible path. Cairns are made from natural stones that have been stacked on top of one another in an unnatural way to catch the hiker's eye. The ancient world had something similar, but it had nothing to do with hiking. In the ancient world, a single stone or pile of stones set up in an unnatural way was called a *maṣṣēbâ* in

The unique appearance of this trail cairn summons the attention of hikers. Sacred stones rely on the same attention-getting strategy.

Hebrew. This word is translated in a variety of ways, including "pillar," "standing stone," and "sacred stone."

A single *maṣṣēbâ* could function as either a memorial stone that invited the viewer to recall a past event or a sacred stone that was employed in worship. The memorial pillar could function in three different ways. First, it could mark the last resting place of a person who died. For example, Jacob set up a pillar at the tomb of Rachel (Gen. 35:20). Second, the pillar or memorial stone could invite the viewer to recall an important event that happened near its location. Jacob set up such a memorial stone as a reminder of the theophany he experienced at Bethel (Gen. 28:18, 22; 31:13; 35:14). And Samuel set up a stone to commemorate the victory God gave Israel against the Philistines (1 Sam. 7:12). Third, the memorial stone could be put in place to commemorate an agreement that was struck near its location (Gen.

31:45–47, 51–52; Exod. 24:4; Josh. 24:26–27).

Most often, however, it appears that a *maṣṣēbâ* was set up as a sacred stone.[6] In this case, the unnaturally placed stone or series of stones provided worshipers with a physical location at which to meet their deity. To this day, surviving sacred stones break the natural contours of the landscape, inviting us to come in for a closer look. The outdoor sanctuary was often marked by stones in groups of seven to nine upright monoliths that faced east with a courtyard immediately to the west.[7] At times long, thin stones were placed next to shorter stones; some have interpreted the taller sacred stones to be associated with male deities and the shorter ones with female deities.[8] In general, the sacred stones that survive in the Promised Land have no message or features carved into them. Some scholars presume that the stones themselves were believed to not just represent the deity but to actually contain the essence of the deity. If that is the case, the raucous

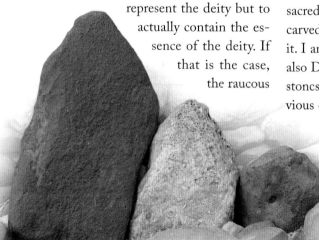

The god Hadad rides a bull on this basalt stela.

carving process might have been intentionally avoided in order to avoid disturbing the deity present within the sacred stone.[9]

The large number of surviving sacred stones coupled with the frequent mention of such stones in Old Testament law settings combine to show just how deeply this particular practice was woven into the fabric of ancient Near Eastern culture. As the Israelites met and engaged the people who occupied the Promised Land before them, they might have been tempted to adopt the sacred-stone concept. To be sure, the Lord did allow a certain amount of parity between pagan worship and Israelite worship, such as the use of sacrifice, temple, and priesthood; but the line was drawn at employing sacred stones. "Do not make idols or set up an image or a sacred stone for yourselves, and do not place a carved stone in your land to bow down before it. I am the LORD your God" (Lev. 26:1; see also Deut. 16:22). But what about the sacred stones that had already been built by the previous occupants of the Promised Land? The law was equally clear in respect to the future of these worship installations. The Israelites were to "demolish," "break," and "smash" the sacred stones erected by pagan

This collection of sacred stones was strategically placed outside the gate of Dan.

worshipers (Exod. 23:24; 34:13; Deut. 7:5; 12:3). Please note that this was a far cry from ignoring those stones or even from just tipping them over. They were directed to make them unrecognizable from the rubble around them by breaking them apart. Apparently the act of smashing them destroyed their capacity to represent or hold the essence of the deity any longer, thus preventing any Israelite who was so inclined from assimilating these sacred stones into their worship life.

With the law code establishing these clear directives regarding sacred stones, the biblical authors who came later returned to this topic repeatedly as they evaluated the Israelites' faithfulness to the Lord and their commitment to keep their end of the covenant they had made with him. The evaluation at times took a decidedly negative tone. Rehoboam, the son of Solomon, was the first to have his reign characterized in a more negative way due to the fact that Judah "set up for themselves high places, sacred stones and Asherah poles on every high hill and under every spreading tree" (1 Kings 14:23). This was clearly a case of hyperbole; nevertheless a land that appeared full of what God had forbidden characterized Rehoboam's rule as less than it needed to be. Hoshea of Israel faced a similar indictment, as did Jeroboam II (2 Kings 17:10; Hosea 10:1–2). Because the people of God did not destroy the sacred stones but instead erected more, the Lord himself assumed the role of destroyer of sacred stones (Hosea 10:2; Mic. 5:13).

On the other hand, the biblical authors certified the faithfulness of other rulers, in part by the fact that they removed the sacred stones from the land. Kings like Joram, Jehu, Hezekiah, Josiah, and Asa were all commended for removing pagan worship facilities and destroying sacred stones (2 Kings 3:1–2; 10:25–27; 18:1, 3–4; 23:14; 2 Chron. 14:2–3).

Ancient people frequently employed sacred stones such as these at Gezer, which became part of their pagan worship.

SADDUCEE
(CHIEF PRIEST)

Both Jewish and Christian writers mention the Sadducees as a subgroup of Jewish society whose station in life, values, and theology differed from the Pharisees. The origin of the name Sadducee is debated, though it appears to have a connection to Zadok, the descendant of Aaron who remained loyal to David and Solomon during attempts to wrest the monarchy from them. Zadok became the high priest, and his family supplied Israel with its legitimate high priests for centuries (2 Sam. 15:24, 27, 29; 1 Kings 1:38; 2:35; 1 Chron. 6:12). Between the time of the Old and New Testaments, this office was given as a political favor to office holders who did not have a connection to the family of Zadok, including those in the party of the Sadducees.[10] Though they were not Zadokites, the Sadducees appear to have leveraged the prestige of their name for their own purposes.

The homes of the Sadducees are among the most lavish discovered to date in Jerusalem.

The Baker Illustrated Guide to Everyday Life in Bible Times

To best perceive their status within first-century Judaism, we need to consider their position in society, their worldview, and how they were perceived by others. While Josephus contrasts them with other religious groups, namely the Pharisees and Essenes,[11] it would be a mistake to see them only as a religious group. The aristocratic priests were joined by other people of wealth and influence who were not members of the clergy to form the party of the Sadducees.[12] Nevertheless, their importance to Bible readers is linked to their ability to control the two most powerful religious institutions in first-century Judaism: the temple and the Sanhedrin.[13]

In order to understand their role in the culture, we need to know what they believed and what they valued. But here a word of caution is in order because the only characterization of the Sadducees' worldview we possess comes from their detractors. Like the Pharisees, they looked to the Old Testament and the Torah in particular as their authoritative canon. But unlike the Pharisees, they did not honor the traditions of the later oral law.[14] The Sadducees believed that people were captains of their own destiny, unrestrained by divine providence.[15] They did not believe in the existence of a human soul, in a bodily resurrection, or in life after death (Acts 23:8). The Sadducees were not particularly popular and were even disparaged by later Jewish writers.[16] Nevertheless, what remained important to them was wealth and the influence that wealth and position had to offer (John 11:48).[17] We see evidence of this in the homes they built, which are the most opulent discovered to date in Jerusalem.[18] They did what was necessary to maintain that influence, accommodating themselves to the

Stone vessels were used in the homes of the aristocratic priests because stone did not transmit ritual impurity like clay vessels did.

Romans as necessary but always being cautious about ritual purity. When taking Jesus to Pilate, they were careful to avoid ritual contamination because that would disqualify them from leading the temple services that generated income (John 18:28).

When the biblical authors formally mention the Sadducees, they present them in a very negative light, criticizing both their theology and their opposition to the kingdom of God. When surveying the adjectives applied to and descriptions of the Sadducees, we look in vain for any positive note; rather we encounter a growing list of invectives. Sadducees are called a brood of vipers, a wicked and adulterous generation, unrepentant sign-seekers, people who are ignorant of the Scriptures and of the power of God, and whitewashed walls who only look good on the outside (Matt. 3:7; 16:4; 22:23, 29; Mark 12:18, 27; Acts 23:3). And their claims of influence and power are not-so-subtly mocked when those they put in prison for preaching go missing from the prison, only to reappear in the temple courts, teaching as they had been before (Acts 5:18, 25).

Despite these invectives, it is clear that the Sadducees were capable of wielding their wealth and influence in an effort to derail the advance of the kingdom of God. They saw Jesus as a threat who upset their cash flow both by overturning tables in the temple market and by causing the sort of unrest that could cause the Romans to take away their place of privilege (Mark 11:15–18; John 11:48). When they could not discredit him with their questions, they actively worked to have him tried and executed (Matt. 22:23, 29–33; 26:3–5; Mark 14:53). And after Jesus died, they did all they could to prevent the likes of Peter, John, and Paul from advancing his message through the gospel they preached (Acts 4:1–3, 6; 5:17; 23:6).

Their theology is mentioned by the biblical authors incidentally when it is necessary to contrast their views with the Pharisees (Acts 23:6–9). But we have one instance in which Jesus took on their theology directly, perhaps because the element of theology in view, shared by the Sadducees and Pharisees, had the ability to completely undo the larger assignment Jesus had for the disciples following his ascension. Three times in this brief narrative he cautioned his disciples not to be influenced by the "yeast of the Pharisees and Sadducees" (Matt. 16:5–12). Jesus did not directly describe what this yeast was, but he contrasted it with the feeding of the four thousand and the five thousand. These parallel feeding miracles were done for the benefit of two different communities—one Jewish and one Gentile—in order to illustrate that the kingdom of God was composed of both. This suggests that the dangerous yeast the disciples were to avoid was the notion that the kingdom of God was to be composed only of Jews.

John the Baptist sized up the Sadducees with a message as harsh as the Judean wilderness in which he taught (below): he called them a brood of vipers.

The Baker Illustrated Guide to Everyday Life in Bible Times

SANDALS
(TO REMOVE)

electing and slipping into footwear is such an ordinary part of our daily schedule that we usually don't even notice we have done it. The same was the case for those living in Bible times who wore sandals on a daily basis. When we examine the surviving examples of footwear and look carefully at the artwork from this period, we see that footwear evolved in composition and design. But when we get down to it, the simple sandal worn in most periods was not all that different from the sandals we wear today. It consisted of a sole designed to cover the bottom of the foot that sometimes included a heel cap. The soles were made of wood, reeds, or leather attached to the wearer by a series of leather straps going around the foot and ankle.[19] Sandals like this were worn in order to protect the wearer's foot from the dirt on which he walked and also to provide a modest amount of protection from the sharp stones and thorns on ancient footpaths. Because people traveled from one place to another by walking and because they traveled on those footpaths virtually every day, they donned sandals to protect their feet. And for those who walked more than others, such as soldiers, donkeys loaded with

sandals were sent along to replace sandals that broke or wore out along the way.[20]

Since the norm was to wear sandals, we take particular note of those instances when the biblical authors mention that people had removed their sandals or were walking barefoot. The first of these instances was an occasion when a superior was being shown respect. In Egypt it seems to have been the case that those who received an audience with the king removed their footwear in deference to the leader before whom they stood.[21] Thus it was more than fitting that Moses and Joshua removed their sandals when standing on ground made holy by the presence of the Lord or one of his messengers (Exod. 3:5; Josh. 5:15). This may also be reflected in a much more subtle way by what was not reported in the Bible. The clothing that Israel's clergy had to wear when performing

The sandal of ancient times looked very much like the sandal of today.

their religious rituals is very carefully defined, but no mention is ever made of footwear. It may well be that out of respect for the Lord the clergy who served in his sanctuary did so barefoot.

The second instance in which sandals were removed had to do with mourning. Along with other external markers, those who grieved the passing of a loved one removed their sandals. This is something Ezekiel was explicitly told not to do as part of the enacted message he delivered (Ezek. 24:17, 23). Grief caused by other disturbing circumstances in life was also illustrated by going barefoot. David's flight from Jerusalem ahead of Absalom was made without footwear (2 Sam. 15:30). And Micah poured out his grief over unrepentant Samaria and Jerusalem by weeping and walking about barefoot (Mic. 1:8).

The sole of an ancient sandal could be made of wood, reeds, or leather.

The wearing of sandals helped mark one's station in life as a free person; however, when one's status changed, the footwear disappeared with the freedom. War captives were required to remove their sandals. We read about literal examples of this practice and enacted prophecy that anticipated the coming of this reality (2 Chron. 28:14–15; Isa. 20:2–3). Aside from losing one's freedom in war, people could voluntarily surrender their freedom and become a slave. This undesirable change in status might be precipitated by desperate financial circumstances in which people sold themselves, using their value as a slave to pay the financial debt they owed. Debt slaves, like war captives, were required to remove their sandals. Amos mentioned this as he castigated the wealthy in Israel who were taking advantage of their countrymen during desperate times: "They sell the innocent for silver and the needy for a pair of sandals" (Amos 2:6).

Removing the sandal was also part of the public shaming of a man who refused to live up to his family responsibilities. For example, when a widow had no son to inherit the family property, God's law made special provision

The loss of personal freedom was marked by the removal of one's sandals.

The Baker Illustrated Guide to Everyday Life in Bible Times

by requiring the deceased man's brother to marry the widow and care for her. The first son from this new marriage would become the heir of the deceased man's property. If the brother refused to perform this family role, he was to be shamed by the widow taking the matter to the elders at the city gate, where she would remove and spit into the sandal of the man. From that time on, that man's family line would be known as "The Family of the Unsandaled" (Deut. 25:5–10).

The sandal also played a very important role in the transfer of property. When a piece of property was to be sold or transferred to a new owner, its perimeter was walked by the owner who was wearing a pair of sandals. At the closing when the property was formally transferred to the new owner, one of those sandals that had surveyed the property line of the land parcel became the title for that property. It was given to the new owner as evidence of the transfer of deed.[22] When Boaz acquired the land of Naomi's husband and assumed care of Ruth, he did this very thing (Ruth 4:7–10).

Sandals offered modest protection to the soles of the feet, which were regularly subjected to this rocky and difficult terrain.

SCRIBE
(SECRETARY)

The scribe of the Old Testament went by the title of both secretary and scribe in our English translations, reflecting the changing status of this profession. A look at the scribe of the larger ancient Near Eastern world will help us better understand the need for and nature of this profession before observing the scribe within the culture of the Old Testament and its rhetorical role when mentioned in the Bible.

The fundamental skill associated with this profession is writing, and this fact requires us to briefly visit the notion of literacy in the biblical world.[23] We are prone to conceptualize literacy in terms of our modern experience, but what is considered normal in our era is far from what was normal during Bible times. The reality is that one could function quite well in the ancient world without being fully literate. Some professions required a higher degree of literacy than others, for instance, merchants, landowners, politicians, and clergy. But the reality is that even their level of competence with the written word was questionable when important documentation was required. At such times they hired a scribe. That leaves us with the impression that very few men (less than 10 percent) and virtually no women who

lived in the Promised Land could be regarded as fully literate by our modern definition.[24]

This means that ancient societies needed professional scribes and a way to educate them. While a child could learn the art of writing (Isa. 10:19), official records and correspondence demanded a higher level of skill. "He cuts off his own feet and drinks violence who sends a message by the hand of a fool" (Prov. 26:6 NASB). Whether within a classroom or by apprenticeship, sons of the ancients were educated in the ways of language and composition until they communicated with "the pen of a skillful writer" (Ps. 45:1).[25]

The fundamental skill associated with the scribe was writing.

The array of roles that a scribe played in ancient society can be seen by examining the cultures of ancient Mesopotamia. In general scribes were present whenever formal contracts were drawn up. They witnessed the inception of the agreement and put it into writing. Within the palace, scribes were responsible for maintaining important records that went into the palace archive, including the court history. Royal correspondence was composed and read by these professionals. And in the temple, scribes kept financial records of offerings as well as the all-important records of omens and consequences so that when an omen was repeated, the future consequence could be anticipated.[26]

The stylus and inkwell were among the tools of the scribe.

In Israel, the scribe or royal secretary had many of the same functions. This person was responsible for putting the king's thoughts into words for transmission to others (2 Sam. 19:11; 1 Kings 5:2; 2 Kings 18:14). Temple accounting records related to offerings, their storage, and their distribution involved the secretary (2 Kings 12:10; 22:3–4; 2 Chron. 34:13; Neh. 13:13). The military also needed written records, which required the practiced hand of a scribe (2 Kings 25:19; 2 Chron. 26:11; Jer. 52:25). Because various roles in Israel, such as king and clergy, were limited to a specific family line, the scribes also meticulously recorded genealogies (1 Chron. 24:6).

The Old Testament itself also has a very intimate connection to this profession, given that God chose to communicate with us using written words. Jeremiah was one of the many inspired authors who used the services of a scribe to put the Word of God he received into writing (Jer. 36:4, 32). As centuries passed, the original manuscripts of the Bible eventually

Writing played an important role in the lives of Qumran's residents. This cave adjacent to the ruin contained 550 documents written by its scribes.

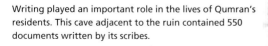

succumbed to deterioration or to intentional destruction. For that reason copies of the original documents had to be made, and once again skilled scribes were the ones who accomplished that task (Deut. 17:18). Realizing this fact allows us to fully capture the irony of an event set during the time of Josiah. The high priest carried a copy of the books of the Law—recently found among the ruins of the temple—to a scribe. This scribe then set about reading the document as if it was the first time he had laid his eyes on it (2 Kings 22:8–11).

This role of writer gave way to the role of scholar during the time of Ezra, which developed into the New Testament scribes who became the "teachers of the law" we encounter frequently in Matthew (Matt. 2:4; 5:20; 7:29). In one ancient piece of poetry, we encounter an ode to this profession that champions the importance of the ancient scribe-scholar over others who work with their hands alone.[27] The book of Ezra gives us a shorter description of the scribe when it describes him as "a teacher well versed in the Law of Moses" and "a man learned in matters concerning the commands and decrees of the LORD for Israel" (Ezra 7:6, 11). Thus the role of the scribes is defined not just by their ability to read but by their ability to teach others how best to think and live (Neh. 8:1–9).

The biblical authors made use of the connotations of this profession in two different ways. First, the inclusion of the scribe in the lists of members of the royal administration helped legitimize and define those administrations as sophisticated states akin to the ancient Near Eastern empires that organized themselves in a similar way (2 Sam. 8:17; 20:25; 1 Kings 4:3). Second, when the secretaries played a formal role in the story, we can assume that a very important matter was under consideration because it deserved the attention of these high palace officials (2 Kings 18:18, 37; 19:2; Ezra 4:8–9, 17, 23; Jer. 36:11–26).

A scribal palette with separate wells for red and black pigment.

Scribes are often depicted as writing while sitting on the floor.

SHAVE

Contemporary trends and personal preference have a lot to say about how we wear our hair and whether a man has a beard. The diversity in style we see today is also apparent in the art of the ancient Near East. In some cultures like ancient Egypt, it was common for men to be clean-shaven; in others like the Israelite culture, it was common for men to boast a full beard and longer hair. Consequently, a shaved head or face among the Israelites was an indication that something was not normal. Here we explore what those unusual circumstances were and how the biblical authors employed them in communicating with us.[28]

Shaving of the head, beard, or one's entire body was a religious imperative in certain circumstances. Those who had recovered from a bout with an infectious skin disease were required to shave all the hair from their bodies as part of the ritual cleansing process. This would clearly demonstrate that no portion of their body was still impacted by the skin abnormality that had tainted them (Lev. 14:8–9). Purity was also the underlying theme behind the legislation that required Levites to shave their entire body as part of the purification rituals in advance of serving in the sanctuary (Num. 8:5–7).[29] Again the removal of all their hair may have been to demonstrate that these

men had no physical abnormality that would disqualify them from office. Divine law governing the Nazarite vow dictated that the man or woman who wanted to make a time-limited vow before the Lord had to avoid cutting his or her hair during the time of the vow (Num. 6:5; with only one exception noted in Num. 6:9). Once that vow had been fulfilled, however, the person shaved his or her head and burned the hair that had grown during the vow together with a fellowship offering (Num. 6:18).

In addition to these religious rites, shaving became the mark of an

In Assyria, the ideal was for men to have full, thick beards.

individual who was in great distress. That distress could be related to the death of a loved one or to some form of national crisis (Job 1:20; Jer. 41:5). For example, victorious soldiers shaved their captives as a way of both humiliating them and marking their new station in life. This practice is mentioned in Israelite law governing the circumstances in which an Israelite man found a non-Israelite young woman whom he wished to make his bride. She had to go about with her head shaved for one month before the marriage was finalized (Deut. 21:12–13).

When the biblical authors mention shaving, they draw our attention to a person in a unique situation. It became a signature component of Samson's story. Even before his birth, Samson was defined as a lifelong Nazarite whose hair was never to be cut (Judg. 13:5). Not in a magical way but in a symbolic way, Samson's hair illustrated his connection to the Lord and to the strength the Lord provided.[30] When it was removed, so was the

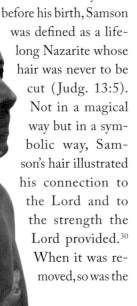

Ancient Egyptians shaved with bronze razors.

Lord's gift of exceptional strength (Judg. 16:17, 19, 22).

The rudeness of Hanun became clear in the forced shaving he did. King David sent envoys to offer Israelite condolences on the passing of the Ammonite king. Hanun, the son of the deceased king, did not receive those condolences graciously but instead shaved off half the beards of each of David's envoys, mocking the very nature of the mission that had brought these men to Ammon (2 Sam. 10:4).

The prophets of God mentioned shaving with some frequency as they warned the Israelites or their neighbors of divine judgment to come. Sometimes this reflected the shaving imposed on captives and other times the shaving associated with mourning about a national crisis (Isa. 7:20; 15:2; Jer. 47:5; 48:37; Amos 8:10). "Shave your head in mourning for the children in whom you delight; make yourselves as bald as the vulture, for they will go from you into exile" (Mic. 1:16). The Lord called on Ezekiel to enact a warning prophecy in which he shaved his head and beard so that he looked like a captive. But the analogy is even more complex because the hair also symbolized Israel being severed from the Lord. The prophet was to burn one-third, strike one-third with a sword, and scatter one-third to the wind.

In art, Egyptian men are typically presented without beards, apparently reflecting the norm in this culture.

Only a few strands were tucked into his garment, illustrating the remnant that would restore the fortunes of Israel (Ezek. 5:1–17).

Finally, Paul raised the issue of a woman's shaved head in his correspondence with the Christians in Corinth (1 Cor. 11:5–6). Jewish women accustomed to life in the synagogues were experiencing many new freedoms in the Christian church, including the opportunity to pray and prophesy. While

This striking image of a divine hero illustrates that even male deities were thought to have beards.

Paul acknowledged those freedoms, he warned about exercising them without wearing a veil. This created an immodest show that distracted from the worship in the same way that a woman whose head was shaved would be a distracting spectacle in the culture of Corinth.[31]

Hanun, who ruled from this Ammonite citadel, deeply embarrassed David by shaving off half the beard of each of David's envoys sent to deliver condolences.

SHEAR

Every mature sheep produces more than two pounds of wool that helps to regulate its body temperature and then provides its owner with a very valuable commodity. The garments that most of the people in the Bible wore were produced from this wool (Lev. 13:47, 59; Deut. 22:11). Beyond the pages of the Bible, wool was such an important product throughout the ancient Near East that it became the most significant component of that land's economy.[32] This is aptly illustrated by the fact that Moab paid its tribute to Israel in part by delivering "the wool of a hundred thousand rams" (2 Kings 3:4).

The value of the wool says volumes about the importance of the process by which that wool was obtained during the sheep-shearing season. The skin and fat of the sheep could not sustain its temperature during the colder winter months of the year, so they naturally produced a thick, insulating blanket of wool around themselves. The warmer weather of spring triggered a physiological change, and the sheep began to shed that heavy winter coat, losing clumps to the thornbushes and shrubs they walked past. This was the time when the

As winter turns to summer, the wool of sheep begins to drop off naturally, marking the start of the shearing season.

The Baker Illustrated Guide to Everyday Life in Bible Times

shepherds gathered their animals and began the shearing process. Because dirty sheep were much harder to shear, the first step in the process was to wash the sheep. If faster-moving water could be secured to wash the sheep, this washing not only cleaned the animals but also began to remove some of the wool. The shepherds continued the process by plucking the wool from the sheep or using a sharp instrument to cut the valuable fibers from the animals, all the while taking great care to avoid injury to the sheep.[33]

The impression we have of this shearing season is that it was both celebrative and bawdy. The Bible formally describes it as "a festive time" (1 Sam. 25:7–8), but it also links this season with prostitution and drunkenness (Gen. 38:12–15; 1 Sam. 25:4, 36; 2 Sam. 13:24, 28). It was a season when men left their families behind, lightening the grip on the moral reins as they sought to forget about life's troubles for a while. These connotations helped create the mood for the four Bible events that were linked to the shearing season.

First, during Jacob's stay with Laban's family, he not only founded a family with Laban's daughters but also obtained a large herd of livestock of his own. Nevertheless, Jacob's destiny was to reside in the Promised Land, not in Paddan Aram. Waiting for just the right moment when the excitement and commotion of the shearing season distracted Laban, Jacob gathered his wives, children, and livestock and fled from

A spindle was used to turn clumps of wool into the yarn from which garments were woven.

Laban's household (Gen. 31:19–21). Laban was completely duped by this plan. Ironically, Jacob's son Judah was about to have the same experience when the shearing season brought him troubles of his own.

The second event during shearing season was when Judah made a dubious decision to spend time with his Canaanite friends and invest some time with a prostitute on the way. Judah thought he was getting away from home and its troubles; but as it turns out, a problem from home had followed him. His daughter-in-law Tamar, who was owed family security in the form of a marriage partner, had grown tired of being rebuffed by Judah, who had failed to provide a new husband for her as promised. So she dressed as a prostitute and used the mood of this festival to dupe Judah and conceive a child with him (Gen. 38:11–26).

The third event involved Nabal. The heady excitement of the shearing festival and its wine caused Nabal to overestimate his military skills. While David was on the run from Saul, he and his men had provided security services for Nabal's shepherds and his three thousand sheep. The shearing festival was the time when such an act of kindness was typically repaid; but Nabal rebuffed David with a bravado that only the sheep-shearing festival might elicit. If it were not for the quick-thinking intercession of Abigail, Nabal's wife, this man would have died at David's hand (1 Sam. 25:2–31).

Amnon is the fourth person who fell victim to the distractions of the sheep-shearing festival. His brother Absalom had two things against this half brother: (1) Amnon had raped his sister Tamar, and (2) Amnon was the oldest son in the family and therefore stood to succeed David as king. Absalom addressed both these matters by specifically inviting Amnon to join him for the sheep-shearing festival, and then, taking advantage of their distance from Jerusalem, the distractions of the festival, and the free flow of wine, he executed Amnon (2 Sam. 13:23–29).

The biblical authors also mention the process of sheep shearing in two metaphors that strike a more positive tone. First, the smile of the female love interest in the Song of Solomon is celebrated with these words: "Your teeth are like a flock of sheep just shorn, coming up from the washing" (Song of Sol. 4:2). But the second and most powerful metaphor

that employs this image comes to us in Isaiah 53:7. With divinely inspired eyesight, Isaiah foresees the last moments of Jesus's life on earth.[34] "As a sheep before its shearers is silent, so he did not open his mouth." We can only imagine that every mortal inclination within Jesus was to defend himself as he stood before judge and accusers who plotted his death. But so he could fulfill this prophecy, the quiet resolve of Jesus spoke louder than any words he could have said (Matt. 27:12–14; Mark 14:60–61; John 19:8–9).

Swiftly flowing water was used to clean sheep and begin the process of removing their wool.

SHIPWRECK

*A*uthors and poets alike have long exploited the tension that exists between the romance of sailing the high seas and the perils that attend these adventures. Fiction and poetry largely reflect the reality we read about in the Bible; but the Bible uses shipwrecks to teach an important lesson about the economy of God's world.

As early as the time of Moses, the nations around the Mediterranean Sea had begun to conduct both commerce and war on the sea.[35] Each of these enterprises called for a ship uniquely designed to maximize its efficiency. Warships were light, sleek, and deadly (Num. 24:24; Isa. 33:21; Dan. 11:30, 40). By contrast, merchant ships were much less nimble but could carry tons of cargo with room to spare for passengers.[36] The early merchant ships followed the coastline so they could navigate effectively and be prepared to dash into safe harbor when severe weather threatened. As early as the first millennium BC, however, the Phoenicians had developed a more sophisticated knowledge of the sea and celestial navigation skills that permitted them to cross the open water. Taking advantage of the direct route and predictable Etesian winds of late May to early September, a ship could sail the distance between Greece and the Promised Land in as little as three to five days.[37] But things changed dramatically during the winter months when storm systems turned friendly winds into hostile adversaries. In modern times, the most severe of these cyclonic storms have been dubbed "Medicanes," hurricane-like storms with a defined eye.[38] These Mediterranean super storms pack winds that can exceed eighty miles per hour, and they might be the type of storm encountered by Jonah and Paul (Jon. 1:4; Acts 27:14).

Severe windstorms created a cascading series of problems for ancient sailors. Assuming they navigated the open waters by celestial navigation, the cloud cover prevented them from maintaining orientation. While the ships were designed for propulsion by wind, there was a point at which the wind became so violent that it threatened to destroy sail and mast. And in the worst cases, the pounding

Assyrian war ships were sleek, nimble, and deadly.

taken by the ship's hull could exceed the structural limits of the vessel, causing it to break apart in the water. The dire nature of these circumstances was captured from the sailor's perspective by the inspired poet: "They mounted up to the heavens and went

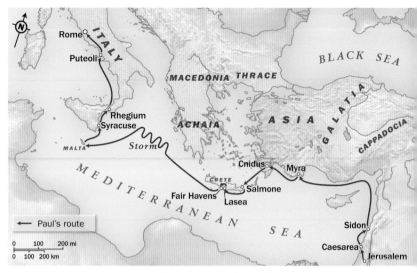

Paul's trip to Rome, depicted on this map, was interrupted by a divinely sponsored shipwreck.

down to the depths; in their peril their courage melted away. They reeled and staggered like drunkards; they were at their wits' end" (Ps. 107:26–27).

Sailors on a storm-tossed ship could not just pull to the side of the road, get out, and wait for assistance. Their survival depended on taking immediate actions, many of which are noted in the storm narratives of Jonah 1 and Acts 27. As the timbers of the vessel creaked under the strain of the storm, the sailors passed ropes under the vessel and bound them tightly to keep its timbers from breaking apart. If the frothing waves were threatening to swamp the ship, the sailors' only option was to lighten it by first jettisoning the cargo and then the ship's tackle. As best they could, the sailors guided the ship closer to shore, slowing its progress by dropping anchors. With cargo and tackle gone, they were then ready to sacrifice the

ship to save their own lives, grounding it on the most inviting piece of land they could find.

The biblical authors mention three specific instances in which a ship or fleet of ships was ruined by a storm. In each case we find men who arrogantly presumed they were wise and strong enough to subdue the sea on their own. And in each case the Lord used a storm and shipwreck to show that he, not they, controlled their fate on the water. First, Jehoshaphat, king of Judah, displayed arrogance when he unwisely joined with the

These sea anchors discovered in the area of Caesarea Maritima bear mute testimony to the shipwrecks along this section of the coast.

The Baker Illustrated Guide to Everyday Life in Bible Times

northern kingdom of Israel in order to fashion a sailing fleet at Ezion Geber (2 Chron. 20:35–37; see also 1 Kings 9:26). The Lord had promised that "every trading ship and every stately vessel" that represented the arrogance of its owner would meet ruin (Isa. 2:16–17). In this case, the fleet was wrecked before it could set sail (1 Kings 22:48).

The second example is the arrogance of Jonah that also needed to be corrected as he climbed aboard a trading ship that would carry him far away from the responsibility God had given him in Nineveh. "Then the Lord sent a great wind on the sea, and such a violent storm arose that the ship threatened to break up" (Jon. 1:4). The sailors made it safely to shore on that boat, but shipwreck was narrowly avoided only when their arrogant passenger was removed from the vessel.

The third example is found in Acts 27—the most detailed report of a shipwreck that we have from the ancient world. Paul had been arrested in Jerusalem, and following a hearing in Caesarea Maritima, he was on his way to Rome where he would stand trial before Caesar. Most of the journey took place on a ship, and it was growing late in the sailing season. The risks were running high when the Roman centurion called for the ship to head into open water despite Paul's warning. A "wind of hurricane force" eventually brought the ship to ruin as the Lord demonstrated that he and not the Roman Empire would determine the travel itinerary and schedule of this important gospel preacher (Acts 27:13–44).

In the area of Ezion Geber (below), the Lord wrecked a fleet to temper the arrogance of the king of Judah.

SIEGE
(BESIEGE)

esidents of ancient cities sought to protect themselves from their enemies by building thick, durable walls around their urban centers. Subsequently, invading armies developed siege techniques and tools that they used to overcome those walls. In effect, the siege was part blockade, part wall-busting, and part psychological warfare. It was sometimes directed against a walled city housing a fugitive (1 Sam. 23:8; 2 Sam. 20:14–15), but it was most frequently used against a nation's capital city (2 Sam. 11:1; 1 Kings 20:1; 2 Kings 16:5; 24:10).

The techniques and tools used to place a city under siege are well known from ancient Near Eastern sources.[39] The army planned to arrive at the siege site as close to the harvest season as possible to be certain that it could benefit from the locally grown produce as well as its water supply. Once on the scene, the army surrounded the city with fortified camps in an effort to blockade the residents' access to any food or water supplies that lay outside the defensive walls.[40] Then the waiting began to see who ran out of those vital supplies first. While the army was waiting, it gathered the materials necessary to build a siege ramp across the defensive slope of the city (glacis) that was designed to protect the base of the city wall. This became such an art that formulas were created to

The eroded remains of the Assyrian siege ramp built to attack Lachish.

The Baker Illustrated Guide to Everyday Life in Bible Times

determine how much material, how much time, and how many people were required to build a ramp of a certain height.[41] While the siege ramp was being built, the army constructed other necessary devices such as mobile towers that allowed soldiers to fire down on the defenders, wheeled battering rams that worked to compromise the integrity of the wall, and ladders that

An Assyrian relief depicting the work of sappers.

soldiers could use to scale the wall. And while all this building was under way, the army also sent sappers to work. These daring individuals dug trenches underneath the wall's foundation courses, temporarily supporting their tunnel with wood beams. In the end the wood beams were set on fire; when they collapsed, so did the tunnel and wall. The siege could last for years, and as the residents of the city grew increasingly hungry and fearful, the besieging army taunted them verbally and even tortured captives before them in a bid to collapse the resolve of the city's residents even before the wall collapsed.[42]

Whenever the biblical authors mention a siege in either a literal or a metaphorical setting, it is important to grasp all the connotations linked to this ancient practice. The experience was terror filled. With the most fundamental elements of existence in question, no one really knew whom to trust as they feared for the worst. It is no wonder that in Solomon's prayer at the dedication of the temple he listed the siege among the most dreadful experiences one can have in life (1 Kings 8:37).

The siege was a method of warfare approved for use by the Israelites with certain limitations (Deut. 20:10–12, 19–20). The most dramatic and meaningful Israelite siege was not even called a siege by the biblical author, and with good reason. When Joshua came against Jericho, its residents expected a traditional siege. But it ended within days rather than years with the walls falling at the direction of God rather than under the brute force of a battering ram (Joshua 6). The point was clear that as Israel took on that first challenge west of the Jordan River, it would be the Lord's war, won with the tactics and power he provided.

More often than not it was the Israelites who experienced siege rather than delivering it (2 Kings 6:24–29; 18:17–19:37). As Bible readers, we are conditioned early on to ask whether a particular siege was a punitive measure directed at people who had failed to honor their covenant with the Lord. "Because of the suffering your enemy will inflict on you during the siege, you will eat the fruit of the womb, the flesh of the sons and daughters the Lord your

God has given you" (Deut. 28:53; see also 28:49–57). In many cases, the prophets made it clear from the start by characterizing the coming or current siege as divine judgment. Frequently the goal was to use the horrific nature of the siege to halt errant thinking in its tracks and foster penitent reflection. As if speaking to the Babylonian soldiers within earshot of the Israelites, the Lord said, "Cut down the trees and build siege ramps against Jerusalem. The city must be punished; it is filled with oppression" (Jer. 6:6; see also Isa. 29:3; Jer. 19:9; Mic. 5:1). Ezekiel took this a step further by building a model and enacting the coming siege of Jerusalem (Ezek. 4:1–13).

This depiction of the Assyrian siege of Lachish illustrates the last moments before the city's fall.

The image of the siege is also used in biblical metaphors. When life's circumstances become unbearable, it can seem as though God himself is conducting a siege against us (Job 19:12; 30:12; Ps. 139:5). "He has besieged me and surrounded me with bitterness and hardship" (Lam. 3:5). But ultimately it is the believer's confidence in the Lord that lifts the challenge. "Though an army besieges me, my heart will not fear" (Ps. 27:3). "Praise be to the LORD, for he showed me the wonders of his love when I was in a city under siege" (Ps. 31:21).

Wall-building strategies evolved in response to improved siege techniques.

The Baker Illustrated Guide to Everyday Life in Bible Times

SIFT
(WITH A SIEVE)

The grain that people grew in their fields became the daily bread that sustained them. Consequently, those living in Bible times were aware of the dozens of steps required between planting field crops and turning them into food.[43] The ripened grain was carried to the threshing floor where the bond was broken between the grain kernel and the remainder of the plant by the hooves of animals and the threshing sledges they pulled. The mixture on the threshing floor was then thrown into the air by a winnowing fork or shovel so that the wind would carry the lighter by-products away while the heavier grain fell back to the floor. At this point the grain needed to be cleaned so the smaller pieces of straw, dust, and pebbles would not be ground in with the kernels and mixed into the bread dough. This final cleaning was done by sifting the grain with a sieve.

The sieve was typically a reed basket and came in two varieties: one had holes large enough to allow the grain kernel to pass through and the other had smaller holes through which the grain kernel could not pass. The

grain and associated debris were first put into the sieve with larger holes and shaken from side to side as well as with a circular motion. The larger pieces of chaff as well as the pebbles would be flung to the sides of the sieve, opening the middle for the grain to tumble through the holes and back to the threshing floor. In this case the undesirable material stayed inside the sieve. "When a sieve is shaken, the refuse remains."[44] After the first sifting, the grain that fell back to the threshing floor was still contaminated with dirt and tiny pieces of chaff, so it had to be cleaned again with the other sieve that had much smaller openings. This time the sieve was shaken up and down so that the dust and other undesirable elements would fall out the bottom of the container, leaving the desirable grain inside the sieve.[45]

Though this tool and the sifting process were common components in

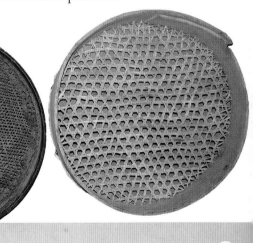

Ancient sieves came in two varieties: those with small openings and those with large openings.

ancient Near Eastern life, the literal sifting with a sieve is not mentioned by the biblical authors. Each of the five occurrences in the Bible of sifting is metaphorical: two associated with rainfall, two with oracles of judgment, and one with an urgent warning.

The first of the two associated with rainfall is found in the poetic verse of 2 Samuel 22:10–12.[46] David expresses his confidence in the Lord, who is capable of assisting him in every form of distress. He pictures the Lord as riding on the thunderstorm; his power is evident in the flashes of lightning, and his blessings are lavished in the rainfall. This rain falls from the sieve-like clouds that the Lord shakes; just as the grain tumbles from the bottom of the sieve with large holes, so the rain tumbles to earth. The same imagery of rainfall appears in Psalm 68:9. Although the word *sieve* does not appear in this verse, the Hebrew verb used in Isaiah 30:28 to describe the motion of the sieve is used here. The inspired psalmist invites us to praise the Lord who *sifts out* abundant showers from the clouds (NIV "gave").

In the next set of metaphors, the prophets Isaiah and Amos use this imagery, likening the judgment of God to the violent shaking of the sieve and to the fate of the cast-off debris. But in order to correctly decode the metaphors, we need to see that two different types of sieve are mentioned. Isaiah 30:28 refers to the sieve with the smaller holes that is shaken up and down. This allows the smaller debris to fall through the openings while keeping the grain within the basket. Isaiah anticipates a day when the nations that have opposed Zion will be judged. In the imagery of the poet, the Lord "shakes the nations in the sieve of destruction." The debris that is hiding among the valuable grain kernels is exposed as it falls from the sieve back to the threshing floor where it can meet its fate without harming the valuable grain kernels. The hostile nations will be exposed by this process and so are identified for destruction.

Amos also employs the image of sifting with a sieve, but this time the type of sieve in view is the one with the larger holes. It is shaken from side to side and in a circular motion,

This sieve with large holes is designed to capture pieces of chaff while allowing the smaller grain kernels to fall through.

The Baker Illustrated Guide to Everyday Life in Bible Times

allowing the valuable grain to fall to the threshing floor while the debris remains in the sieve. "For I will give the command, and I will shake the house of Israel among the nations as grain is shaken in a sieve, and not a pebble will reach the ground" (Amos 9:9 TNIV). The Lord will render judgment against Israel after he has shaken out the faithful. Those who remain in the sieve will stand in judgment before him, and not one "pebble" will escape.

Finally, Jesus uses the imagery of sifting when he offers the disciples in general and Peter in particular an urgent warning: "Simon, Simon, Satan has asked to sift all of you as wheat" (Luke 22:31). This brief sentence is full of Old Testament imagery and reminds us of Satan asking to bring difficulty to the life of Job (Job 1:6–12; 2:1–6). The image of sifting recalls the judgment oracle imagery that links sifting to very difficult circumstances. In the hours ahead after Jesus is separated from them, Peter can expect to be pressed with particularly difficult challenges akin to the testing Job faced—testing that will come with the intensity of violent sifting.

The processing of harvested grain, which included sifting, occurred on a threshing floor such as this one.

SIT

Many of us sit for extended periods of time during our day; in fact you are probably sitting as you read this sentence. Of course, the posture of sitting was also a regular part of the day for the people of the ancient Near East.[47] People sat on the ground, on the floor, and on small, four-legged stools with flexible webbed seats.[48] Here we will explore exceptional types of sitting and their connotations as employed by the authors of the Bible.

First, sitting could be a posture that marked someone as a respected figure of authority; this was true of elders, kings, judges, and teachers. In ancient cities, prominent senior citizens took special seats in the gate of the city to discuss public policy,

witness contracts, and decide legal cases. Lot, Ephron, Job, and others were identified as distinguished elders who sat in the gate (Gen. 19:1; 23:10; Ruth 4:1–2; Job 29:7–8; Prov. 31:23).

The royal throne was a symbol of power and authority, and those who sat on it became connected to those qualities. In that light, the Lord promised David, "You shall never fail to have a successor to sit before me on the throne of Israel" (1 Kings 8:25). As two of David's sons tussled for this honor, the biblical author reminds us of what was at stake by mentioning sitting on David's throne over and over again in 1 Kings 1–2. Not just sitting on the throne but also sitting in proximity to it was a sign of honor whether that was at the king's gate, at his right hand, or at his left hand (1 Kings 2:19; Esther 2:19, 21; 5:13; 6:10; Matt. 20:21–23; Mark 10:37–40). But the biblical authors never let us lose sight of the fact that the ultimate honor goes to the Messiah, who will sit at the right hand of his Father to rule forever (Ps. 110:1; Matt. 22:44; Acts 2:34; Heb. 1:3, 13; 8:1; 10:12; 12:2).

The roles of judge and teacher also were marked by sitting. Moses sat to judge the Israelites as Pilate sat to judge Jesus

Respect was accorded to the elders who sat on benches within the city gate.

(Exod. 18:14; John 19:13). But once again the ultimate sitting to judge will fall to the Messiah, who will judge the nations on the last day (Joel 3:12; Matt. 25:31–32). Finally, it was teachers who were also marked for special honor by the posture of sitting. A special seat in the first-century synagogue called the seat of Moses became the spot where the rabbi sat when he interpreted the text that had been read (Matt. 23:2). When Jesus was in Nazareth, Luke tells us that he stood to read from the prophetic scroll and then sat down to teach (Luke 4:16–21). There are many other instances in which the Gospel writers tell us that Jesus sat not because he was tired but because he was teaching (Matt. 5:1; 13:1–2; 15:29; 26:55; Mark 4:1; Luke 5:3; John 6:3; 8:2). We can add here that students, like Mary, also sat to learn from their seated teacher (Luke 10:39). This may explain why Jesus was so emphatic about having the hungry masses sit down before receiving the food he was about to miraculously multiply. Their sitting marked that the diners were also students about to participate in a dramatic lesson served with dinner (Matt. 14:19; 15:35).

When the biblical authors note that someone is sitting, it may also be to draw attention to the person's disposition in life, whether that is contentment or exhaustion. In the Old Testament the ultimate image of contentment is sitting under your own vine and fig tree (1 Kings 4:25; Mic. 4:4; Zech. 3:10). The shade

People in Bible times sat on the ground, on the floor, and on small, four-legged stools.

provided by the large leaves of the fig tree and the nourishment provided within arm's reach made this an ideal place to sit. Perhaps this explains why John emphasized the fact that Nathanael was sitting under a fig tree when Jesus called him. In this abbreviated form of the Old Testament formula, Nathanael was cast as a self-satisfied Israelite whose world was about to be rocked by meeting the Messiah (John 1:48–50).

Like those of us living today, people of the past sat down when they were physically exhausted. After hours of holding up his hands to secure an Israelite victory, Moses needed to sit down, as did Elijah after an exhausting flight from his enemies (Exod. 17:12; 1 Kings 19:4). Sitting can also connote deep grief or stress.[49] The Israelites sat before the Lord and wept in grief over the potential extinction of a tribe (Judg. 21:2–3). Ezra and Nehemiah sat down when confronted by the

Sitting on a royal throne represented the exercising of royal authority.

state of Jerusalem's walls and the impenitence of its residents (Neh. 1:4). And Job sat among the ashes when physical and spiritual exhaustion overwhelmed him (Job 2:8).

At times the biblical authors used the notion of sitting to emphasize the fact that someone had chosen to stand rather than sit. The Lord sent Samuel to the home of Jesse in Bethlehem in order to identify the next king of Israel. After going through all the older sons, Samuel learned there was one more son but that he was some distance away tending the sheep. Samuel could well have taken a seat while waiting for David to arrive, but the urgency of the matter is suggested by his words: "Send for him; we will not sit down until he arrives" (1 Sam. 16:11). Similarly, Paul chose to stand rather than sit when he was speaking in the synagogue at Pisidian Antioch (Acts 13:16). Though his listeners might well have expected him to sit when teaching as he did at other times (Acts 16:13), counter to expectation he stood to emphasize the importance of what he had to say.

The seats in first-century synagogues such as this one in Gamla were simply stone benches located along the walls of the building. Those who gathered to listen as well as those who taught would sit on the benches.

The Baker Illustrated Guide to Everyday Life in Bible Times

SLAVE
(TO BECOME OR TO BE FREED)

We may expect that the idea of one person owning another would be strongly censured in the Bible. What we find instead is a general acknowledgment of the existence of slavery, the use of slavery as a metaphor, and a theological trajectory that moved society in the direction of abolition without formally demanding it.

By definition, a slave is a person who lacks full personal and social autonomy and whose daily work and energy are invested toward improving the well-being of his or her owner.[50] The undesirable life of a slave was imposed when victorious armies took war captives and made them slaves. And as in the case of the Israelites, a strong state could enslave an entire race for centuries (Exod. 1:11; Josh. 9:22–23; Judg. 1:28; 1 Kings 9:20–22; Esther 7:4). Financial problems could also rob a person of his or her freedom. Free people who faced insolvency due to debt could sell themselves or members of their family into servitude, using their value as a servant or slave to pay their debts (Lev. 25:39; 2 Kings 4:1; Neh. 5:1–5; Isa. 50:1).

By definition, slaves lacked personal and social autonomy.

The descriptions of slavery in the Bible paint a somber scene. Slavery began with the indignity that came with living on the lowest end of the social continuum, treated as property that was purchased and inherited (Gen. 9:25–27; Exod. 21:21; Lev. 25:45–46; 2 Sam. 6:20; Lam. 1:1). The most dirty, difficult, and undesirable jobs fell to the slaves. But what may have been most defeating of all was that only death could provide any sustained relief from the master's demands (Exod. 2:23; 3:7; Josh. 9:23; Job 3:18–21). The calloused hands and aching muscles did nothing to change the reality that the very next day it had to be done again; control of their day and destiny resided in the hands of their owner (Gen. 16:6).

The biblical authors resided among people who accepted slavery as the status quo.[51] While they make no formal statement demanding the abolition of slavery, there is clearly a theological trajectory that presses their readers in that direction.[52] The law code of Israel addressed abuses like kidnapping, maiming, sexual abuse, and corporal punishment

War captives were frequently consigned to slavery.

owner to treat his runaway "no longer as a slave, but better than a slave, as a dear brother" (Philem. 1:16).

The idea of slavery is a very important image within the theology of (Exod. 21:16, 20, 26–27; Lev. 19:20; Deut. 24:7; 1 Tim. 1:10). The idea that one Israelite could permanently own another was completely ruled out; and though debt slavery was permitted, it was limited in duration to six years (Exod. 21:1–4; Lev. 25:39–55). What is more, each slave was invited to participate in the religious life of God's people, including Passover and the Sabbath day of rest (Exod. 12:43–44; 23:12). This took on an even more mature tone when Paul taught that slavery was not a barrier to becoming a Christian: "There is neither Jew nor Gentile, neither slave nor free, nor is there male and female, for you are all one in Christ Jesus" (Gal. 3:28). While slaves were encouraged to pursue their freedom, the Epistles urged nothing short of a grand transformation in the slave-master relationship (Eph. 6:6–8; Col. 3:22–4:1; 1 Tim. 6:1; 1 Pet. 2:18–21). This is particularly evident in the book of Philemon where Paul urged this slave

both Old and New Testaments. When the Israelites left behind their servitude in Egypt, the biblical authors quickly seized on the image, using it to describe Israel's relationship to the Lord: "I am the Lord your God, who brought you out of Egypt, out of the land of slavery" (Deut. 5:6; see also 6:12). The Israelites, however, had not been freed to run wild but were freed to better serve the Lord, who assumed the role of their new, benevolent master (Deut. 6:13; Jer. 34:8–11). Israel's relationship to him was defined by the covenant, and if they failed to honor that covenant, an ironic reversal of fortunes would follow that

Slaves were assigned mundane tasks such as the daily grinding of grain with hand mills.

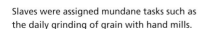

would literally return them to slavery. "I will enslave you to your enemies in a land you do not know" (Jer. 15:14).

In the New Testament the movement from sinner to saint is described as a change in ownership. Jesus declared that everyone who commits a sin becomes a slave to sin (John 8:34). This is the place to insert the horrible and difficult pictures of literal slavery into the metaphor. Only then will the amazing purchase from slavery take on its full meaning. "You were bought at a price; do not become slaves of human beings" (1 Cor. 7:23). With Jesus as the new, loving owner, the believer should look for every way possible to honor him and avoid being a slave to sin (Rom. 6:6, 16–18; 8:15). This means that believers must also abandon the path back to the law as the path to righteousness. Paul treats it within an extended metaphor featuring Hagar and Sarah, the slave woman and the free woman (Gal. 4:21–31). But he captures the essence in one statement: "It is for freedom that Christ has set us free. Stand firm, then, and do not let yourselves be burdened again by a yoke of slavery" (Gal. 5:1).

Finally, the model for Christian leadership is also housed within this imagery. When the disciples began to argue about their social status in the kingdom of God, Jesus reminded them that true leaders in his kingdom assume the attitude of a slave (Matt. 20:27). That is why Paul said, "Though I am free and belong to no one, I have made myself a slave to everyone, to win as many as possible" (1 Cor. 9:19).

Yokes like these could be worn by either animals or slaves and became synonymous with unrelenting hours of labor. Paul employs this image when he calls for those who know freedom in Christ to avoid a return to legalism characterized by "a yoke of slavery" (Gal. 5:1).

SLEEP

The scientific study of human sleep has yielded no consensus on why it is important for people to sleep; yet no one who has gone without a good night's sleep doubts its importance. Sleep lifts our energy levels, sharpens our cognition, and sweetens our disposition. The fact that Adam slept prior to the fall into sin and that the sinless Son of God slept in the stern of a boat indicates that our need for sleep is not the product of our sinfulness but rather is how God created us (Gen. 2:21; Matt. 8:24). That makes sleep as much a part of an ordinary day as eating and drinking (Judg. 19:4).[53]

In the ancient Near East it was widely believed that sleep was the time one received divine revelation. In fact temples both inside and outside Canaan are known to have had special rooms in which worshipers could sleep in the hope of incubating revelatory dreams.[54] When Balaam invited the elders of Moab to "spend the night" before he provided them with an answer to their invitation to curse Israel, he likely expected to find the answer during his sleep (Num. 22:8). These pagan practices in no way diminish the fact that the one true God chose to communicate with mortals while they slept on a number of noteworthy occasions (Gen. 15:12–16; 28:11–17; 1 Kings 3:5–15; Dan. 8:18; Matt. 1:20–24).

Real sleep reported by the biblical authors carries three distinct connotations. First, real sleep is associated with the believer who has uncompromised trust in the Lord: "In peace I will lie down and sleep, for you alone, LORD, make me dwell in safety" (Ps. 4:8; see also 3:5; Prov. 3:24). This may best explain why the Gospel writers note that Jesus was asleep in the stern of the storm-tossed ship (Matt. 8:24; Mark 4:38). The fear of the disciples contrasted sharply with the confidence Jesus had in his heavenly Father—a perfect trust that allowed him to sleep while others shuddered in fear.

The second connotation associated with sleep is lethargic complacency that gives too much attention to resting and too little attention to hard work. Proverbs repeatedly links this kind of unhelpful slumber with the sluggard whose lifestyle leads to poverty: "How long will you lie there, you sluggard? When

A tomb. The biblical authors use sleep as a euphemism for death.

will you get up from your sleep? A little sleep, a little slumber, a little folding of the hands to rest—and poverty will come on you like a thief and scarcity like an armed man" (Prov. 6:9–11; see also 10:5; 19:15; 20:13; 24:33–34).

Finally, sleep is also associated with the unfortunate habit of letting one's spiritual guard down. Samson, Saul, and Jonah were alike in that their time of spiritual inattention was highlighted by the fact that they slept when they really needed to be awake to the danger around them (Judg. 16:13–14, 19–20; 1 Sam. 26:12; Jon. 1:5–6). This is the connotation that best explains why the Gospel writers put so much emphasis on the fact that the disciples kept falling asleep in Gethsemane. Jesus asked these men to keep watch and pray, but like Samson, Saul, and Jonah they let their spiritual guard down, sleeping when they needed to remain alert. Their embarrassing sleep is mentioned four times in five verses (Mark 14:37–41). And lest we follow in the footsteps of these sleepers, the Bible summons us to leave behind our spiritual inattentiveness as well: "If he comes suddenly, do not let him find you sleeping" (Mark 13:36). "The hour has already come for you to wake up from your slumber, because our salvation is nearer now than when we first believed" (Rom. 13:11). Paul urged the believers in Ephesus to live lives worthy of their calling, apparently drawing words from an early Christian hymn: "Wake up, sleeper, rise from the dead, and Christ will shine on you" (Eph. 5:14; see also 1 Thess. 5:7).

The biblical authors also employ the idea of sleeping in two figures of speech. In the first, sleep is likened to divine inactivity and to physical death. In the ancient Near East, pagan deities had periods of time in which they must sleep.[55] Thus Elijah asked the Baal prophets to consider the possibility that their unresponsive god was sleeping (1 Kings 18:27). In contrast, the psalmist celebrated the ever-attentive nature of the Lord: "He will not let your foot slip—he who watches over you will not slumber; indeed, he who watches over Israel will neither slumber nor sleep" (Ps. 121:3–4). But there were times when the Lord *seemed* inattentive, and in those moments the biblical authors describe the Lord's failure to intervene on behalf of Israel as though he were sleeping. "Awake, Lord! Why do you sleep? Rouse yourself! Do not reject us forever" (Ps. 44:23; see also 78:65; Isa. 51:9).

The second figure of speech is one that lives today as a common euphemism; like the ancients, we describe death as sleep (Ps. 7:5; 13:3; 76:5; 90:5). This seems natural enough given the fact that someone who has recently died appears to be sleeping. But the Bible does something wonderful with this image; it creates the expectation that those who die will also reawaken just as if they were only sleeping physically (Dan. 12:2; John 11:12–13; 1 Cor. 15:51). Death looks and feels permanent, but when we reconstruct it as sleep, we will not "grieve like the rest of mankind, who have no hope" (1 Thess. 4:13).

Pagan temples often had special rooms in which worshipers might sleep and incubate revelatory dreams.

SLING
(A PROJECTILE)

As early as 8000 BC, the ancients discovered that slinging rather than merely throwing a projectile at a perceived threat was much more effective.[56] Such slinging added distance and power to the throw because centrifugal force was added to arm strength. No weapon of the ancient Near Eastern world was quite so simple, elegant, and lethal.

The sling and slingshot have similar sounding names, but the latter device must not be confused with the appearance and operation of the former. The sling consisted of two cords that were made of leather, woven wool, or twisted palm fiber. One end of each cord was attached to a small pouch in which the projectile was placed. The projectile varied in shape from round to elliptical, typically two to three inches in diameter and fashioned from clay, lead, or stone.[57] High-velocity rotation was the key to this weapon's effectiveness, and this rotation was achieved with a set of well-practiced motions. After placing the projectile in the pouch, the operator pinched the free end of both cords between his fingers. The weapon was then rotated either parallel to the ground, over the slinger's head, or perpendicular to the ground at his side. One rotation would set the projectile firmly in the pouch before one or two more rotations created the force required. The slinger then released one of the two cords while continuing to hold the other, sending the projectile from the pouch at one hundred to one hundred fifty miles per hour on its way to the target that could be as much as two hundred yards away.[58]

The sling was utilized by soldiers and shepherds for the same reason: it allowed them to engage a threat at great distance. In Bible times shepherds tending flocks in the countryside had to deal with large predators—animals a human would prefer to deter at hundreds of yards rather than at dozens of feet (1 Sam. 17:34). As the ancient armies developed, a segment of the soldiers honed their skills in slinging stones. The slingers are most often

An ancient sling consisted of a pouch and two cords.

The Baker Illustrated Guide to Everyday Life in Bible Times

pictured in ancient art beside the archers; they joined to engage an opposing army from the greatest range. Slingers are also depicted when cities were under siege, picking resistors off the wall and even from behind the wall. This was achieved by slinging the stones skyward at a sharp angle. Just as a Frisbee thrown in a similar way returns toward the thrower, so the slung projectile with the correct trajectory would return and strike those out of sight behind a wall.

Mention of literal slinging by the biblical authors was used to certify the military competence of an army and to confirm the intelligence of David as Israel's future king. The capability of an ancient army was defined in terms of both its numbers and its weapon technology. Having a corps of soldiers who were skilled in slinging projectiles was the mark of a well-crafted fighting force. When the biblical authors formally mention this technology, the connotation of military competence is in view, particularly if the slingers could "sling a stone at a hair and not miss" (Judg. 20:16; see also 2 Kings 3:25; 1 Chron. 12:2; 2 Chron. 26:14).

In 1 Samuel 17, the inspired author is at work convincing us that David had the combination of faith and intelligence that Saul lacked. We get to hear David's faith in the powerful statements he made as he prepared to fight Goliath; but it was his choice of weapon that highlighted his intelligence. The weapons Goliath carried into the valley all had a modest effective range. The biblical author generates this list of Goliath's weapons and emphasizes David's choice of weapon at the expense of all others because it illustrates that this man of faith was also a man of great wisdom (1 Sam.

Assyrians employed slingers when putting a city under siege.

17:40, 50). David's sling had the ability to dispatch Goliath long before he was in range of the Philistine's spear.

The sling also appears in figurative settings. The great velocity and force with which the projectile leaves the pocket of the sling is in view in two instances; in each case God is the one doing the metaphorical slinging. First, when David's anger at the insult delivered by Nabal was about to boil over in an act of violence, the wife of Nabal reminded David, "the lives of your enemies he [the Lord] will hurl away as from the pocket of a sling" (1 Sam. 25:29). And second, when a later generation of Israelites had wandered far from the faithful example David offered, Jeremiah warned of an exile so sudden and dramatic that it would be as if the Lord had loaded his chosen people into a sling and slung them from the land (Jer. 10:18; NIV "hurl").

Zechariah's figurative use of the sling assumes an understanding of the slingers' role in the timeline of the battle. Typically, the slingers were the first to engage an advancing army in order to create injuries and disruption before the infantry engaged the enemy. When the Lord fought with Israel, slingers would not just begin but end the battle, having to use only this long-range weapon. Zechariah said, "They will destroy and overcome with slingstones" (Zech. 9:15).

Finally, we have the comical picture painted in Proverbs 26:8: "Like tying a stone in a sling is the giving of honor to a fool." In order for the sling to be effective, the projectile had to be slung from the pocket. If it was tied in the pocket, the projectile would do no good. Honor is like the stone fastened securely in a sling; it will be worthless if given to a fool.

As early as 8000 BC, the ancients discovered that slinging a stone was more effective than throwing it.

SMELT
(TO REFINE METAL)

Applications for metal are found in everything from jewelry to tools to weapons. But the copper, silver, gold, and iron ore extracted from the earth cannot immediately be shaped for practical use; first the dross must be separated from the desirable metal. No gentle tap on the ground, no combination of hammer blows has sufficient force to excise the metal from the ore. The bond between the metal and slag within the ore is so powerful that it cannot be broken by mechanical force; it requires extreme heat. Whether by calculation or by accident, the ancients found that when they heated the ore sufficiently to liquefy it, the metal and slag flowed apart from one another, allowing the precious metal to be harvested. The process is called *cupellation*. In the case of gold and silver, the ore is heated within a cupel—a crucible made from bone ash.[59] When sufficiently heated, the slag either is absorbed into the cupel or floats to the top of the crucible from which it can be skimmed. After this process is repeated a number of times, the pure metal remains.[60]

Apart from knowledge of the process, the metallurgist in ancient times had to secure the necessary fuel and tools for the job. Smelting required a great deal of fuel, so the refining centers were located near adequate supplies of wood and charcoal. The tremendous

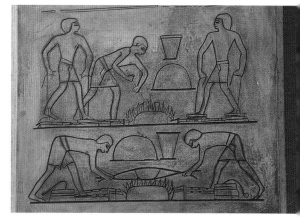

A special furnace was used to smelt mined ore.

temperatures necessary for cupellation (about 1,640°F for silver) required a furnace to assist in gathering and focusing the heat on the crucible (Ps. 12:6). The wood or charcoal fire burning with just a natural draft did not stoke the smelting fire to the necessary temperatures, so air had to be blown onto the fire by either compressing bellows or aggressively exhaling through long pipes. Finally, a crucible had to be made that could contain the molten metal and withstand the extreme temperatures of the smelting process.

Not everyone was involved in smelting metals, but the idea and procedures were known well enough that the biblical authors could assume their readers were familiar with them. The earliest evidence of smelting in western Asia dates to the fifth millennium BC, and by the third millennium the process had become commonplace.[61] The product but never the process is mentioned in literal descriptions within the Bible. For example, the raw materials collected for building the temple in Jerusalem included refined gold and silver (1 Chron. 28:14–18; 29:4). Certainly no expense was spared when selecting materials for use in the temple; and precious metals that had been smelted were rare and expensive. But it may be the purity of the metal that says the most about its inclusion in the sanctuary. These impurity-free metals aptly reflected the purity of the God whose house they adorned.

Most often the mention of this process resides within a figure of speech that focuses on one of the connotations of smelting. In some cases, it is the idea of separation that takes the lead. For example, the Lord wanted to reduce the number of Israelite soldiers who had come to fight the Midianites, so he directed Gideon to take them to the spring so he could smelt them (Judg. 7:4 TNIV "sift"; NIV "thin them out"). Kings were encouraged to separate the wicked advisers from the righteous

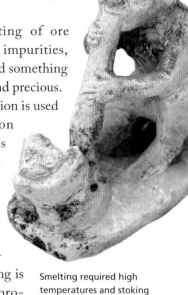

advisers as the dross is removed from the silver (Prov. 25:4).

The smelting of ore removes the impurities, leaving behind something that is pure and precious. This connotation is used in connection with God's Word and his people. No matter how hard one may try, mortal thinking and writing is always compromised by sinful impurity. That is not the case, however, with God's Word. It was written by men but allowed their words to be refined of all mortal impurity (2 Sam. 22:31; Pss. 18:30; 119:140; Prov. 30:5; NIV "flawless" and "thoroughly tested"). "And the words of the LORD are flawless, like silver purified in a crucible, like gold refined seven times" (Ps. 12:6).

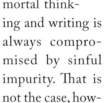

Smelting required high temperatures and stoking a fire by blowing air into it with a bellows or a pipe.

In other places the bond that unites sinful attitudes or actions with people is likened to the bond between dross and metal; only a rigorous smelting process will break that bond. The trials and difficulties that the Lord allows into the lives of his people are designed to melt us down so that the undesirable qualities can flow away. The Israelites experienced this refining

A piece of ore. No gentle tap on the ground or series of hammer blows was sufficient to extract metal from ore.

in Egypt—the "iron-smelting furnace" that refined them as God's chosen people (Deut. 4:20; Jer. 11:4). And when it came time to do so again, the Lord did not hesitate to repeat the process. "I will turn my hand against you; I will thoroughly purge away your dross and remove all your impurities" (Isa. 1:25; see also 48:10; Jer. 9:7; Zech. 13:9). As painful and difficult as the process is, believers can celebrate the end product. "For you, God, tested us; you refined us like silver" (Ps. 66:10).

There are times in real-world smelting, however, that the process fails and no pure metal results. In two figurative applications of this image, refining takes on a very ominous tone. In each the Lord's smelting process has failed to produce the desired results and the unrefined ore will be discarded like dross. "The bellows blow fiercely to burn away the lead with fire, but the refining goes on in vain; the wicked are not purged out" (Jer. 6:29; see also Ezek. 22:17–22).

Ore was extracted from the ground by means of tunnels dug at Timnah (below).

STIFF-NECKED

Stubbornness is so much a part of the human condition that a variety of very colorful terms have developed to describe it. In English we may speak of someone as bull-headed, hard-nosed, or even pigheaded. In Hebrew, the seriously recalcitrant can be called *qĕšēt ʿōrep*, which is translated "stiff-necked." Here we will explore the image that lies behind this Hebrew term, observe the connotations linked to it, and track the ways in which the biblical authors infrequently but strategically put it to work.

There is not complete agreement on whether the real-world image behind the term *stiff-necked* is derived from the human or the animal world. Some suggest that the neck of woman is in view. Females depicted in ancient Near Eastern art often have long and exquisitely decorated necks; hence the female neck became a symbol of self-confidence and pride.[62] Certainly the Song of Solomon pays a great deal of attention to this feature of the young woman (Song of Sol. 1:10; 4:4; 7:4), and it becomes a matter of concern for Isaiah when he criticizes the women of Zion who are "haughty, walking along with outstretched necks" (Isa. 3:16). The more likely source for the image, however, is associated with steering a draft animal. The demanding tasks of plowing, threshing, and pulling carts and chariots employed the strength of horses, donkeys, and oxen. Through the use of harness, yoke, and rein the rider or driver put pressure on the draft animal's neck in order to turn it this way or that.[63] An animal that resisted these commands was said to have a stiff neck. So when humans exhibit resistance, they too can be called stiff-necked.

The idea of stubbornness falls along a continuum that stretches from reticence to full-out rebellion. Where does stiff-necked fit? We

Strong neck muscles allow animals such as the camel (left), donkey, and ox to resist the guidance of their handlers.

turn to the first mention of this condition in the Bible to better understand its connotations. Moses had just received the two tablets that contained the Ten Commandments. Meanwhile below the mountain, the Israelites were breaking the very first of those commandments by worshiping a golden calf. The Lord called the Israelites a "stiff-necked people" and said he was ready to destroy them all and start afresh with Moses (Exod. 32:9–10). Moses intervened, and the people were spared; but just before they left Mount Sinai, the expression surfaced again conveying a similar connotation. The Lord said he was afraid to personally accompany the Israelites to the Promised Land because they were stiff-necked and so he might destroy them on the way (Exod. 33:3–5). These first uses of the expression reveal just how serious this condition is: stiff-necked people are thoroughly rebellious people who live within a hair's breadth of divine destruction.

Stephen said the ultimate example of stiff-necked people were those who had brought about the execution of the Son of God.

From here on out the biblical authors use the term quite infrequently; but when it is used, it marks critical moments in Israel's history, moments in which the Lord was brought to the very edge of unleashing his anger. Moses used the term three times in Deuteronomy. First he looked back, recalling how rebellious stubbornness nearly brought the Israelites to an end (Deut. 9:13–14). Then he looked ahead, urging them to step away from this condition as they prepared to step into the Promised Land. The final use of the adjective in the Pentateuch foreshadows an ominous future. As Moses prepared to hand leadership off to Joshua, this aging leader observed that the Israelites would all too often be characterized by this stiff-necked disposition in the future (Deut. 31:27).

This gloomy prediction hangs in the air as we turn past many pages of the Bible. Though there are many rebellions between the time of Joshua and the exile of Israel, the term is put away by the biblical authors until the history of rebellion reaches its climax. In the summary that explains the unthinkable defeat and deportation of the northern kingdom, the biblical author brings back the expression to illustrate how bad things had gotten: "But they would not listen and were as stiff-necked as their ancestors, who did not trust in the LORD their

God" (2 Kings 17:14). The southern kingdom trailed behind, but not so very far behind. Jeremiah punctuates his criticism of Judah and threatens extreme judgment by employing this expression repeatedly (Jer. 7:26; 17:23; 19:15). In the end, the exile of Judah is explained with the rare but powerful description of their last king as stiff-necked: "He became stiff-necked and hardened his heart and would not turn to the Lord, the God of Israel" (2 Chron. 36:13).

Eventually the Lord brought a remnant of his chosen people back from the exile and began to reestablish them in the Promised Land. As Ezra read the book of the law of Moses, urging them to adopt a pattern of living that was different from their ancestors (Neh. 8:2), it elicited both joy and confession from the gathered Israelites. In a lengthy prayer that was offered as the people confessed their sins, they remembered and eschewed those moments in history marked by the stiff-necked rebellion of their ancestors that led to dramatic divine judgments (Neh. 9:16–17, 29).

The rare but powerful language was set aside once again for a time, only to appear one last time in Scripture, spoken by Stephen. When this witness to the work of the Lord Jesus was brought before the Sanhedrin, he offered a remarkable testimony and history lesson. Stephen summarized the history of the Israelites, getting as far as the building of the temple that he had been accused of desecrating (Acts 6:13–14; 7:1–50). At this point, Stephen showed just how serious his detractors' rejection of Jesus was. In language that was meant to show the gravity of their rebellion, he shouted, "You stiff-necked people! Your hearts and ears are still uncircumcised" (Acts 7:51). That expression recalled all the serious rebellion of the past and led to the immediate execution of Stephen.

In ancient Near Eastern art, females are often portrayed with long necks.

STONING
(AS A FORM OF EXECUTION)

Though stoning is virtually unmentioned in other ancient Near Eastern literature,[64] it is the method of execution mentioned most often in the Bible and the primary form of state execution mentioned in Old Testament law.[65] The Bible spares us the gory details of the stoning event, but the traditional writings of early Judaism help us understand a bit more of what was involved. Those who witnessed the infraction were directly involved in delivering the penalty for it (Lev. 24:14). According to the Jewish traditional writings, the condemned person was taken to the execution site, which was to be an elevation at least twice the person's height. The first witness then pushed the individual face-first off this elevation that could be either the edge of sharply rising terrain (Luke 4:29) or the edge of a cistern that had been dug into the ground (Lam. 3:53). If the fall brought death, the matter was done. If not, the second witness had to turn over the accused and drop a large stone on his or her chest. If this action did not bring about death, then the rest of the gathered assembly had to pick up stones and pummel the condemned until he or she died.[66]

According to the law and practice during the earliest periods of Old Testament history, this grisly punishment awaited those who had compromised Israel's singular devotion to the one true God. Public stoning was to end the

In the Promised Land (below), there is no shortage of stones that might be used for stoning, a grisly form of capital punishment.

life of those who openly worshiped or encouraged others to worship false gods, who dabbled in the dark arts, or who blasphemed (Lev. 20:2, 27; 24:13–16; Deut. 13:10; 17:2–5). Stoning

This ridge is the most likely location for Jesus's attempted execution by the citizens of Nazareth.

was also the penalty for Sabbath violation, for a persistently rebellious son, for certain sexual sins, and for violation of God's directive to destroy all people and property during a holy war battle (Num. 15:32–35; Deut. 21:18–21; 22:20–24; Josh. 7:22–25).[67]

This form of execution served three purposes when it was actually put into practice. First, it prevented the family of the condemned from retaliating against any single member of the community since the community as a whole participated in the execution. Second, this punishment was designed to purge the person and his or her influence from the midst of God's chosen people (Deut. 17:7; 21:21; 22:21–22, 24). And finally, given that the sight, sound, feel, and smell of the execution would linger in the community, the punishment became a deterrent to anyone tempted to follow in the condemned person's path of sinning (Deut. 13:10–11). These laws sound rigid and austere in their proclamations, and we cannot say for sure how often this particular punishment was employed. What we can say for sure is that exceptions were allowed, as illustrated by Jesus. He did not demand that the woman caught in adultery be executed but instead disarmed her executioners and urged her to leave her life of sin (John 8:3–11).

When the biblical authors formally mention stoning in action, they do so to characterize people's faith, illustrate the power of God's Word, or indicate that a mob was out of control. In a few cases, the Israelites followed the letter of the law and literally stoned a person to death (Lev. 24:23; Num. 15:36; Josh. 7:25). In each of these cases, there appears to have been a specific directive from God to apply the ultimate penalty; consequently, when the Israelites stoned the offender, they are characterized

According to Israelite law, offering incense on a pagan altar was grounds for execution by stoning.

This hill outside Jerusalem may have been the terrain for Stephen's stoning.

as faithful. But the opposite impact on characterization of those stoning someone is shown with Ahab and Jezebel, who used the stoning of Naboth not in the interest of justice but for personal gain (1 Kings 21:8–15; see also the example of Joash in 2 Chron. 24:20–21).

The New Testament writers mention stoning to show the power of God's Word. People had no desire to die, particularly by the painful death associated with being stoned, but those empowered by God's Word proclaimed their message even in the face of those who wanted to stone them. Jesus expressed his frustration over Jerusalem because its people had so often stoned the divine messengers sent to it (Matt. 23:37); and when he arrived in the city, he too faced the prospect of being stoned by those who found his divine claims to be nothing short of blasphemy (John 8:59; 10:31–33; 11:8). After Jesus's death on the cross, the Jewish religious leaders tried to quiet

those who shared his gospel. With stones in hand, they muted the voice of Stephen (Acts 7:59). But as Stephen entered heaven, new witnesses arose, like Paul and so many others who were stoned and died or were left for dead (Acts 14:5, 19; 2 Cor. 11:25; Heb. 11:37). In no instance do we find that the threat of stoning was effective in halting the advance of the gospel.

Finally, there is one more way the biblical authors make use of stoning: to illustrate that a crowd was out of control. In these cases, we are not talking about stoning that came at the close of a judicial process but instead stoning that resulted from unrestrained mob violence. Angry, frustrated, disappointed people stood before Moses, Joshua, Caleb, David, and Rehoboam. In each case the mob is characterized by the fact that they were on the verge of stoning these leaders (Exod. 17:4; Num. 14:10; 1 Sam. 30:6; 1 Kings 12:18).

STRANGER
(ALIEN)

The terms *stranger* (or *foreigner*) and *alien* are likely to conjure pictures and connotations in the Western mind that are quite different from what the biblical authors expected. In order to understand the idea in the Bible, we need to start with the importance of land ownership in the culture of the biblical world. Land ownership was intimately linked to the growing of crops and the pasturing of animals that in turn created a more certain food supply as well as resources for making clothing and building shelters. The lack of land ownership put these fundamentals at risk. In the ancient world, the stranger or alien did not own land and had to either

hire out to a landowner or rely on uncertain access to public land (Gen. 15:13; Deut. 24:14).[68] Old Testament examples of those who lived this life include Abraham, Moses, Rahab, and Ruth (Gen. 23:4; Exod. 2:22; Josh. 6:25; Ruth 1:15–16).

The Old Testament law code gives us a detailed perspective on what it meant to be a stranger living in the Promised Land, particularly when we compare what it says to other ancient Near Eastern law codes. What is most striking in this comparison is the frequency with which the foreigner or alien is mentioned in the biblical law code in contrast to the lack of mention in other law codes.[69] This silence strongly suggests that living as a foreigner in any other country meant living outside the rights and protection afforded by the law. Thus since Ruth was an alien, she was surprised when she was treated well (Ruth 2:10).

The resident alien living in the Promised Land had responsibilities, privileges, and protection that nearly equaled those of the Israelites. For example, God's law prescribed that they avoid the consumption of blood and abhorrent sexual behaviors (Lev. 17:10–13; 18:23–26). They were to practice circumcision and

A woman gleaning in a grain field. God's law extended gleaning rights to strangers who were living among his people.

The Baker Illustrated Guide to Everyday Life in Bible Times

then could join in the worship festivals, even bringing sacrifices to the sanctuary (Exod. 12:48; Lev. 16:29; 17:8; Num. 9:14; 15:13–15). They rested on the Sabbath and could seek asylum in the cities of refuge (Exod. 20:10; Num. 35:15; Deut. 5:14). The penalties for blasphemy or pagan worship applied to Israelite and alien alike (Lev. 20:2; 24:16). They enjoyed gleaning rights and the right to seek redress for wrongs in the courts (Lev. 19:10; 23:22; Deut. 1:16; 24:17). And lest they be ignorant about such matters, all aliens were invited to the public reading of the law code (Deut. 31:12; Josh. 8:33–35). All these legal details led to one controlling premise: "The same laws and regulations will apply both to you and to the foreigner residing among you" (Num. 15:16).

This unique and highly honorable treatment of the stranger within Israelite culture was used by the biblical authors to define the nature of the Lord and his people. The Lord defined himself as the one who "loves the foreigner residing among you, giving them food and clothing" (Deut. 10:18). And the psalmist celebrated the way in which his God attends in particular to the disadvantaged members of society: "The LORD watches over the foreigner and sustains the fatherless and the widow" (Ps. 146:9). As this is a characteristic of the Lord, he instructed his people to make it a fundamental principle governing how they lived. The Israelites had lived the life of the landless foreigner in Egypt. This experience not only helped them appreciate what it meant to enter the land that the Lord gave them but also led them into a more sympathetic treatment of the foreign-born who lived among them. "Do not mistreat or oppress a foreigner, for you were foreigners in Egypt" (Exod. 22:21; see also 23:9; Lev. 19:33–34). When the Israelites wandered from this fundamental dimension of whom they were to be, the prophets delivered words of correction (Jer. 7:3, 6; Ezek. 22:7; Zech. 7:10; Mal. 3:5). Lest there be any doubt that kindness extended to strangers was part of a New Testament ethic, Matthew quoted the clear words of Jesus: "I was a stranger and you invited me in" (Matt. 25:35–46). And later the writer to the Hebrews instructed, "Do not forget to show hospitality to strangers, for by so doing some people have shown hospitality to angels without knowing it" (Heb. 13:2).

While we think of extended family as living in different physical homes, households in Bible times were linked to physical compounds such as this one. Paul says that Gentiles are no longer strangers but fellow citizens united by the gospel and members of a single, divine household (Eph. 2:19).

Apart from defining the uniqueness of the Lord and the uniqueness of his people, the biblical authors also describe some people as strangers or aliens in order to emphasize their humble faith. Abraham and his family realized the Lord's promise of land only in a very limited way and so truly were aliens in the Promised Land (Gen. 17:8; 28:4; 47:9, 11; Exod. 6:4). The uncertain life of the alien, however, forced the eyes of these wanderers to the certainty of the Lord's provision. "By faith he made his home in the promised land like a stranger in a foreign country" (Heb. 11:9). This faith of the alien living in a foreign land became the model for Christians to follow (Heb. 11:13).

Following the trajectory from Abraham to the present, being a stranger in the world

In contrast to ancient law codes such as this one, those of the Old Testament afforded strangers nearly the same rights, responsibilities, and protection that were extended to Israelites.

becomes part of the Christian worldview. In the economy of God in the new era, there is a uniting that means old labels like *foreigner* and *citizen* go away because we are all members of God's single household (Eph. 2:19). Yet on this earth, we remain strangers in a world ruined by sin, ever reluctant to become attached to a place that is only a temporary residence for us (1 Pet. 1:1, 17; 2:11). Ultimately, believers in Jesus know that the home they live in and the property to which they have a land deed does not change the fact that they are strangers "longing for a better country—a heavenly one" (Heb. 11:16).

TAX COLLECTOR

During the Roman era, tax collectors and the manner in which taxes were collected evolved and varied from one region to the next. Here we offer a general picture of the process that will allow us to appreciate the role tax collectors played in the Gospels.[1] Taxes were paid to both the temple and the state, each of which established its own tax code without consideration of the other. First-century Jews paid a religious tithe of their produce, herd, and flock (Lev. 27:30–32); they were also required to pay the half-shekel or two-drachma tax for sanctuary upkeep (Exod. 30:13; Matt. 17:24). The state demanded taxes that included a poll tax levied on males fourteen to sixty-five years of age and females twelve to sixty-five, real estate tax, customs tax collected at road and harbor stations, a tax on produce that amounted to 10 percent on grain and 20 percent on wine, fruit, and oil, a 1 percent income tax, and sales and inheritance taxes. In the end, Jews of the first century carried a combined tax burden that was near or slightly exceeded 50 percent of their income.[2]

Within certain regions, a portion of these taxes was collected by tax farming. In this case, the state collected bids from enterprising individuals who contracted to pay the taxes owed by a region. The chief tax collector with the highest bid was awarded the contract, and he then hired a second-tier staff of regular tax collectors to do the actual collection from the residents in that region. The state largely remained on the sidelines, allowing the tax farming system to provide the income they demanded.[3]

A denarius of Tiberius. The Roman poll tax had to be paid annually at the rate of one denarius per person.

Tax collectors had always faced a public relations challenge, but the tax farming system and the connotations linked to it really made it difficult for Jewish tax collectors to find sympathy from the general public. They were perceived as dishonest (Luke 3:12–13), and their strong-arm tactics used to collect and even over-collect what was due made them feared. What is more, and maybe worse, their business required regular contact with Gentiles; thus they were perceived as collaborators with the Romans who occupied the Promised Land. Matthew had personally felt the unpopularity of his position as tax collector. Yet in his Gospel he attempted no repair of the tax collectors' reputation; he lumped them in with abusers of alcohol, gluttons, pagans, public sinners, and prostitutes (Matt. 9:10; 11:19; 18:17).

Tax collectors were part of the real-world life of Jesus's day; they also became an important element in the communication of the Gospel writers. Jesus used their low social status to make a point on several occasions. Because they were seen as such disreputable characters, little good was expected of them. Consequently, Jesus taught that if the way we love does not exceed that of tax collectors, then we have learned little about the kind of love he encourages us to show. "If you love those who love you, what reward will you get? Are not even the tax collectors doing that?" (Matt. 5:46). On another occasion, Jesus outlined a procedure for calling attention to the danger of impenitence. The final and most dramatic step requires us to treat the recalcitrant person in the same way an observant Jew of the first century would

An Egyptian tax receipt.

treat a tax collector (Matt. 18:17). We also find Jesus using the perceptions linked with tax collectors to jolt the Jewish leaders from their complacency. While he was teaching in the temple courts during the final week of his life on earth, Jesus frequently clashed with the Jewish leaders, who questioned his authority and resisted his invitations to know him as

Zacchaeus was a chief tax collector in Jericho (below) when Jesus entered his home and his life.

their Savior from sin. In this context, Jesus offered this stunning appraisal: "Truly I tell you, the tax collectors and the prostitutes are entering the kingdom of God ahead of you" (Matt. 21:31).

But perhaps the largest rhetorical role that tax collectors play in the Gospels is linked to our understanding of just how large the kingdom of God is and consequently just how far the forgiveness of Jesus extends into the culture of a sin-ruined world. From the world's perspective, Jesus was going about building a popular following in all the wrong ways. Instead of courting popular leaders, he courted those of lowest social status, spending considerable time with and even eating with the likes of tax collectors and other publicly shunned sinners (Matt. 9:10–12; Luke 19:5–7). Jesus then invited Matthew, a tax collector, to become one of his disciples. The Gospel of Matthew does not hide the fact but parades it about for all to see (Matt. 9:9; 10:3). And in Luke 19 it is Zacchaeus, a chief tax collector in Jericho, who seems to get all the attention.

Jesus invited him to come down from the sycamore tree and then invited himself into Zacchaeus's home for dinner, much to the chagrin of all the people who muttered about Jesus going to be the guest of a sinner. Yet it was this sinner in whom we see a remarkable change. Zacchaeus promised to give half of his possessions to the poor and repay those whom he had defrauded at a rate of 400 percent.[4] Of all those in Jericho, Jesus called this chief tax collector a "son of Abraham" (Luke 19:9). Why did the Gospel writers give all this attention to Jesus's connection with tax collectors like Zacchaeus? Because it says something about the kingdom of God; if they are in, there is no one who is ruled out.

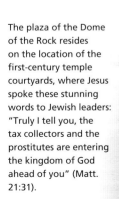

The plaza of the Dome of the Rock resides on the location of the first-century temple courtyards, where Jesus spoke these stunning words to Jewish leaders: "Truly I tell you, the tax collectors and the prostitutes are entering the kingdom of God ahead of you" (Matt. 21:31).

TEAR A GARMENT

If we tear our clothing, it is generally by accident unless we are tearing up an old garment for rags. This was not true in the culture of Bible times where the tearing of one's garment was an external sign of one's internal pain. The average person of this era did not have multiple changes of clothing like we do in our closets and dressers;[5] consequently, they took great care to prevent accidental tearing of their clothing (Exod. 28:32; Matt. 9:16; Mark 2:21). But there was "a time to tear and a time to mend" (Eccles. 3:7); the time to intentionally tear was a time of intense grief that might have included repentance.

At the personal level, there is broad evidence in the ancient Near East that people tore their garments as part of the mourning ritual associated with death (Gen. 37:34; 2 Sam. 3:31; 13:31; 2 Kings 2:12).[6] Other personal tragedies such as rape, loss of position, or the suffering of a friend also precipitated the tearing of

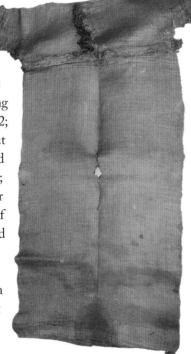

The intentional tearing of one's garment was an external sign of deep internal pain.

one's garment (2 Sam. 13:19; 2 Kings 11:14; Job 2:12). But in the Bible we most often hear about Israel's leaders literally tearing their garments as they faced some form of national calamity and its associated spiritual failure that put the nation at grave risk. For example, Joshua tore his garment after the Israelite army was defeated by Ai; King Hezekiah did the same in the face of an Assyrian siege of Jerusalem; and Ezra tore his clothing in the face of a return to behavior that had caused the exile from the Promised Land (Josh. 7:6; 2 Kings 19:1; Ezra 9:3, 5; see also Num. 14:6; 2 Sam. 1:11; 15:32; 2 Kings 5:7–8; 6:30; 18:37; 22:11; Esther 4:1).

When the biblical authors mention this cultural practice, they expect us to see the intensity of the moment. But there are other instances when the literal tearing of a garment plays a larger rhetorical role in the narrative. Within the story of Joseph, clothing is a very important literary element.[7] Tearing of garments marks two important turning points in this narrative: (1) Reuben and Jacob tore their garments, highlighting the loveless behavior of Joseph's brothers who sold him as a slave (Gen. 37:29, 34), and (2) the subsequent turning point in Joseph's story, when Joseph's brothers tore their garments (Gen. 44:13).

The motif of the torn garment is linked to political changes in Israel as well. When Saul was rejected as king, he tore the hem of Samuel's garment just before hearing "the LORD has torn the kingdom of Israel from you today and has given it to one of your neighbors" (1 Sam. 15:27–28; see also 28:17). Later when David's son Solomon harbored sins that were not appropriate for a leader of God's people, the Lord promised to tear the kingdom away from him and give it to one of his subordinates (1 Kings 11:11–13). This is illustrated just verses later when the prophet Ahijah tore his new cloak into twelve pieces and invited Jeroboam to take ten of them. Those ten scraps represented the ten tribes of Israel that would form a kingdom and break away from the Davidic dynasty (1 Kings 11:29–36; see the image referenced in 14:8; 2 Kings 17:21).

Tearing also plays a rhetorical role in Jeremiah 36. The Lord had directed Jeremiah to write his message on a scroll that was then read at the Lord's temple. When King Jehoiakim got word of the troubling content, he confiscated it and had it read to him. After a segment had been read, the king cut (Hebrew, *yiqĕrā'ehā*, "tore") it off and burned it (Jer. 36:23). Jeremiah was quick to note that they were tearing the wrong thing: "The king and all his attendants who heard all these words

At the time of Jesus's death, the curtain in the temple was torn in two.

showed no fear, nor did they tear their clothes" (Jer. 36:24).

We trace the literal mention of tearing during the passion of Jesus. When Jesus linked himself to the messianic prophecy of Daniel 7:13, the high priest tore his clothes to emphasize his declaration of blasphemy (Mark 14:63). At the cross, the soldiers refused to tear up the seamless garment of Jesus but instead cast lots for it, fulfilling Old Testament prophecy (John 19:24). With his mission accomplished, Jesus surrendered his life—a moment marked by the tearing of the curtain in the temple (Matt. 27:50–51). That tearing of the curtain might be symbolic of both the grief of a father at the death of his son and the dawning of the new era marked by divine accessibility (Heb. 10:19–20).[8]

Finally, the biblical authors used tearing metaphorically. Joel called for God's people to repent of their sins and return to the Lord. But mere external demonstrations of grief would not do; the Lord demanded something more: "Rend your heart and not your garments" (Joel 2:13). And last are two instances in which the heavens were torn. Isaiah longed for the day in which the Lord would make his presence physically known on earth: "Oh, that you would rend the heavens and come down, that the mountains would tremble before you!" (Isa. 64:1). There was a powerful parallel to which Mark calls our attention at the time of Jesus's baptism; for on that momentous day the heavens were torn open (Mark 1:10).

The intentional tearing of one's garment is often mentioned in connection with grieving for a loved one whose remains had been carried to a family tomb.

TENT PEG/STAKE
(TO DRIVE)

*T*hose who have spent a stormy night in a tent appreciate how important well-driven tent stakes are. Careless fixing of these tent pegs virtually guarantees time spent outside the tent at the height of the storm to reset the stakes. Driving tent stakes was a real part of the biblical world, and they also were used as part of God's communication with us in the Bible. We hear about tent stakes because God delivered many of his first direct promises to people who lived in tents. Permanent structures were out of the question for people who were constantly on the move securing sources of food and water, so they needed a portable sanctuary in which to worship. Therefore, before the time of Solomon's temple, God's people came to worship him at the tent-like

The Lord delivered many of his first promises to people who lived in tents secured by pegs.

tabernacle that also was secured by tent pegs. Eventually the mobile lifestyle of the Israelites became more settled, but that did not extinguish the memory of the previous tent culture, particularly since Israelite soldiers used tents and tent stakes when campaigning.

The tents the Bible has in view were made from the hair of goats or camels that was woven into three-foot-wide sheets. Multiple sheets were sewn together in order to achieve the desired size of the tent.[9] No such tents survive from Bible times, but the manner of constructing and erecting them continues in the Bedouin culture. The ridge of the roof sheet of such a tent was defined by vertically set ridgepoles. The two ridgepoles—one at the front and one at the back of the dwelling—were secured by angled guylines that were held in place by carefully driven tent pegs. The edges

of the roof were elevated on shorter poles and stretched taut; these were also held in place by guylines and pegs.

The composition and securing of the tent pegs were critical to the entire operation. The pegs had to meet two design criteria: (1) They had to be strong so that when a storm threatened to lift the tent from its moorings, the pegs would hold fast. (2) They had to be light so they could be more easily transported. The material that best met these design goals was wood from a sturdy tree (Ezek. 15:2–3). An experienced hand then established the guy ropes at just the right angle and similarly drove the tent pegs at an angle into the ground to achieve maximum holding power.

Tent pegs are mentioned seven times in Exodus and Numbers as references to the tent stakes that held up the tabernacle and secured the curtain-like wall around it. While some people have found allegorical meaning in the stakes themselves,[10] we are most struck by the fact that they were made of bronze (Exod. 27:19; 38:20, 30–31; see also 35:18; 39:40; Num. 3:37; 4:32). Wooden tent pegs would

have served the purpose and made the job of the Merarites who had to carry this equipment a bit easier (Num. 3:36–37), but the sanctuary tent was to be unique from all the other tents in the Israelite camp, right down to the way in which it was fixed to the ground with bronze, not wood, stakes.

The book of Judges also mentions a literal tent peg in connection with Jael killing Sisera. When the Israelite general Barak hesitated to engage the battle as God had directed through Deborah, God promised that a woman would be the one to dispatch this Canaanite general (Judg. 4:9). The tent peg was mentioned so prominently (Judg. 4:21–22; 5:26) because the hammer and tent peg were part of the women's world. Traditionally women were responsible for erecting the tent, and so when Jael drove the tent peg into the head of Sisera, she put a female signature on the event, thus highlighting the promise that God had made to Barak.

The other instances in which tent pegs or stakes are mentioned in the Bible are all metaphorical. With hope-filled words that speak of the reestablishing of Zion following its destruction by foreign invaders, Isaiah likens that

The tabernacle had tent pegs made of bronze.

The Baker Illustrated Guide to Everyday Life in Bible Times

Jerusalem to a tent whose tent pegs will not fail: "Look on Zion, the city of our festivals; your eyes will see Jerusalem, a peaceful abode, a tent that will not be moved; its stakes will never be pulled up, nor any of its ropes broken" (Isa. 33:20).[11]

A second figurative use of the tent peg is linked to the expansion of Jerusalem. Abraham was promised a great nation that would have an impact on all the nations of the world (Gen. 12:3). But this tent-dwelling man may have had difficulty contemplating just how large the kingdom of God would become. Isaiah pictures the realization of this promise with the image of an expanding tent. With more tent panels to hold in place, improved staking techniques would be necessary. "Enlarge the place of your tent, stretch your tent curtains wide, do not hold back; lengthen your cords, strengthen your stakes" (Isa. 54:2).

Finally, the prophets also use the tent stake as a metaphor for important people. During the time of Isaiah, Eliakim was destined to replace the foreigner, Shebna, as palace administrator (Isa. 22:15–19). The Lord says that he will "drive him like a peg into a firm place" (Isa. 22:23; but see 22:25). As Zechariah lifts our eyes to the ultimate leader whose holding power will not fail, he likens the Messiah to a cornerstone or tent peg that will permanently secure the well-being of the kingdom of God (Zech. 10:4).

Figurative tent pegs are mentioned in the prophecy about Jerusalem (right). As the city expanded like a tent, its tent pegs required strengthening (Isa. 54:2).

THRESH

When we purchase our food from a grocery store, it is easy to lose sight of the tremendous battle that attends the process of extracting the seeds we consume from the seed-bearing plants that are loath to surrender them. This mechanical bond between seed and plant is broken through the process of threshing. People in Bible times used various methods to thresh their field crops.[12] When the amount of seed to be processed was small or when the seed itself was delicate and could easily be harmed by aggressive threshing, family members beat the harvested plant with a flail or stick (Ruth 2:17; Isa. 28:27). The threshing of large quantities of wheat and barley required another strategy; the harvested grain was taken to a threshing floor where the processing occurred in one of three ways:[13]

1. Some farmers tied cows or oxen together and walked them about the threshing floor. As they ambled, the plants were crushed beneath their plodding hooves (Deut. 25:4; Jer. 50:11).
2. A second method involved the use of the threshing sledge, which was composed of several boards fastened together with an upturned front like a sled (2 Sam. 24:22). The bottom of the sledge was impregnated with sharp rocks so that when oxen pulled the weighted sledge over the threshing floor, it twisted this way and that as it masticated the grain.
3. Though not as well documented, a third alternative involved pulling a cart over the threshing floor so that its wheels threshed the grain (Prov. 20:26).

The predominant connotations associated with the process are hope, celebration, and destruction. The positive connotations of hope and celebration are linked to the fact that the threshing season was the one in which the fundamental grain reserves for the year

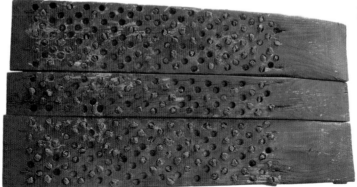

A threshing sledge was one tool used to break the bond between harvested plant and seed.

were secured. Threshing season was a time to be optimistic and to celebrate (Deut. 16:13; Jer. 50:11; Joel 2:23–24). By contrast, the news was not so good for the personified grain plants and the threshing floor. Both were pummeled and crushed as the plant was shredded beneath hoof, cart, or wheel. The biblical authors made use of all these connotations as they wrote.

Narratives linked with threshing usually resonate with hope and celebration; the threshing season added to the optimism they reveal. Perhaps the best example is the book of Ruth. The listless worry of Naomi over her fate and the fate of her widowed daughter-in-law Ruth began to give way to hope and celebration as Ruth threshed the barley she had gleaned from the field of Boaz and as she lingered at the threshing floor near Boaz, raising the possibility of the marriage that would provide security for Ruth and Naomi (Ruth 2:17; 3:1–18). In part, this may also explain why the biblical authors are so insistent that we understand that Solomon's temple was built on a threshing floor—a place of celebration and hope (2 Sam. 24:18, 21–22, 24; 1 Chron. 21:15, 18, 20–23, 28; 2 Chron. 3:1).

By contrast, there were times when sad and difficult events occurred in connection with threshing. In such cases, the tragedy was amplified by the irony of its association with the happy season of threshing. For example, a threshing floor was the setting for the seven days of mourning Jacob's death (Gen. 50:11). Gideon threshed wheat in a winepress to conceal his efforts and produce from the Midianites who had overrun the land (Judg. 6:11).

Grain was threshed each spring on the uneven surface of a threshing floor like the one below.

And it was Saul's failure to provide adequate defense that resulted in the Philistines raiding the threshing floors of Keilah and taking the grain for themselves (1 Sam. 23:1).

In addition to these literal instances in which threshing is mentioned, the biblical authors also use threshing as a metaphor. In some cases, the violent and destructive nature of threshing is likened to the violent treatment of one person by another. When Jehoahaz of Israel was soundly defeated by Aram, the army was threshed so badly that there was little left of it. They became "like the dust at threshing time" (2 Kings 13:7). A wise king was said to drive the threshing wheel over the wicked (Prov. 20:26). The Babylonian invasion of Israel left them in a sorry state, "crushed on the threshing floor" (Isa. 21:10). And Damascus "threshed Gilead with sledges having iron teeth" (Amos 1:3).

To advance his kingdom, at times God threshed the nations who stood in the path of his plan. So it is that the Lord "will thresh from the flowing Euphrates to the Wadi of Egypt" (Isa. 27:12). And Babylon in particular would feel the pain that a personified threshing floor felt when it was trod on (Jer. 51:33). At a time when Israel was feeling much misfortune in life, Micah offered the hope that things would turn around so that the nations opposing God's people would be threshed:

The front of this threshing sledge was curved upward like the front of a sled so that it could be pulled more easily across the threshing floor.

"But they do not know the thoughts of the LORD . . . who gathers them like sheaves to the threshing floor. 'Rise and thresh, Daughter Zion, for I will give you horns of iron; I will give you hooves of bronze, and you will break to pieces many nations'" (Mic. 4:12–13 TNIV).

When the Lord spoke of such judgment falling on his own people, he offered them a word of warning and comfort. He would thresh them for their covenant violations, but he reminded the people that "one does not go on threshing it [grain] forever" (Isa. 28:28). Threshing was a vital part of breaking the bond between plant and seed; but if it continued for too long a time, the seed itself could be harmed. In this image, God promised measured judgment that would correct but not destroy his people.

TRAP/SNARE

Ancient hunters used four different trapping devices to catch game animals and birds: the pit trap, the snare, the entangling net, and the fowler's net.[14] In the case of the *pit trap*, the hunters dug a hole on a game trail that was big enough to hold the animal and deep enough to prevent its escape once it had fallen in. A net was stretched over the top of the pit and disguised so that it looked like solid ground. When an animal stepped on the net, the apparently solid ground collapsed, trapping the animal (Ps. 35:7; Jer. 18:22). The *snare* was also set along a game trail. It consisted of a cord with a loop on one end that could tighten around an animal's foot. The hunter bent a springy sapling or branch, locked it in position, and then tied the cord to it. When an animal placed its foot into the loop, the hiding hunter pulled the cord, which released the energy stored in the bent branch, which tugged the loop of the snare tightly around the animal's foot (Amos 3:5).[15] The *entangling net* frequently was used to capture the fleet-footed deer. The hunters identified a location where the natural lay of the land created a funnel and erected and camouflaged a vertical net at the narrow end of the funnel. Then hunters caused the animals to panic and run into the wide end of the funnel. Distracted by the threat from behind them, the fleeing animals ran headlong into the net and became entangled (Isa. 28:13). The *fowler's net* used to capture birds was often suspended above the capture zone by using the branches of a tree. Birds were lured into the danger zone with bait and decoys. When they were in place,

An Assyrian relief depicting deer being trapped in a net.

An Assyrian hunting relief. "As fish are caught in a cruel net, or birds are taken in a snare, so people are trapped by evil times that fall unexpectedly upon them" (Eccles. 9:12).

the waiting hunter released the weighted net, which fell and entrapped the animals (Jer. 5:26).[16]

All these trapping mechanisms are mentioned by the biblical authors in figures of speech. Because these devices are often referenced with the same Hebrew or Greek term, we look to the larger context, which may be helpful in determining exactly which type of trapping device is in view. Whether or not we can identify the specific type of trap, three connotations linger that imbue the figure of speech with meaning: (1) The trap captured those who were not expecting it. (2) Once the animal was trapped there was virtually no chance of escape. (3) Because

the trapping mechanism was camouflaged, what at first glance appeared to be harmless resulted in death.

A wide range of sinful choices became effective traps that could harm God's people; consequently, the Lord offered early warnings about them. For example, the Lord repeatedly warned that the Canaanites and their pagan worship were deadly traps for the Israelites (Josh. 23:13; see also Exod. 23:33; 34:12–13; Deut. 7:16, 25; Judg. 2:3). Unfortunately, the Lord's warning about such traps often went unheeded and "they worshiped their idols, which became a snare to them" (Ps. 106:36). Apart from the choice to engage in false worship, inappropriate words and sinful actions became traps. This image is particularly prominent in the book of Proverbs (6:2–3; 18:7; 20:25; 23:27). Note the trap-laden imagery linked to the warning about following a wayward wife into the sin of adultery: "All at once he followed her like an ox going to the slaughter, like a deer stepping into a noose till an arrow pierces his liver, like a bird darting into a snare, little knowing it will cost him his life" (Prov. 7:22–23). In the same way,

The Baker Illustrated Guide to Everyday Life in Bible Times

"those who want to get rich fall into temptation and a trap" (1 Tim. 6:9).

Times of misfortune are also likened to the unexpected and in-escapable nature of a trap: "Moreover, no one knows when their hour will come: As fish are caught in a cruel net, or birds are taken in a snare, so people are trapped by evil times that fall unexpectedly upon them" (Eccles. 9:12). These harsh times could be the product of their own making, as in the case of the exile of God's people from the Promised Land that entrapped them (Isa. 42:22; Lam. 4:20; Ezek. 19:8).

As hunters used trapping mechanisms to capture animals, so the wicked ruthlessly pursued the righteous in a bid to surprise them with traps and ensnare them. This image is particularly evident in the Psalms: "The arrogant have hidden a snare for me; they have spread out the cords of their net and have set traps for me along my path" (Ps. 140:5). "Since they hid their net for me without cause and without cause dug a pit for me, may ruin overtake them by surprise—may the net they hid entangle them, and may they fall into the pit, to their ruin" (Ps. 35:7–8; see also 31:4; 57:6; 64:5; 119:85; 141:9; 142:3; Jer. 5:26; 9:8; 18:20).

A Canaanite idol. God warned the Israelites that the pagan practices of their Canaanite neighbors would become a trap for them.

Finally, we come to those topics to which we give little thought in our daily life: death and the arrival of the end times. Death can be just like a snare hidden along the path of life. We stroll along with our attention given to so many other things when the cords of the grave coil around us and we are confronted by the snares of death (Ps. 18:5). Along the way we do well to live cautiously, avoiding behaviors and attitudes that are unhelpful to our eternal cause, because the last day will "close on you suddenly like a trap" (Luke 21:34).

An Egyptian tomb painting depicting birds being trapped in a net.

VINEYARD
(TO ESTABLISH)

Growing grapes was not a hobby but a necessity in Bible times; the grapes, raisins, and wine that grew in the family vineyard were essential to daily living, and laws were established in Israel to ensure everyone had access to this vital commodity (Lev. 19:10; Deut. 23:24; 24:21).[1] In order to appreciate the connotations associated with establishing a vineyard as well as the literal and figurative references to it in the Bible, we will review the incredible investment of time and energy required to establish a vineyard.[2]

The process began by creating a terrace on the steep, eroded slopes of the hill country in the Promised Land where grapes grew well. The family started by constructing a blocking wall that would prevent the growing bed they were establishing from washing back into the valley floor. With the blocking wall in place, it was time to carry bag after bag of soil uphill the hundreds of feet from the valley floor to create an ideal growing medium. Such terraces were not built over a weekend but required months, even years of effort. Unlike grain, the vineyard was not established by planting seeds but by planting cuttings in the terraces. These cuttings were excised from successful vines, and once planted, the cuttings required at least four years before they were mature enough to produce good-quality grapes.[3] During those maturing years, the family invested a great deal of time and effort in the maintenance of the vineyard. In order to eliminate competition from weeds for precious water and nutrients, the vineyard required constant cultivation. During the fall, the vines were inspected for

The process of establishing a vineyard in the mountains of Judah began with building a terrace.

branches that showed little promise of producing good fruit, and they were pruned away. The family also dedicated time to maintain the terrace wall lest the hydraulic pressure of a heavy rain burst the soil dam and destroy years of effort.

Establishing a vineyard also meant creating other infrastructure needed to safeguard and process the grapes; these included a watchtower, wall, and pressing floor. In order to prevent unauthorized harvesting of the grapes as they ripened, members of the farm family constructed and then lived in an agricultural watchtower located in sight of the vineyard. They also built a wall of either thornbushes or stone to prevent animals from feasting on the ripening grapes. And in order to prevent unintentional damage to the grapes that were going to be pressed to make wine, a pressing floor was cut into the stone near the vineyard.[4]

Because it took so many years and so much effort to establish a vineyard, it was linked to the notions of permanence and stability (Mic. 4:4; Zech. 3:10). Furthermore, the vineyard was considered a highly valued asset; it was protected by law and sadly became an asset of such value that some would kill to take it away from its rightful owner (Exod. 22:5; Num. 20:17; Deut. 20:6; Matt. 21:33–39). Given all of that, it was unthinkable that one would invest so much time and effort in establishing a vineyard only to sell it to another or allow it to fall into disrepair (1 Kings 21:2; Prov. 24:30–31).

A pressing floor such as the one depicted here was built near the vineyard, where the grapes could be stomped to obtain their precious juice.

The biblical authors expect us to carry this understanding into our reading of texts in which establishing a vineyard is formally mentioned or assumed. Established vineyards project the connotation of normalcy. Thus a return to normalcy is suggested when Noah plants a vineyard shortly after exiting the ark (Gen. 9:20). But we barely get to enjoy the moment before Noah returns to the ways of pre-flood sinful behavior, getting drunk on the produce from the vineyard.

As the author of 1 Kings describes the paganism that characterized the rule of Ahab and Jezebel, he gives significant time to telling the story of Naboth's vineyard. Not only is the royal family criticized for their cavalier attitude toward divinely sanctioned land ownership in the Promised Land, but they also are subjected to satire. Only a fool would reverse the energy expended in establishing a vineyard by turning it into an ordinary vegetable garden (1 Kings 21:1–2).

From time to time, the prophets use the vineyard as a metaphor for Israel, but the most sustained use of this figurative speech is in Isaiah 5. Here Isaiah meticulously describes the steps that were required to establish a successful vineyard. Every expectation is that this time and effort would lead to an abundant harvest of grapes. But the Song of the Vineyard leads us to a very different scene—one marred by lackluster vines that produced only bad fruit: "What more could have been done for my vineyard than I have done for it? When I looked for good grapes, why did it yield only bad?" (Isa. 5:4). When we know what the farmers of Isaiah's day knew about establishing a vineyard, we can quickly answer the first question: Nothing—nothing more could have been done for the vineyard. The results were inexplicable, but they also predicted what would happen next both to the hapless vineyard and to the people it represented. "I will take away its hedge, and it will be destroyed; I will break down its wall, and it will be trampled. I will make it a wasteland, neither pruned nor cultivated, and briers and thorns will grow there. I will command the clouds not to rain on it" (Isa. 5:5–6).

Pressing floors were kept as close to the vineyards as possible.

The Baker Illustrated Guide to Everyday Life in Bible Times

WASH CLOTHES

Clean clothing is destined to get dirty, so we regularly take the walk to the local Laundromat or our laundry room to do the laundry. People living in Bible times wore clothes that also collected dirt, stains, and odors, so they too had to wash their clothing. Thanks to some very specific language used by the biblical authors, we can trace mention of the literal and figurative clothes washing in their writing.

The method and frequency with which people washed their clothes varied between the ordinary and elite members of society. Ordinary people carried their soiled clothes to a water source, soaked them in water—often without any soap added—and rubbed them on rocks in an effort to loosen the ground-in dirt before rinsing them and laying them out to dry.[1] The scarcity of water in the Promised Land dictated that ordinary people rarely enjoyed a full body wash; so we presume that clothes washing was an equally rare occurrence.[2]

By contrast, the royalty and the well-to-do had others do this job for them. The pharaoh had a member of his royal court designated as "Chief Launderer of the Palace."[3] Thanks to a new kingdom tomb painting, we have a reasonable idea of how an Egyptian commercial laundry worked. The laundry was first soaked in a cold tub before immersion in a second tub that contained warm, soapy

water. If dirt or stains remained, the workers rubbed and beat the clothes on rocks before rinsing them in the river and hanging them up to dry.[4] Though we lack this sort of detail in the Bible, it seems the Washerman's Field, mentioned several times as a Jerusalem landmark, may have been a commercial laundry that served those who could afford it (2 Kings 18:17; Isa. 7:3; 36:2). We presume that the elite members of Israel's society washed their clothes more frequently than ordinary folks. Mephibosheth shunned this luxury during the time David fled the capital city (2 Sam. 19:24).

The great majority of instances in which the biblical authors mention people washing their clothing or being directed to do so link this activity to ritual and worship. Because clothing that people wore was not regularly washed, the command to wash one's clothing marked a day as quite extraordinary. For example, Moses directed the Israelites to prepare themselves to receive divine communication at Mount Sinai by washing their clothing

The most desirable place for people to wash their clothing was near running water such as the Jordan River (right).

(Exod. 19:10, 14). The law they received from the Lord gave very specific instances when the Israelites were to wash their clothing as part of purification rituals—from touching the carcass of a clean animal that had died to touching something a person had touched who was having a natural discharge (Lev. 11:25, 28, 40; 13:6, 34, 54–58; 14:8–9, 47; 15:5–6, 8, 10–11, 21–22; 17:15–16). The clergy and their assistants were to wash their clothing in connection with specific duties they performed (Lev. 6:27; 16:26, 28; Num. 8:7, 21; 19:7–8, 10, 19, 21). Again, because the washing of one's clothing was done less frequently, the direction to do so was more arresting for those living in that era.

The biblical authors also use the image of clothes washing in figures of speech. In one instance we come upon the notion of washing clothing in wine. As his life was coming to a close, Jacob summoned his sons to receive his blessing. Speaking of Judah, Jacob said, "He will wash his garments in wine, his robes in the blood of grapes" (Gen. 49:11). The direct mention of the vine, choicest branch, grapes, and wine are used to call our attention to the family vineyard. Because the vineyard provided such a critical commodity to those living in the Promised Land, no one would think of using wine as if it were merely wash water. The arresting image promises Judah a landscape filled with producing vineyards that create a surplus of wine so great that one could use it as if it were wash water.

In other instances, the figure of speech likens the taint of sin to the dirt and stains that impregnate clothing. Using the Hebrew verb that otherwise is used for washing clothing, David prayed, "Wash away all my iniquity and cleanse me from my sin. . . . Cleanse me with hyssop, and I will be clean; wash me, and I will be whiter than snow" (Ps. 51:2, 7). The Lord warned the Israelites that their penchant for rebellion had made them like a filthy garment that simply could not be washed clean even though soap was used. "Although you wash yourself with soap and use an abundance of cleansing powder, the stain of your guilt is still before me" (Jer. 2:22; see also 4:14).

The ultimate clothes-cleaning experience is linked to the Messiah, who will use "launderer's soap" to purify the people of God (Mal. 3:2). This leads to the tender and comforting image that we find in the book of Revelation—an image that has brought comfort and hope to so many at the graveside of their loved ones. During his tour of heaven, John saw a great multitude standing before him, representing all nations of the world, each person wearing a white robe. John's heavenly tour guide explained who they were: "These are they who have come out of the great tribulation; they have washed their robes and made them white in the blood of the Lamb" (Rev. 7:14). We are inclined to think of bloodstains as harmful to a garment, but here we learn of the cleansing power of Jesus's blood that washes away all our sins.

God commanded the Israelites camped on these plains below Mount Sinai to wash their clothing before receiving the law.

WATER
(TO ACQUIRE OR TO DRAW)

Water is absolutely vital for life. It sustains humans not only by directly hydrating us but also by watering the agricultural fields and pastures that supply our food. Yet this fundamental element of life was in very short supply in the Promised Land. When we compare the per capita water supply available to the average resident of the West to the per capita supply available to the ancient resident of the Promised Land, we find them living with less than 10 percent of the water to which Western moderns have access.[5] In addition to being in short supply, the water of the Promised Land was difficult to acquire. Lakes and water courses of that land were too low in elevation, too laden with chemicals, or too itinerant in flow to be of value. Consequently, the eyes of all turned to the heavens and the rainfall that supplied the water of their land (Deut. 11:11). During the rainy months, water could be collected directly. But during most of the year, the rain that had already fallen and resided as groundwater had to be accessed.

The three most common places to get water were the spring, well, and cistern.[6] Getting water from a spring involved the least effort and promised tasty, naturally filtered water. Springs required little to no excavation or development because they occurred naturally where the elevation of the surface coincided with the elevation of the local water table. When the water table lay beneath the surface, it was sometimes practical to excavate a shaft to reach it—by definition, a well. The typical well consisted of a shaft from four to six feet in diameter that was sunk one hundred feet or more to intersect the water table. This kind of deep well is pictured in Proverbs 20:5: "The purposes of a person's heart are deep waters, but one who has insight draws them out." As

Wells were shafts dug to the water table and then covered by a stone cap to limit evaporation and contamination.

the water seekers excavated where they hoped to find the water table at a reasonable depth, they shored up the sides of the shaft with fieldstones to prevent the walls from collapsing. Eventually the developed well would also include a permanent cover with a removable cap to limit contamination and prevent evaporation. The third method of acquiring water was the cistern. It might look similar to a well, but it was designed to capture and hold surface water that ran off after it rained rather than intersect the water table.[7] In profile, cisterns often had a bell-like shape that terminated near the surface in a narrow neck that, like the well, was fit with a cap and cover. Unlike the well, however, the sides of the cistern were plastered to prevent the captured water from leaking out.

Because springs were less common in the Promised Land, water was largely obtained from wells and cisterns. This meant that a considerable part of a person's year was invested in identifying, developing, maintaining, and defending these water sources. And that does not begin to take into account the daily labor of lifting that water to the surface and carrying it home. Nevertheless, the connotation of hard work was offset by the connotation of pure joy in being able to draw water from a reliable source. This euphoria was so strong that poets liken it to the joy-filled sexual intimacy a man shares with his wife (Prov. 5:15).

The hard work of drawing water from such sources is sometimes mentioned by the biblical authors to help characterize the industriousness of a person. Genesis 24 gushes over Rebekah, who drew water not only for her family but also for Abraham's servant, who was visiting, and for his ten camels. Moses did something similar when he drove off competitors and then watered the flock of Jethro (Exod. 2:15–19). And David's three mighty men traveled to Bethlehem, battled a Philistine garrison, drew water, and carried it back to David so he could have a drink from his hometown well (2 Sam. 23:15–16).

The biblical authors also employ the drawing of water in two starkly different figures of speech. First, the Lord compares drawing life-giving water to unfortunate spiritual decisions being made by the Israelites: "My people have committed two sins: They have forsaken me, the spring of living water,

A Nabatean dam used to slow and direct runoff

This cistern at Arad was designed to collect surface water and make it available to residents of the city.

and have dug their own cisterns, broken cisterns that cannot hold water" (Jer. 2:13). Their apostasy was as unthinkable as passing up a spring in order to draw water from the less desirable cistern that was itself out of service.

On the other hand, the biblical authors also see the life-giving drawing of water as an apt metaphor for the salvation the Lord provides. Isaiah's song of praise brims with optimism and hope that includes this image: "With joy you will draw water from the wells of salvation" (Isa. 12:3). Perhaps this is the image that lingered in Jesus's mind as he spoke to the Samaritan woman at the well. When the woman hesitated to give him a drink from the physical well that hosted their conversation, Jesus spoke of another and better well: "Everyone who drinks this water will be thirsty again, but whoever drinks the water I give them will never thirst. Indeed, the water I give them will become in them a spring of water welling up to eternal life" (John 4:13–14).

Water from a flash flood races to the Dead Sea after a rainstorm in the Judean wilderness.

WEAVE

The typical family of Bible times had its own looms and some family members who were skilled at the art of weaving (Prov. 31:13). At its most fundamental level, weaving involved the interlocking of threads at right angles to one another in order to create a piece of cloth that could function as a garment, tent curtain, or even carrying sack. The threads were derived from wool, flax, or goat hair that could be left in their original, subtle tone or be dyed radiant colors.

Two types of looms were used to create cloth from such threads: the horizontal loom (or ground loom) and the vertical loom.[8] Both types allowed the weaver to tie a series of threads in tension and parallel to one another so that another set of threads could be interlaced between them at a ninety-degree angle. The threads held in tension are called the *warp* and those interlaced are the *woof* (or *weft*). The earliest form of the loom was the horizontal or ground loom. The weaver made this loom from two branches to which the warp threads were tied. The weaver separated the branches and then staked them to the ground to hold the warp in tension so the loom lay parallel to the ground before the weaver. The simplicity and portability of this loom made it the loom of choice for those on the move. All one had to do was pull up the stakes and roll up the

uncompleted cloth. Alternatively, some weavers constructed vertical looms. This loom consisted of three branches—one horizontal and two vertical—that allowed this loom to stand upright in an inverted *U* shape when leaning against a wall. The weaver tied the threads of the warp to the horizontal branch and used clay loom weights to create tension on those threads.

The process of weaving required the weaver to methodically separate the threads of the warp from one another so that the woof threads could be woven over and under them

The vertical loom was one of the two common looms used during Bible times.

consecutively. Innovations were used to speed up the process. For example, a flat heddle rod was woven between the threads of the warp. It could be turned one direction and then another in order to separate alternate threads of the warp. The weaver could then use a shuttle—a narrow wooden stick with a leather leash attached—to quickly shoot the thread of the woof through the shed opened in the warp. Once through, the weaver changed the position of the heddle rod, creating a new pathway through the warp. Using the leather leash of the shuttle, the weaver could quickly return the thread through the new passageway.

The clothing worn by both commoners and clergy was made from cloth woven on a loom.

Weaving was a very creative process that allowed the weavers to express themselves in a variety of ways. In extreme cases, alteration in thread colors and interlacing technique could produce cloth that was intricately designed and had a unique texture. The only limitation on this creative process for the Israelites was the requirement that they not mix different types of thread when making clothing (Lev. 19:19; Deut. 22:11). Cloth was also woven to play a role in the worship life of God's Old Testament people. During their early years, the worship facility they used had to be light and portable because they were traveling so often. Consequently, the walls and screens of the tabernacle were made of woven cloth (Exod. 26:1, 31, 36; 27:16; 35:35; 36:8, 35, 37; 38:18).

The garments worn by the clergy were also carefully defined and then woven by skilled artists (Exod. 28:4, 8, 32, 39; 29:5; 31:10; 35:19; 39:1, 3, 5, 8, 22, 29, 41) who were specifically trained for the task (Exod. 35:34–35; 38:23). These unique and beautiful items continually reminded God's people at worship that they had entered a sacred space.

But these frequent and positive mentions of weaving contrast with two instances of weaving that have a darker side. The Lord had given Samson great strength in order to liberate his people from the oppression of the Philistines. But one evening he teased his beloved Delilah with the notion that if only she would weave the seven braids of his hair into a loom, he would become as weak as any other man (Judg. 16:13). And worse yet, we hear of Israelite women who, prior to the reforms of Josiah, took it on themselves to weave in service to the pagan goddess Asherah (2 Kings 23:7).

Weaving also appears in figures of speech related to creation and the end of life. The cloth created by the weaver was both highly

personalized in design and carefully shaped by the attentive hands of the artist. This makes weaving an apt metaphor for God's creation of individuals. David described his beginning in this elegant fashion: "My frame was not hidden from you when I was made in the secret place, when I was woven together in the depths of the earth. Your eyes saw my unformed body" (Ps. 139:15–16; see also Job 10:11).

Clay loom weights held the vertical threads taut while the horizontal threads were woven between them.

The poetry of the Bible also describes the end of life with imagery that links it to the art of weaving. Feeling his life ebbing to a close all too soon, Job likened the passing of his days to the swift movement of the weaver's shuttle as it raced back and forth: "My days are swifter than a weaver's shuttle, and they come to an end without hope" (Job 7:6). When Hezekiah faced death, he also expressed his feelings with images of weaving: "Like a weaver I have rolled up my life, and he has cut me off from the loom" (Isa. 38:12). When it was time for the shepherd to move to a new pasture, the ground loom's stakes were pulled up and the cloth was rolled up for transport. And when the cloth's creation had come to a close, the weaver cut the warp threads from the loom.

WEIGH

The coins that we take out of our purse or pants pocket to make a purchase were unknown through most of the Old Testament era. The first evidence of minted coins in the region dates to the middle of the seventh century BC.[9] Nevertheless, people in this coinless era needed to pay for things using precious metals. During such transactions, a scale and weights were pulled out so the metal could be weighed, assuring sellers that they were getting the amount of precious metal they were expecting to receive. In the early books of the Bible we read about a great variety of things that were paid for in this way. The scale came out and metal was weighed when paying for property, grain, taxes (tribute), wages, a fine, and even when giving an offering at the Lord's sanctuary (Gen. 23:16; 43:15, 20–21; Exod. 30:16; Num. 3:47; 18:16; 31:52; 1 Kings 10:14; 20:39; Ezra 8:25–26, 34; Isa. 46:6; Jer. 32:9).

The scale that was used to weigh the precious metal was a balance scale that consisted of two flat pans that were attached by cords to each end of a beam that rested on a fulcrum. An honest scale would balance with empty pans. When the negotiations ended and it was time for the exchange to take place, the weight of the precious metal promised in the transaction would be placed in one of the pans and certified by placing a stone weight of known value in the other pan. If the scale balanced

A balance was used to confirm the weight of precious metals that a person was offering in exchange for goods or services.

again, the weight of the metal was certified and the exchange was completed.[10]

Such a scale was used so regularly by God's people in their daily living that it became a way to demonstrate their integrity. There were a number of ways to cheat when conducting a purchase with a scale. Some had two sets of weights, one heavier and one lighter, to give them the advantage; others rigged the scale itself. But we repeatedly hear the Lord calling his people to demonstrate their sturdy character by weighing things honestly: "Do not use dishonest standards when measuring length, weight or quantity. Use honest scales and honest weights, an honest ephah and an honest hin" (Lev. 19:35–36; see also Deut. 25:13–15). The poetic verses of Proverbs also call for God's people to show good faith during transactions that involve weighing: "The Lord detests the use of dishonest scales, but he delights in accurate weights" (Prov. 11:1 NLT; see also 16:11;

20:10, 23). Israel's failure to honor this fundamental direction became a sign of their apostasy (Mic. 6:11).

A known weight such as this one was placed on one pan of the balance while the item whose weight was being verified was placed on the other pan.

The biblical authors formally mention weighing or the weight of an item when they wish to impress us with value, size, or integrity. In the case of Abraham's servant, the author wishes us to be impressed with the weight and value of the jewelry he offered Rebekah (Gen. 24:22). When 1 Kings summarizes the wealth of Solomon, we are invited to marvel at the weight in gold that Solomon received on an annual basis (1 Kings 10:14). The weight of an object is also presented to impress us with its size. The weights of some of Goliath's weapons are given to confirm the size of this Philistine warrior, and the weight of the crown David took from Rabbah gives us an impression of its size (1 Sam. 17:5–7; 2 Sam. 12:30). A similar impression of size and value is delivered when the biblical authors tell us that the amount of precious metal in view is so large that it cannot be effectively weighed (1 Kings 7:47; 1 Chron. 22:3, 14). Finally, one biblical author also mentions weighing in the interest of marking integrity. Ezra had been entrusted with a great deal of precious metal to use in rebuilding the temple in Jerusalem. Despite the long trip and many months, all of the precious metal was accounted for. The final weighing of the material confirmed his integrity (Ezra 8:34). This stands in stark contrast to Absalom, who made an effort to impress people by weighing his hair (2 Sam. 14:26)—an act that decidedly fails to impress us with anything but his vanity.

In the Bible we also find weighing used metaphorically. The pain and mental

In this Egyptian judgment scene, the heart of the deceased is weighed in a balance against the feather of truth.

anguish that Job experienced during his trials were so intense that he struggled to find language that would adequately communicate them. We can almost see the pain in his eyes when he says, "If only my anguish could be weighed and all my misery be placed on the scales! It would surely outweigh the sand of the seas" (Job 6:2–3). Weighing can also be a metaphor for measuring personal integrity. In that light, the frustrated Job made this request: "Let God weigh me in honest scales and he will know that I am blameless" (Job 31:6). Belshazzar, the Babylonian king who had failed to humble himself before the Lord, did not ask to be weighed but was anyway. Daniel offered the verdict: "*Tekel*: You have been weighed on the scale and found wanting" (Dan. 5:27).

God does not need a scale to know something's weight, but when Isaiah tried to communicate the incredible ability of the Lord, he put a scale in the divine hand to show that he can measure what we cannot: "Who has held the dust of the earth in a basket, or weighed the mountains on the scales and the hills in a balance?" (Isa. 40:12). We cannot but God can, just as "he weighs the islands as though they were fine dust" (Isa. 40:15).

WIDOW

In the ancient Near East, it was common for the groom to be somewhat older than his bride, which means that he would often die sooner than his bride and leave her as a widow. The Bible acknowledges the physical and emotional pain experienced by the widow (Lam. 1:1–2; Ruth 1:20), but it is her economic peril that is most often in view.[11] While it was possible for a woman to own property following the death of her husband, it was property that was linked to her dowry. Whether in Mesopotamia, Egypt, or Israel, widows generally did not inherit property from their husband's estate.[12] The man's property generally transferred directly to sons or the nearest male relative of the deceased (Num. 27:8–11). This means that the economic well-being of the widow was in the hands of the children who inherited the estate. If there were no children, she could seek remarriage using the stipulations of the levirate marriage law and hope to produce a son who could then come to own the property and care for her (Deut. 25:5–6). Or she might return to her extended family in the hope that they would

In the small village of Nain on the flanks of Mount Moreh (below), Jesus raised a widow's son from the dead.

spread a blanket of economic security over her (Gen. 38:11; Lev. 22:13). But if these options failed, the widow found herself facing a life of great uncertainty that in the extreme forced some women into prostitution and others to sell their own children as debt slaves.[13]

The Bible stories that mention widows co-opt this tragic vulnerability in a couple of ways. The devastating circumstances of a disadvantaged widow can enhance the dramatic reversal of circumstances delivered by a divine miracle. We see this in the case of the widow of Zarephath, whom we meet preparing a final meal for herself and her son; the prophet's widow who was about to lose her sons as debt slaves to a creditor; and the widow at Nain, who was going about the sad task of burying her only son (1 Kings 17:7–24; 2 Kings 4:1–7; Luke 7:11–17). The miracles that freed them from their plight appear all the more spectacular given their sad circumstances. At other times we meet disadvantaged widows who seize our attention because they demonstrate special acumen in escaping their circumstances or remarkable faith in the midst of their circumstances. These include Tamar, Ruth, Naomi, Abigail, and Anna (Gen. 38:6–26; Ruth 1–4; 1 Sam. 25:14–42; Luke 2:36–38). But Jesus delivered the accolades personally when a nameless widow dropped a seemingly insignificant amount of money in the donation horns at the temple: "Truly I tell you, this poor widow has put more into the treasury than all the others. They all gave out of their wealth; but she, out of her poverty, put in everything—all she had to live on" (Mark 12:43–44).

The moral instruction in the Bible also mentions widows. This instruction is animated by the underlying premise that God and his followers are cut from the cloth of great compassion; they will make it their business to take care of the disadvantaged in society. The Lord declares in unmistakable language that he will personally care for the disadvantaged widow (Deut. 10:18; Pss. 68:5; 146:9; Prov. 15:25). He subsequently demands that those who call themselves his followers replicate this concern in their lives. Various Old Testament laws were meant to serve as a social safety net for widows, who would not have the essentials for living or might fail to find justice in the courts (Exod. 22:22; Deut. 14:28–29; 24:17–22; 26:12; 27:19). The needs of certain widows did not expire with the change to the New Testament

In the biblical world, the role of a wife was typically limited to household support roles such as churning butter. Therefore, the death of a husband spelled economic peril for his widow.

This relief carved into a sarcophagus depicts Jesus raising a widow's son from the dead at Nain.

the oppressed. Defend the cause of the fatherless, plead the case of the widow" (Isa. 1:17 TNIV). And Jesus himself harangued the Jewish leaders who walked about piously but failed to honor the Lord by caring for widows. He described the teachers of the law as those who "devour widows' houses and for a show make lengthy prayers" (Luke 20:47). James summed up the matter in a premise that should inform the lives of all believers: "Religion that God our Father accepts as pure and faultless is this: to look after orphans and widows in their distress and to keep oneself from being polluted by the world" (James 1:27).

In the majority of instances, the biblical authors had literal widows in mind when they deployed this language; but in two instances widowhood became a figure of speech. In the first, Isaiah was delivering a stern judgment speech against Babylon, anticipating its fall from power. This nation, which never imagined itself to be an unfortunate, suffering, poor widow, would become exactly that. "Both of these will overtake you in a moment, on a single day: loss of children and widowhood" (Isa. 47:9). But before this happened, Jerusalem itself would know the pain of being a widow. The poetic lament of her fall begins with these words: "How deserted lies the city, once so full of people! How like a widow is she, who once was great among the nations" (Lam. 1:1).

era, so we find this fundamental principle functioning there as well (Acts 6:1; 1 Tim. 5:3–10; James 1:27).

In both testaments when the people of God drifted in their relationship with the Lord, a bellwether of that failure was the mistreatment of the most vulnerable members of society, widows in particular. The Old Testament prophets addressed this matter frequently with strong and pointed language (Isa. 1:23; 10:1–2; Jer. 7:6; 22:3; Ezek. 22:7; Zech. 7:10; Mal. 3:5). Seeing injustice all around, Isaiah sounded the warning: "Seek justice, encourage

WINNOW

Winnowing was very well known to those living in Bible times; it happened on a yearly basis, often within sight of their homes. It was part of the larger process of harvesting and processing grain; in particular, its goal was to isolate the valuable grain kernels from the rest of the plant. In order to accomplish this feat, the harvested grain was carried uphill to the threshing floor where the tenacious bond between the grain kernel and the remainder of the plant was overcome through threshing. The threshing process left a mixture of grain and straw on the threshing floor, and winnowing was the first step in isolating the valuable grain kernels from the straw. [14]

Winnowing took advantage of two realities. The first is that the grain kernels weighed more than the by-products from which they needed to be separated. Second, when the mixture was tossed upward into the wind, the heavier grain kernels fell into a discrete pile while the lighter by-products were deposited on the threshing floor farther downwind. The ideal wind for doing this occurred during the harvest season. [15] During the late days of spring and early summer, the warm air over the Promised Land heated quickly while the water of the Mediterranean Sea kept the air over it somewhat cooler. As the air over the land warmed and rose, a Mediterranean Sea breeze pushed inland. This was the cool air of the sea surging in to replace the air rising over the land. This predictable westerly sea breeze determined the location of threshing floors, which were located just below the crest of a hill on its eastern side.

The process of winnowing began with a threshing fork—a wood fork with five to seven tines that was used to throw the mixture of grain kernels and straw high enough to get it into the wind blowing over the hill from the west. With each toss of the mixture, the heavier grain kernels were increasingly isolated from the chaff; and once on the threshing floor, the kernels were isolated from the wind so they would not blow away. This process was repeated again and again with the fork until the chaff mixed with the grain consisted of smaller pieces. Then the winnower shifted to the threshing shovel and

The tines of the winnowing fork were used to throw the threshed grain plant up and into the wind.

continued the process.[16] Though the work was hard and dusty, the spirits of those processing the grain were high. The connotation of joy attached itself to the entire process, including the winnowing, because it spelled survival for another year in a culture fully dependent on bread as a staple food.

This common cultural practice is mentioned as a literal event only once by the biblical authors, when we find Boaz winnowing barley on the threshing floor (Ruth 3:2). In all other instances, the words *winnowing* or *scatter* or the phrase *scatter to the wind* are used as a figure of speech. In a few instances, the winnowing is presented in a positive light. Kings judged effectively when they winnowed out evil from their kingdom (Prov. 20:8, 26). The successful restoration of Israel is also shown with a surreal picture of winnowing. Here the mountains are the figurative obstacles that stand in the way, but God promises, "You will thresh the mountains and crush them, and reduce the hills to chaff. You will winnow them, the wind will pick them up, and a gale will blow them away" (Isa. 41:15–16).

The majority of cases where threshing is referenced, however, are found in judgment speeches of the prophets. Here it is people who are being winnowed so that the undesirable are blown away. This image occurs in judgment speeches delivered against Hazor, Elam, Babylon, and Egypt (Jer. 49:32, 36; 51:2; Ezek. 30:26). But most often this image signals judgment against God's chosen people. He warned them early on that this would be the price to be paid for covenant infidelity: "I

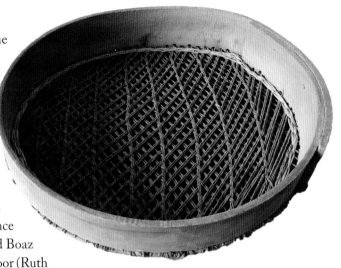

Using the sieve was the last step in the process of winnowing or cleaning the grain.

will scatter [winnow] you among the nations and will draw out my sword and pursue you" (Lev. 26:33). The prophets seized the image and repeated it as they spoke of judgments that would blow the Israelites from the Promised Land. "I will winnow them with a winnowing fork at the city gates of the land" (Jer. 15:7; see also 1 Kings 14:15; Pss. 44:11; 106:27; Jer. 31:10; Ezek. 5:10; 6:8; 12:14–15; 20:23; 36:19; Zech. 1:21).

This image might be repeated so often because it is effective and evocative in several ways. First, it employs a well-known image that would have stuck with those living in Bible times. Second, it takes the positive connotations of that image and reverses them. While real winnowing is a happy time, divine winnowing of Israel is about as far from that as one can get. The dramatic reversal in connotation found in these figures is what makes them powerful. And finally, the figure of speech characterizes those who are experiencing winnowing in a very negative way. The people who

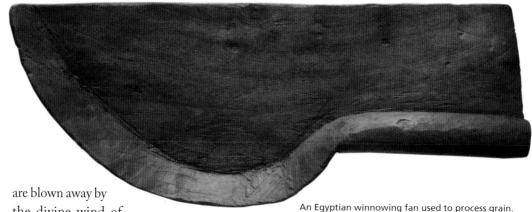
An Egyptian winnowing fan used to process grain.

are blown away by the divine wind of judgment are pictured as the dry and relatively worthless chaff that blows away during the winnowing process.

John the Baptist seized on this imagery in his ministry. In doing so, he linked himself to the prophets of an earlier era and demonstrated that the need for his listeners to change was just as urgent as it was for their ancestors. He pictured the Lord with his winnowing fork in hand ready to clear the threshing floor, gathering the wheat into barns while burning up the chaff with unquenchable fire (Matt. 3:12; Luke 3:17).

YOKE
(TO WEAR A)

*I*n a world without electric motors or internal combustion engines, the farmers and generals of the ancient world turned to draft animals when they needed to pull a cart, chariot, plow, or threshing sledge. The yoke provided the strong link between the powerful shoulders of the draft animal and the device that needed to be pulled.

The design of the yoke was personalized in size to fit the pulling team and generally was built from hardwood in order to keep the weight of the device down without compromising on strength. In both agriculture and military applications, the yoke had the same general design.[1] It was shaped to lie across the base of the draft animal's neck, held in position by ropes, staves, or *U*-shaped oxbows. When the powerful legs of the animal pulled forward, its shoulders made contact with the yoke, which, in turn, was connected to the device being pulled. Thus the yoke allowed the strength of multiple draft animals to be drawn from their shoulders and delivered to the necessary device while keeping the animals side by side and in line with the device being pulled.

Wearing a yoke carried two strong connotations. First, it meant that one's day was going to be difficult. Putting on a yoke meant that the time of relaxation and easy living was about to be traded for hours of hard, physical labor. The difficulty of that physical labor was compounded by the fact that the one wearing the yoke lacked autonomy in deciding how long or how hard the tasks ahead were going to be. The second connotation associated with putting on a yoke was that one became part of a team. The yoke itself was designed to create symmetry of effort and direction by those conjoined by the device.

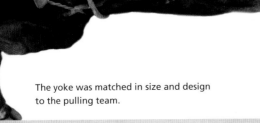

The yoke was matched in size and design to the pulling team.

The biblical world was filled with draft animals and yokes, so it is not surprising that we find them mentioned literally in a number of contexts in both law and narrative sections of the Bible (Num. 19:2; 1 Sam. 6:7; 2 Sam. 24:22; Luke 14:19). For example, there was an injunction that prohibited plowing with two animals unmatched in size and pulling ability: "Do not plow with an ox and a donkey yoked together" (Deut. 22:10). And we read that Elisha was plowing with oxen under yoke when Elijah called him to special service (1 Kings 19:19).

But in the majority of cases, we meet those wearing a yoke in figures of speech. Here the biblical authors take advantage of the two connotations noted above in order to artfully communicate their intended point. On the one hand, wearing a yoke symbolized a hard life of servitude that was imposed by one human being on another; to wear a yoke was a figure of speech for suffering under foreign domination. When the Lord permitted nations like Egypt, Assyria, or Babylon to impose their will on his chosen people, they were pictured as residing under the yoke of oppression that those nations lowered onto their shoulders (Exod. 6:6–7; Isa. 10:27; 14:25; 47:6; Jer. 27:8, 11–14; 28:14; Hosea 10:11; Nah. 1:13). For example, "I am the Lord your God, who brought you out of Egypt so that you would no longer be slaves. . . . I broke the bars of your yoke and enabled you to walk with heads held high" (Lev. 26:13).

Understanding the yoke image helps explain the repeated reference to the yoke in the exchanges between Solomon's son Rehoboam and his subjects from the northern tribes who were less than convinced about giving their loyalty to him (1 Kings 12:4, 9–11, 14).

At Shechem (below), the northern tribes of Israel sought relief from the heavy yoke that Solomon's administration had placed on them. Rehoboam told them to expect a heavier yoke during his administration.

The Baker Illustrated Guide to Everyday Life in Bible Times

They spoke of the heavy yoke Solomon had placed on them and asked that Rehoboam replace that more difficult life they had known with a lighter yoke. The united kingdom broke apart when Rehoboam said that instead of lightening the yoke, he would make it heavier. Given the fact that wearing a yoke was a figurative way of expressing foreign political dominance in the ancient Near East,[2] we get a clearer picture of the charge being leveled

The biblical authors employed the yoke as an image of domination. Egyptian prisoners could be pictured with a stylized yoke around their necks.

against Solomon and what the tribes of the north could expect from his son. The choice of symbolic language indicates the northern tribes felt they were being ruled by oppressive outsiders; Rehoboam said that they had better get used to it.

The second connotation associated with wearing a yoke was that it linked two entities together in a close relationship. The ancestors of God's people were criticized for the way in which they "yoked themselves to Baal of Peor" (Ps. 106:28); and Paul used the same imagery when he warned the Corinthians not to be "yoked together with unbelievers" (2 Cor. 6:14). But the conjoining under a symbolic yoke could also be positive. One of the ways in which God's Old Testament people were linked to him was through their obedience to the law, though they were often pictured trying to throw that yoke off themselves (Jer. 2:20; 5:5; Acts 15:10). But what happened with that conjoining device during the New Testament era? Jesus did not say that there would be no more yoke for those who lived in this new age, but he invited his followers to see that he offered a different way of connecting to him: "Take my yoke upon you and learn from me, for I am gentle and humble in heart, and you will find rest for your souls. For my yoke is easy and my burden is light" (Matt. 11:29–30).

NOTES

A

1. Olive oil was consumed as food, was used as medicine, provided fuel for lamps, and functioned as a base for cosmetics. Philip J. King and Lawrence E. Stager, *Life in Biblical Israel*, Library of Ancient Israel (Louisville: Westminster John Knox, 2001), 97.

2. John H. Walton, ed., *Zondervan Illustrated Bible Backgrounds Commentary*, vol. 2 (Grand Rapids: Zondervan, 2009), 278–79.

3. John H. Walton, Victor H. Matthews, and Mark W. Chavalas, *The IVP Bible Background Commentary: Old Testament* (Downers Grove, IL: InterVarsity, 2000), 125.

4. Ibid., 347.

5. For a similar request by an Assyrian king, see Daniel David Luckenbill, ed., *Ancient Records of Assyria and Babylon*, vol. 2 (Chicago: University of Chicago Press, 1926), 312, 815.

6. For a more complete discussion of the ancient bow and arrow see King and Stager, *Life in Biblical Israel*, 226–27.

7. Note the contrast. Not only will the Assyrians fail to enter the city, but they will not even get close enough to fire the long-range arrow in the direction of Jerusalem.

8. Alfred Edersheim, *The Life and Times of Jesus the Messiah*, vol. 2 (Grand Rapids: Eerdmans, 1971), 381–82.

9. Joachim Jeremias, *Jerusalem in the Time of Jesus* (Philadelphia: Fortress, 1969), 235–36.

10. For a further discussion, see James C. Martin, John A. Beck, and David G. Hansen, *A Visual Guide to Gospel Events* (Grand Rapids: Baker, 2010), 40–41.

B

1. John J. Rousseau and Rami Arav, *Jesus and His World: An Archaeological and Cultural Dictionary* (Minneapolis: Fortress, 1995), 8.

2. Jack M. Sasson, ed., *Civilizations of the Ancient Near East*, vol. 1 (Peabody, MA: Hendrickson, 1995), 195.

3. For a more complete discussion, see Philip J. King and Lawrence E. Stager, *Life in Biblical Israel*, Library of Ancient Israel (Louisville: Westminster John Knox, 2001), 67.

4. Willem A. VanGemeren, ed., *New International Dictionary of Old Testament Theology and Exegesis*, vol. 1 (Grand Rapids: Zondervan, 1997), 344.

5. Ibid., 267.

6. John H. Walton, ed., *Zondervan Illustrated Bible Backgrounds Commentary*, vol. 2 (Grand Rapids: Zondervan, 2009), 353.

7. Oded Borowski, *Daily Life in Biblical Times*, Archaeology and Biblical Studies, vol. 5 (Atlanta: Society of Biblical Literature, 2003), 81.

8. King and Stager, *Life in Biblical Israel*, 41.

9. Leland Ryken, James C. Wilhoit, and Tremper Longman III, eds., *Dictionary of Biblical Imagery* (Downers Grove, IL: InterVarsity, 1998), 99.

10. For a summary of loans in the ancient Near Eastern economy, see John H. Walton, Victor H. Matthews, and Mark W. Chavalas, *The IVP Bible Background Commentary: Old Testament* (Downers Grove, IL: InterVarsity, 2000), 185.

11. For a discussion of loans and securities in the ancient world, see Roland de Vaux, *Ancient Israel: Its Life and Institutions*, Biblical Resource Series (Grand Rapids: Eerdmans, 1997), 170–71.

12. Some regard this as a ceremonial act that became part of the lending process indicating the goodwill that existed between creditor and lender. VanGemeren, *New International Dictionary of Old Testament Theology and Exegesis*, 3:176.

13. Ibid., 2:43.

14. This very protocol is noted in the El Amarna texts from Egypt (fourteenth century BC) where Canaanite vassals bow seven times before the pharaoh. Walton, *Zondervan Illustrated Bible Backgrounds Commentary*, 1:116.

15. For a complete discussion of bread making, see King and Stager, *Life in Biblical Israel*, 65–67.

16. Sasson, *Civilizations of the Ancient Near East*, 1:195.

17. For a discussion of marriage in ancient Israel, see ibid., 644–45.

18. de Vaux, *Ancient Israel*, 27.

19. Ibid., 56–57.

20. For illustration and discussion of the evolving nature of tombs during the biblical period, see King and Stager, *Life in Biblical Israel*, 363–72; Jack Finegan, *The Archeology of the New Testament*, rev. ed. (Princeton: Princeton University Press, 1992), 292–318.

21. This perspective is offered by Byron R. McCane, "Let the Dead Bury Their Own Dead: Second Burial and Matthew 8:21–22," *Harvard Theological Review* 83, no. 1 (1990): 40–41.

C

1. Robert James Forbes, *Metallurgy in Antiquity: A Notebook for Archaeologists and Technologists* (Leiden, the Netherlands: Brill, 1950), 324.

2. Jack M. Sasson, ed., *Civilizations of the Ancient Near East*, vol. 2 (Peabody, MA: Hendrickson, 2000), 1546–47.

3. Willem A. VanGemeren, ed., *New International Dictionary of Old Testament Theology and Exegesis*, vol. 4 (Grand Rapids: Zondervan, 1996), 474.

4. John H. Walton, ed., *Zondervan Illustrated Bible Backgrounds Commentary*, vol. 1 (Grand Rapids: Zondervan, 2009), 89.

5. Egyptians circumcised by cutting a dorsal incision that left the foreskin in place. Jack M. Sasson, "Circumcision in the Ancient Near East," *Journal of Biblical Literature* 85, no. 4 (1966): 474.

6. This event is recorded in 1 Maccabees 1:48, 60–63.

7. These insights are summarized together with illustrations from ancient Near

Eastern art in Nili S. Fox, "Clapping Hands as a Gesture of Anguish and Anger in Mesopotamia and Israel," *Journal of the Ancient Near Eastern Society* 23 (1995): 46–60.

8. Walton, *Zondervan Illustrated Bible Backgrounds Commentary*, 1:384.

9. Sailhamer is particularly helpful in building the bridge between the purity laws of Leviticus and the narratives of Genesis. John H. Sailhamer, *The Pentateuch as Narrative: A Biblical-Theological Commentary*, Library of Biblical Interpretation (Grand Rapids: Zondervan, 1992), 332–41.

10. The Lord is not physically present with us in the same way that he was present with the Israelites. VanGemeren, *New International Dictionary of Old Testament Theology and Exegesis*, 4:478.

11. Sasson, *Civilizations of the Ancient Near East*, 1:624–25.

12. Hennie J. Marsman, *Women in Ugarit and Israel: Their Social and Religious Position in the Context of the Ancient Near East*, Oudtestamentiche Studiën 49 (Leiden, the Netherlands: Brill, 2003), 140–41.

13. For an insight-filled look into this narrative, see Paul H. Wright, *Greatness, Grace, and Glory: Carta's Atlas of Biblical Biography* (Jerusalem: Carta, 2008), 55–58.

14. David A. Dorsey, *The Roads and Highways of Ancient Israel*, ASOR Library of Biblical and Near Eastern Archaeology (Baltimore: Johns Hopkins University Press, 1991), 33–37.

15. Viscount Montgomery, *A History of Warfare* (New York: World Publication, 1968), 56–57.

16. Dorsey, *Roads and Highways of Ancient Israel*, 39.

17. John A. Beck, "Why Do Joshua's Readers Keep Crossing the River? The Narrative-Geographical Shaping of Joshua 3–4," *JETS* 48, no. 4 (2005): 689–99.

18. Roland de Vaux, *Ancient Israel: Its Life and Institutions*, Biblical Resource Series (Grand Rapids: Eerdmans, 1997), 103.

19. The only exception to this list of wedding crowns within Proverbs can be found in 27:24, in which the allusion is to a royal crown.

20. John J. Rousseau and Rami Arav, *Jesus and His World: An Archaeological and Cultural Dictionary* (Minneapolis: Fortress, 1995), 74. For an example of a Jewish king using crucifixion, see Josephus, *Antiquities*, 13.14.2.

21. John McRay, *Archaeology and the New Testament* (Grand Rapids: Baker Academic, 1991), 205–6.

22. Rousseau and Arav, *Jesus and His World*, 75.

23. For additional thoughts on the details that attend Jesus's crucifixion, see James

C. Martin, John A. Beck, and David G. Hansen, *A Visual Guide to Gospel Events* (Grand Rapids: Baker, 2010), 176–81.

D

1. Jack M. Sasson, ed., *Civilizations of the Ancient Near East* (Peabody, MA: Hendrickson, 2000), 1:370, 2:2610.

2. Willem A. VanGemeren, ed., *New International Dictionary of Old Testament Theology and Exegesis*, vol. 2 (Grand Rapids: Zondervan, 1996), 45.

3. Song of Solomon 6:13 mentions the "dance of Mahanaim," literally "the dance of two camps." This may imply a dance that employs two groups of women.

4. Sasson, *Civilizations of the Ancient Near East*, 2:2611.

5. As many as ten different Hebrew verbs are used to describe dancing in the Old Testament. See VanGemeren, *New International Dictionary of Old Testament Theology and Exegesis*, 2:45–46.

6. Philip J. King and Lawrence E. Stager, *Life in Biblical Israel*, Library of Ancient Israel (Louisville: Westminster John Knox, 2001), 299.

7. The same vocabulary is used for the Assyrian practice (2 Kings 19:11) and in the ninth century BC inscription on the Moabite Mesha. See VanGemeren, *New International Dictionary of Old Testament Theology and Exegesis*, 2:276.

8. For a detailed and thorough treatment of this topic, see Frederick H. Cryer, *Divination in Ancient Israel and Its Near Eastern Environment* (Sheffield, UK: Sheffield Academic, 1994).

9. Sasson, *Civilizations of the Ancient Near East*, 2:2071–72.

10. Ibid., 1:45, 358, 480.

11. G. K. Beale and D. A. Carson, eds., *Commentary on the New Testament Use of the Old Testament* (Grand Rapids: Baker Academic, 2007), 23–24.

12. Note how Paul draws upon and then applies this principle in the circumstances being faced by the Corinthians (1 Cor. 7:10–16).

13. Sasson, *Civilizations of the Ancient Near East*, 2:2055.

14. Ibid., 1:52.

15. Alfred J. Hoerth, *Archaeology and the Old Testament* (Grand Rapids: Baker, 1998), 70.

16. Sasson, *Civilizations of the Ancient Near East*, 1:197–99.

17. King and Stager, *Life in Biblical Israel*, 101.

18. For a more detailed discussion, see John A. Beck, *The Land of Milk and Honey: An Introduction to the Geography of Israel* (St. Louis: Concordia, 2006), 148–50.

19. This may be an ancient Near Eastern motif as well for the Assyrian ruler, Sennacherib, who sought to impress us with his great power by claiming to have "dried up all the streams of Egypt" (2 Kings 19:24).

20. Sailhamer notes the thematic connection between the creation and exodus narratives. John H. Sailhamer, *The Pentateuch as Narrative: A Biblical-Theological Commentary*, Library of Biblical Interpretation (Grand Rapids: Zondervan, 1992), 91, 127.

E

1. Leland Ryken, James C. Wilhoit, and Tremper Longman III, eds., *Dictionary of Biblical Imagery* (Downers Grove, IL: InterVarsity, 1998), 226.

2. For a broader discussion of engraving tools and receiving media, see Philip J. King and Lawrence E. Stager, *Life in Biblical Israel*, Library of Ancient Israel (Louisville: Westminster John Knox, 2001), 304–10.

3. For a discussion of such seals and imagery linked to them, see John A. Beck, ed., *Zondervan Dictionary of Biblical Imagery* (Grand Rapids: Zondervan, 2011), 225–26.

4. John Walton, ed., *Zondervan Illustrated Bible Backgrounds Commentary*, vol. 4 (Grand Rapids: Zondervan, 2009), 163.

5. For a longer discussion of the typical fate of ancient exiles, see D. L. Smith-Christopher, "Reassessing the Historical and Sociological Impact of the Babylonian Exile," in *Exile: Old Testament, Jewish, and Christian Conceptions*, ed. James M. Scott (Leiden, the Netherlands: Brill, 1997), 23–27.

6. For a discussion of the theological dimension of exile from the Promised Land, see Willem A. VanGemeren, ed., *New International Dictionary of Old Testament Theology and Exegesis*, vol. 4 (Grand Rapids: Zondervan, 1996), 595–601.

F

1. For a discussion of drought, see Efraim Orni and Elisha Efrat, *Geography of Israel*, 3rd ed. (Jerusalem: Jewish Publication Society of America, 1971), 148–49.

2. In describing Titus's siege of Jerusalem, Josephus describes the horrific scene in very graphic language, even describing the methods of torture used to compel those who had hidden food to reveal its location. See Josephus, *War of the Jews*, 5.10.3.

3. For an extended treatment of this comparison, see John A. Beck, "Faith in the Face of Famine: The Narrative-Geographical Function of Famine in Genesis," *The Journal of Biblical Storytelling* 11, no. 1 (2001): 58–66.

4. Fasting is mentioned much more frequently in the Bible than in any of the other literature from the ancient Near East. John H. Walton, Victor H. Matthews, and

Mark W. Chavalas, *The IVP Bible Background Commentary: Old Testament* (Downers Grove, IL: InterVarsity, 2000), 275.

5. Fasting certainly may have had its origins in the ancient Near East, based on the fact that those who are deeply troubled by life tend to lose their appetite (see John H. Walton, ed., *Zondervan Illustrated Bible Backgrounds Commentary*, vol. 3 [Grand Rapids: Zondervan, 2009], 492), but the Bible developed fasting into a powerful spiritual discipline.

6. The firstborn enjoyed privileged status in many ancient Near Eastern cultures. For a summary, see Roger Syrén, *The Forsaken First-Born: A Study of a Recurrent Motif in the Patriarchal Narratives*, JSOT Supplement Series 133 (Sheffield, UK: Sheffield Academic, 1993), 88–93.

7. For a discussion of Jesus's dedication at the temple, see G. K. Beale and D. A. Carson, eds., *Commentary on the New Testament Use of the Old Testament* (Grand Rapids: Baker Academic, 2007), 268–69.

8. Archaeological evidence also suggests there may have been another fish market at some distance from the Fish Gate that was located within the City of David. H. Lernau and O. Lernau, "Fish Remains," in *City of David Excavations Final Report*, vol. 3, ed. A. de Groot and D. T. Ariel (Jerusalem: Institute of Archaeology, Hebrew University, 1992), 131–48.

9. For a discussion of the various types of fish in the Sea of Galilee and their role in Israel's culture, see John A. Beck, ed., *Zondervan Dictionary of Biblical Imagery* (Grand Rapids: Zondervan, 2011), 87–88.

10. For a further discussion of fishing in Jesus's day, see John J. Rousseau and Rami Arav, *Jesus and His World: An Archaeological and Cultural Dictionary* (Minneapolis: Fortress, 1995), 93–97.

11. See Midrash, *Makkut* 3.12–13.

12. See also Midrash, *Makkut* 3.10. As a point of comparison, the law code of Hammurabi permitted the administration of sixty blows with an ox whip for insubordination (paragraph 202).

13. See Midrash, *Makkut* 3.12–13.

14. Gerhard Kittel, ed., *Theological Dictionary of the New Testament*, vol. 4 (Grand Rapids: Eerdmans, 1967), 518–19.

15. There is some evidence to suggest that the word *scorpion* may have referred to a form of whip like the Roman *flagellum*, which included metal cutting edges in the thongs. See Walton, *Zondervan Illustrated Bible Backgrounds Commentary*, 3:54–55.

16. Richard P. Hallion, *Taking Flight: Inventing the Aerial Age from Antiquity through the First World War* (Oxford: Oxford University Press, 2003), xvi.

17. For a helpful overview of this ancient cultural phenomenon, see ibid., 3–7.

18. The average distance traveled in a day during Bible times was between seventeen and twenty-three miles. Barry J. Beitzel, *The New Moody Atlas of the Bible* (Chicago: Moody, 2009), 81–84.

19. Jeffrey J. Niehaus, *Ancient Near Eastern Themes in Biblical Theology* (Grand Rapids: Kregel, 2008), 68.

20. These examples are nicely surveyed and illustrated in Silvia Schroer and Thomas Staubli, *Body Symbolism in the Bible* (Collegeville, MN: Liturgical Press, 2001), 184–90.

21. For a discussion of city fortification and its evolution, see Jack M. Sasson, ed., *Civilizations of the Ancient Near East*, vol. 2 (Peabody, MA: Hendrickson, 2000), 1523–37.

22. For a discussion of Rehoboam's systemic placement of such fortified cities, see Beitzel, *New Moody Atlas of the Bible*, 171–72.

23. For a more complete discussion of the foundation-building process, see Aharon Kempinski and Ronny Reich, eds., *The Architecture of Ancient Israel: From Prehistoric to the Persian Periods* (Jerusalem: Israel Exploration Society, 1992), 17–20.

24. Paul H. Wright, *Greatness, Grace, and Glory: Carta's Atlas of Biblical Biography* (Jerusalem: Carta, 2008), 24.

G

1. For an overview of the larger social contract that supported those who were less fortunate, see Oded Borowski, *Agriculture in Iron Age Israel* (Boston: ASOR, 2002), 11.

2. If a family lost their private property as a consequence of hardship, this property was to be returned to them in the Year of Jubilee (Lev. 25:28).

3. Mishnah, *Peah* 4:10, 5:5, 7:3.

4. For an overview of the nonverbal elements associated with greetings in the ancient world, see Mayer I. Gruber, *Aspects of Nonverbal Communication in the Ancient Near East* (Rome: Biblical Institutes Press, 1980), 293–345.

5. When the Israelites did not have access to grain in the wilderness, God provided them with manna. Like the grain kernels, this product was also ground so that it could be used to make bread (Num. 11:8).

6. This grinding mill is also referred to as the *saddle and rider mill*. Philip J. King and Lawrence E. Stager, *Life in Biblical Israel*, Library of Ancient Israel (Louisville: Westminster John Knox, 2001), 95.

7. This development is evident later in the period of the Old Testament. Borowski, *Agriculture in Iron Age Israel*, 90n4.

8. Possibly a reference to the common household task assigned to the female

members of the household but in context is more likely a sexual innuendo. Athalya Brenner, *On Gendering Texts: Female and Male Voices in the Hebrew Bible* (Leiden, the Netherlands: Brill, 1993), 143.

H

1. We find similar examples in the literature and art of extrabiblical sources in the ancient Near East. John H. Walton, ed., *Zondervan Illustrated Bible Backgrounds Commentary*, vol. 4 (Grand Rapids: Zondervan, 2009), 56; Mayer I. Gruber, *Aspects of Nonverbal Communication in the Ancient Near East* (Rome: Biblical Institutes Press, 1980), 32–33, 60–64.

2. For example, the Syrian storm god is pictured with a lightning bolt in a raised hand. Alberto R. W. Green, *The Storm-God in the Ancient Near East*, Biblical and Judaic Studies from the University of California, vol. 8 (Winona Lake, IN: Eisenbrauns, 2003), 156.

3. Willem A. VanGemeren, ed., *New International Dictionary of Old Testament Theology and Exegesis*, vol. 2 (Grand Rapids: Zondervan, 1996), 403.

4. The Philistine recollection of this event led them to apply the Lord's raised hand to the plagues they experienced (1 Sam. 6:3, 5–6).

5. A limestone plaque dating to the tenth century BC (from approximately the time of Solomon) called the Gezer calendar summarizes the rhythm of the agricultural year. For a description and translation, see Philip J. King and Lawrence E. Stager, *Life in Biblical Israel*, Library of Ancient Israel (Louisville: Westminster John Knox, 2001), 87–88.

6. The sickle allowed the harvesters to cut the plant higher up on the stalk and so limit the amount of straw that was managed on the threshing floor. See Oded Borowski, *Agriculture in Iron Age Israel* (Boston: ASOR, 2002), 58–59.

7. A helpful overview of hunting techniques described and illustrated can be found in Othmar Keel, *The Symbolism of the Biblical World: Ancient Near Eastern Iconography and the Book of Psalms* (Winona Lake, IN: Eisenbrauns, 1997), 89–95.

8. Jack M. Sasson, ed., *Civilizations of the Ancient Near East*, vol. 1 (Peabody, MA: Hendrickson, 2000), 370.

9. Note how the description of the land in Isaiah 7:24 suggests ways in which the populated land will revert into a more wild landscape, again supporting more widespread hunting.

I

1. See the chapter titled "Succession and Inheritance" in Roland de Vaux, *Ancient*

Israel: Its Life and Institutions, Biblical Resource Series (Grand Rapids: Eerdmans, 1997), 53–55.

2. Jack M. Sasson, ed., *Civilizations of the Ancient Near East*, vol. 2 (Peabody, MA: Hendrickson, 2000), 1395.

K

1. A helpful overview of the ancient Near Eastern evidence on location of the kiss is found in Admiel Kosman, "Ancient Foundations for Religious Homilies," in *Self, Soul, and Body in Religious Experience*, ed. Albert I. Baumgarten (Leiden, the Netherlands: Brill, 1998), 107–8n38.

2. Amélie Kuhrt, *The Ancient Near East: c. 3000–330 BC*, vol. 1 (New York: Routledge, 1995), 148.

3. Gerhard Kittel and Gerhard Friedrich, eds., *Theological Dictionary of the New Testament*, vol. 9 (Grand Rapids: Eerdmans, 1974), 139.

L

1. For a discussion of the lamp and its imagery, see John A. Beck, ed., *Zondervan Dictionary of Biblical Imagery* (Grand Rapids: Zondervan, 2011), 152–54.

2. See Varda Sussman, *Oil-Lamps in the Holy Land: From the Beginning to the Hellenistic Period*, BAR International Series (Oxford: Archaeopress, 2007).

3. For an argument on the distinction of one-hand or two-hand placement and the employment of this gesture in the Hittite culture, see David P. Wright, "The Gesture of Hand Placement in the Hebrew Bible and in Hittite Literature," *Journal of the American Oriental Society* 106 (1986): 433–86.

4. Gerhard Kittel and Gerhard Friedrich, eds., *Theological Dictionary of the New Testament*, vol. 8 (Grand Rapids: Eerdmans, 1974), 160.

5. Note how this image reappears in 2 Sam. 18:12. Joab chastised one of his soldiers for failing to take Absalom's life. But echoing the words of David, the soldier declared that he "would not lay a hand on the king's son."

6. Ada Taggar-Cohen, "The Casting of Lots among the Hittites in Light of Ancient Near Eastern Parallel," *Journal of Ancient Near Eastern Studies* 29 (2002): 101.

7. Anne Marie Kitz, "The Hebrew Terminology of Lot Casting and Its Ancient Near Eastern Context," *Catholic Biblical Quarterly* 62 (2000): 201–14.

8. Jack M. Sasson, ed., *Civilizations of the Ancient Near East*, vol. 2 (Peabody, MA: Hendrickson, 2000), 2072.

9. Philip J. King and Lawrence E. Stager, *Life in Biblical Israel*, Library of Ancient Israel (Louisville: Westminster John Knox, 2001), 330.

10. Kitz, "The Hebrew Terminology of Lot Casting and Its Ancient Near Eastern Context," 203.

M

1. Roland de Vaux, *Ancient Israel: Its Life and Institutions*, Biblical Resource Series (Grand Rapids: Eerdmans, 1997), 199. For comparative values, see Willem A. VanGemeren, ed., *New International Dictionary of Old Testament Theology and Exegesis*, vol. 1 (Grand Rapids: Zondervan, 1997), 385–86.

2. For comparative values, see VanGemeren, *New International Dictionary of Old Testament Theology and Exegesis*, 1:421–22.

3. Jack M. Sasson, ed., *Civilizations of the Ancient Near East*, vol. 2 (Peabody, MA: Hendrickson, 2000), 1810.

4. John H. Walton, Victor H. Matthews, and Mark W. Chavalas, *The IVP Bible Background Commentary: Old Testament* (Downers Grove, IL: InterVarsity, 2000), 799–800.

5. Craig S. Keener, *The IVP Bible Background Commentary: New Testament* (Downers Grove, IL: InterVarsity, 1993), 817.

6. Dominique Collon, *Near Eastern Seals: Interpreting the Past* (Berkeley: University of California Press, 1990), 11.

7. Leland Ryken, James C. Wilhoit, and Tremper Longman III, eds., *Dictionary of Biblical Imagery* (Downers Grove, IL: InterVarsity, 1998), 547.

8. Nathan MacDonald, *What Did the Ancient Israelites Eat? Diet in Biblical Times* (Grand Rapids: Eerdmans, 2008), 35.

9. Oded Borowski, *Daily Life in Biblical Times*, Archaeology and Biblical Studies (Atlanta: Society of Biblical Literature, 2003), 66.

10. Barry J. Beitzel, *The New Moody Atlas of the Bible* (Chicago: Moody, 2009), 61–62.

11. VanGemeren, *New International Dictionary of Old Testament Theology and Exegesis*, 2:136. Some have expressed concerns about the way this ancient text has been interpreted. See John H. Walton, ed., *Zondervan Illustrated Bible Backgrounds Commentary* (Grand Rapids: Zondervan, 2009), 1:246.

12. For a discussion of this palace and its purposes, see Ehud Netzer, *The Architecture of Herod, the Great Builder* (Grand Rapids: Baker Academic, 2006), 179–201.

13. Midrash, *Abodah Zara* 3:3, 9.

14. Sackcloth was made from the coarse hair of goats or camels and was very itchy compared to the softer wool. For its connection to other mourning rituals, see Philip J. King and Lawrence E. Stager, *Life in Biblical Israel*, Library of Ancient Israel (Louisville: Westminster John Knox, 2001), 373.

15. Some but not all of these laments were written with a special poetic cadence called the *qînâ*. For a brief introduction to the topic, see VanGemeren, *New International Dictionary of Old Testament Theology and Exegesis*, 4:867–68.

N

1. William James Hamblin, *Warfare in the Ancient Near East to 1600 B.C.: Holy Warriors at the Dawn of History* (Abingdon: Routledge, 2006), 85–88.

2. Nakedness could be a symbol of heroism or dominance. Julia M. Asher-Greve, "Images of Men, Gender Regimes, and Social Stratification in the Late Uruk Period," in *Gender Through Time in the Ancient Near East*, ed. Diane R. Bolger (Lanham, MD: Altamira, 2008), 139.

3. John H. Walton, ed., *Zondervan Illustrated Bible Backgrounds Commentary* (Grand Rapids: Zondervan, 2009), 14–15, 159.

4. George W. Ramsey, "Is Name-Giving an Act of Domination in Genesis 2:23 and Elsewhere?" *Catholic Biblical Quarterly* 50 (1988): 24–35.

5. Jan Assman, *The Search for God in Ancient Egypt* (Ithaca, NY: Cornell University Press, 2001), 83–84.

6. Genealogies and genealogical registers played very important roles in maintaining obedience to divine law and in maintaining social order. See James C. Martin, John A. Beck, and David G. Hansen, *A Visual Guide to Gospel Events* (Grand Rapids: Baker, 2010), 12–13.

O

1. Legislation that addresses the well-being of orphans can be found in many ancient Near Eastern cultures. For a detailed treatment, see F. Charles Fensham, "Widow, Orphan, and the Poor in Ancient Near Eastern Legal and Wisdom Literature," in *Essential Papers on Israel and the Ancient Near East*, ed. Frederick E. Greenspahn (New York: New York University Press, 1991), 176–92.

2. This is a value represented in many ancient Near Eastern cultures. See Jack M. Sasson, ed., *Civilizations of the Ancient Near East*, vol. 2 (Peabody, MA: Hendrickson, 2000), 2044–45.

P

1. For a summary of their origins and early history, see Richard L. Niswonger, *New Testament History* (Grand Rapids: Zondervan, 1988), 34–37; Ben Witherington III, *New Testament History: A Narrative Account* (Grand Rapids: Baker Academic, 2001), 45–48.

2. Joachim Jeremias, *Jerusalem in the Time of Jesus* (Philadelphia: Fortress, 1969), 235–36.

3. Alfred Edersheim, *The Life and Times of Jesus the Messiah*, vol. 2 (Grand Rapids: Eerdmans, 1971), 281–82.

4. Philip J. King and Lawrence E. Stager, *Life in Biblical Israel*, Library of Ancient Israel (Louisville: Westminster John Knox, 2001), 93–94.

5. For a chart that illustrates the time of year for planting various commodities in Israel, see Oded Borowski, *Agriculture in Iron Age Israel* (Boston: ASOR, 2002), 34.

6. For use of the seed drill, see ibid., 54–55.

7. The Bible does not mention the age of children when their parents arranged a marriage contract. Jewish traditional writings mention that young men were married by the age of eighteen and girls by the time they were thirteen. See Midrash, *Aboth* 5:21, and Talmud, *Pesachim* 113.

8. King and Stager, *Life in Biblical Israel*, 54.

9. See the Code of Hammurabi no. 155, in James B. Prichard, ed., *The Ancient Near East: An Anthology of Texts and Pictures* (London: Oxford University Press, 1958), 155–56.

10. The importance of this operation and familiarity with it are quietly but powerfully affirmed by the numerous Hebrew terms used to describe the different types of furrows and even parts of furrows left in the wake of the plow. See Borowski, *Agriculture in Iron Age Israel*, 48.

11. King and Stager, *Life in Biblical Israel*, 92.

12. For an example from the Hittite culture, see William James Hamblin, *Warfare in the Ancient Near East to 1600 B.C.: Holy Warriors at the Dawn of History* (Abingdon: Routledge, 2006), 303.

13. The laws in Deuteronomy provide some clear direction regarding the collection of plunder and the treatment of captives, differentiating between those defeated within the bounds of the Promised Land and those defeated outside those boundaries (Deut. 20:10–18; 21:10–14).

14. John H. Walton, Victor H. Matthews, and Mark W. Chavalas, *The IVP Bible Background Commentary: Old Testament* (Downers Grove, IL: InterVarsity, 2000), 167.

15. While there is some evidence that professional potters were banned from operating their kilns within Jerusalem at the time of Jesus due to the smoke they produced, the presence of a potter's house and Potsherd Gate in Jerusalem at the time of Jeremiah gives credence to their presence near if not within the city (Jer. 18:1–6; 19:2). Jeremias, *Jerusalem in the Time of Jesus*, 6.

16. Sirach 38:29–30.

17. For an overview, see Jack M. Sasson, ed., *Civilizations of the Ancient Near East*, vol. 2 (Peabody, MA: Hendrickson, 2000), 1545.

18. A more detailed treatment of the manufacturing process is available in King and Stager, *Life in Biblical Israel*, 133–39.

19. In each of the instances cited here, the active participle of the Hebrew verb *ytsr* is employed. This verb form doubles as the Hebrew word for *potter*, though not all English translations show evidence of this relationship.

20. Sasson, *Civilizations of the Ancient Near East*, 2:2529.

21. For a discussion, see Hennie J. Marsman, *Women in Ugarit: Their Social and Religious Position in the Context of the Ancient Near East*, Oudtestamentiche Studiën 49 (Leiden, the Netherlands: Brill, 2003), 497–501.

22. Leland Ryken, James C. Wilhoit, and Tremper Longman III, eds., *Dictionary of Biblical Imagery* (Downers Grove, IL: InterVarsity, 1998), 677.

Q

1. In this article we will be exploring the use of two Hebrew verbs, *khtsf* and *psl*, which are most frequently translated as *hew* or *quarry*.

2. For a discussion of the ashlar stone as used in construction, see Aharon Kempinski and Ronny Reich, eds., *The Architecture of Ancient Israel: From the Prehistoric to the Persian Periods* (Jerusalem: Israel Exploration Society, 1992), 3–5.

3. Ibid., 3–4, and Marc Waelkens, "Bronze Age Quarries and Quarrying Techniques in the Eastern Mediterranean and Near East," in *Ancient Stones: Quarrying, Trade and Provenance*, ed. Marc Waelkens, Norman Herz, and Luc Moens (Leuven, Belgium: Leuven University Press, 1992), 5–12.

R

1. For a more complete treatment of each of these forms of transportation, see the appropriate entry in John A. Beck, *Zondervan Dictionary of Biblical Imagery* (Grand Rapids: Zondervan, 2011).

2. While these other modes of transportation were primarily used to get to and from the battlefield, chariots played two important roles in the battles themselves: (1) they were used to move archers from one critical location to the next, and (2) they were used to induce panic when they made a direct charge at the enemy infantry. Jack M. Sasson, ed., *Civilizations of the Ancient Near East*, vol. 1 (Peabody, MA: Hendrickson, 2000), 295.

3. John H. Walton, ed., *Zondervan Illustrated Bible Backgrounds Commentary*, vol. 1 (Grand Rapids: Zondervan, 2009), 521.

4. For a more complete discussion of this momentous event, see James C. Martin, John A. Beck, and David G. Hansen, *A Visual Guide to Bible Events* (Grand Rapids: Baker, 2009), 194–95.

5. Larry R. Helyer, "'Come What May, I Want to Run': Observations on Running in the Hebrew Bible," *Near East Archaeology Society Bulletin* 48 (2003): 1.

6. Barry J. Beitzel, *The Moody Atlas of the Bible* (Chicago: Moody, 2009), 81.

7. This article traces the use of the two most common verbs in the Old and New Testaments for the word *running—ruts* and *trhechô*—even though modern English translations use various terms to represent the word.

S

1. Willem A. VanGemeren, ed., *New International Dictionary of Old Testament Theology and Exegesis*, vol. 4 (Grand Rapids: Zondervan, 1996), 1158.

2. Josephus, *War of the Jews*, 4.9.12.

3. Roland de Vaux, *Ancient Israel: Its Life and Institutions*, Biblical Resource Series (Grand Rapids: Eerdmans, 1997), 482.

4. See 1 Maccabees 2:29–38.

5. Mishnah, *Shabbat* 7:2.

6. For a more detailed discussion, see Augustine Pagolu, *The Religion of the Patriarchs* (Sheffield, UK: Sheffield Academic, 1998), 145–70.

7. Richard S. Hess, *Israelite Religions: An Archaeological and Biblical Survey* (Grand Rapids: Baker Academic, 2007), 198.

8. Ibid., 199.

9. Pagolu, *Religion of the Patriarchs*, 148.

10. See 2 Maccabees 4:7, 23–24. Onias, who lost the position in Jerusalem, traveled to Egypt to continue the contribution of the Zadokites at a rival temple built in Leontopolis. Josephus, *Antiquities*, 13.3.1–3.

11. Ibid., 13.5.9.

12. Joachim Jeremias, *Jerusalem in the Time of Jesus* (Philadelphia: Fortress, 1969), 230.

13. The high priest and captain of the temple guard were Sadducees, and Sadducees represented the majority of votes in the Sanhedrin. Josephus, *Antiquities*, 20.9.1.

14. Ibid., 13.10.6.

15. Ibid., 13.5.9.

16. Midrash, *Erubim* 6:2; *Niddah* 4:2.

17. Josephus, *Antiquities*, 13.10.6

18. John McRay, *Archaeology and the New Testament* (Grand Rapids: Baker Academic, 1991), 78.

19. Philip J. King and Lawrence E. Stager, *Life in Biblical Israel*, Library of Ancient Israel (Louisville: Westminster John Knox, 2001), 272–73.

20. William James Hamblin, *Warfare in the Ancient Near East to 1600 B.C.: Warfare and History* (New York: Routledge, 2006), 389.

21. John H. Walton, ed., *Zondervan Illustrated Bible Backgrounds Commentary*, vol. 1 (Grand Rapids: Zondervan, 2009), 174.

22. John H. Walton, Victor H. Matthews, and Mark W. Chavalas, *The IVP Bible Background Commentary: Old Testament* (Downers Grove, IL: InterVarsity, 2000), 280.

23. For a more detailed introduction to this topic, see King and Stager, *Life in Biblical Israel*, 310–15.

24. Jack M. Sasson, ed., *Civilizations of the Ancient Near East*, vol. 2 (Peabody, MA: Hendrickson, 2000), 2395.

25. Ibid., 2:2215.

26. Ibid., 2:2272–74.

27. Sirach 38:24–39:11.

28. For a more detailed treatment of shaving in the ancient Near East, see Saul M. Olyan, "What Do Shaving Rites Accomplish and What Do They Signal in Biblical Ritual Contexts?" *Journal of Biblical Literature* 117 (1998): 611–22.

29. Egyptian priests performed all their religious duties only after removing all their head and body hair. Sasson, *Civilizations of the Ancient Near East*, 2:1733.

30. At least two tales from the Aegean world link a leader's hair to his invincibility. When that leader's hair was cut, his power left him. Assuming the Aegean origins of the Philistines, we can see why this explanation for Samson's strength may have had merit in the Philistines' eyes. Walton, *Zondervan Illustrated Bible Backgrounds Commentary*, 2:203.

31. Lucille A. Roussin, "Costume in Roman Palestine: Archaeological Remains and the Evidence of Mishnah," in *The World of Roman Custom*, eds. Judith Lynn Sebesta and Larissa Bonfante (Madison: University of Wisconsin Press, 2001), 188.

32. King and Stager, *Life in Biblical Israel*, 147.

33. Jonas Carl Greenfield, *Al Kanfei Yonah: Collected Studies of Jonas C. Greenfield on Semitic Philology*, vol. 2 (Jerusalem: Hebrew University Magnes Press, 2001), 98–101.

34. For a discussion on the messianic nature of this passage, see G. K. Beale and D. A. Carson, eds., *Commentary on the New Testament Use of the Old Testament* (Grand Rapids: Baker Academic, 2007), 573–75.

35. A helpful summary of shipping and ships of the ancient Near East is found in Sasson, *Civilizations of the Ancient Near East*, 2:1425–31.

36. The Alexandrian grain ship on which Paul was traveling carried 276 people (Acts 27:37).

37. Paul H. Wright, *Greatness, Grace, and Glory: Carta's Atlas of Biblical Biography* (Jerusalem: Carta, 2008), 233.

38. Maria-Carmen Llasat, "Storms and Floods," in *The Physical Geography of the Mediterranean*, ed. Jamie C. Woodward (Oxford: Oxford University Press, 2009), 534.

39. For a more comprehensive treatment of the siege as it developed in Mesopotamia, see Hamblin, *Warfare in the Ancient Near East to 1600 B.C.*, 226–36.

40. The horrific hunger that led to cannibalism within a city under siege is graphically reported in 2 Kings 6:24–29.

41. Hamblin, *Warfare in the Ancient Near East to 1600 B.C.*, 227.

42. See an example in 2 Kings 18:19–36 as well as in Ephraim Stern, *Archaeology of the Land of the Bible: The Assyrian, Babylonian, and Persian Periods*, Anchor Bible Reference Library (New York: Doubleday, 2001), 6.

43. Sasson, *Civilizations of the Ancient Near East*, 2:2724.

44. Sirach 27:4.

45. Oded Borowski, *Agriculture in Iron Age Israel* (Boston: ASOR, 2002), 66–67.

46. Here the NIV follows the Septuagint translation with "dark rain clouds" rather than with "sievelike rain clouds." The idea of darkness, however, appears to be an attempt to harmonize the poetry of this verse with Psalm 18:11. For a discussion, see VanGemeren, *New International Dictionary of Old Testament Theology and Exegesis*, 2:319–20.

47. Note its mention in the ordinary postures that filled the day in Deuteronomy 6:7; 11:19.

48. For a discussion of the ancient chair and imagery associated with it, see John A. Beck, *Zondervan Dictionary of Biblical Imagery* (Grand Rapids: Zondervan, 2011), 226–29.

49. Mayer I. Gruber, *Aspects of Nonverbal Communication in the Ancient Near East* (Rome: Biblical Institutes Press, 1980), 460–62.

50. See the summary in John J. Rousseau and Rami Arav, *Jesus and His World: An Archaeological and Cultural Dictionary* (Minneapolis: Fortress, 1995), 253–57.

51. James S. Jeffers, *The Greco-Roman World of the New Testament Era: Exploring the Background of Early Christianity* (Downers Grove, IL: InterVarsity, 1999), 235.

52. William J. Webb, "Slavery," in *Dictionary for Theological Interpretation of the Bible*, ed. Kevin J. Vanhoozer (Grand Rapids: Baker Academic, 2005), 751–53.

53. For a discussion of the vocabulary of light versus heavy sleeping, see VanGemeren, *New International Dictionary of Old Testament Theology and Exegesis*, 2:534.

54. Sasson, *Civilizations of the Ancient Near East*, 2:2055.

55. Mark S. Smith, *The Early History of God: Yahweh and the Other Deities in Ancient Israel*, 2nd ed. (Grand Rapids: Eerdmans, 2002), 69.

56. VanGemeren, *New International Dictionary of Old Testament Theology and Exegesis*, 3:930.

57. Peter Roger Stuart Moorey, *Ancient Mesopotamian Materials and Industry: The Archaeological Evidence* (Winona Lake, IN: Eisenbrauns, 1994), 166.

58. King and Stager, *Life in Biblical Israel*, 228–29.

59. Walton, *Zondervan Illustrated Bible Backgrounds Commentary*, 4:15.

60. In the case of iron, the temperature required to melt the ore is much too high for the ancients to achieve. Instead, an iron smelting furnace was heated with coal in order to carburize the iron, making it more malleable. King and Stager, *Life in Biblical Israel*, 169.

61. Wolfram von Soden, *The Ancient Orient: An Introduction to the Study of the Ancient Near East* (Grand Rapids: Eerdmans, 1994), 117.

62. Silvia Schroer and Thomas Staubli, *Body Symbolism in the Bible* (Collegeville, MN: Liturgical Press, 2001), 91–93.

63. For a complete discussion of the topic through various historical periods, see M. A. Littauer and J. H. Crouwel, *Wheeled Vehicles and Ridden Animals of the Ancient Near East* (Leiden, the Netherlands: Brill, 1979).

64. The Mesopotamian cultures do not mention this brutal form of punishment at all. Moses mentioned his concern that it might be used by Egyptians against Israelites (Exod. 8:26). Another possible reference to the practice is found in the Syrian Hadad Inscription, which condemns members of the royal household who commit acts of treason to be pounded with stones. See Walton, *Zondervan Illustrated Bible Backgrounds Commentary*, 1:320.

65. Beth A. Berkowitz, *Execution and Invention: Death Penalty Discourse in Early Rabbinic and Christian Cultures* (Oxford: Oxford University Press, 2006), 125.

66. This is according to Deuteronomy 17:7 and Mishnah, *Sanhedrin* 6:4.

67. An ox that had gored a person was also to be stoned to death (Exod. 21:28–32).

68. de Vaux, *Ancient Israel*, 74–76.

69. The foreigner and alien are only mentioned in the prologues and epilogues of these codes if they are mentioned at all. Christiana Van Houten, *The Alien in Israelite Law* (Sheffield, UK: Sheffield Academic, 1991), 34–35.

T

1. For an overview, see James S. Jeffers, *The Greco-Roman World of the New Testament Era* (Downers Grove, IL: InterVarsity, 1999), 145–46; Peter Schäfer, *The History of the Jews in the Greco-Roman World* (New York: Routledge, 2003), 106–7.

2. John J. Rousseau and Rami Arav, *Jesus and His World: An Archaeological and Cultural Dictionary* (Minneapolis: Fortress, 1995), 278.

3. Gerhard Kittel and Gerhard Friedrich, eds., *Theological Dictionary of the New Testament*, vol. 8 (Grand Rapids: Eerdmans, 1972), 94–105.

4. In the case of tax collection fraud, the law required repayment at the rate of 200 percent. Ibid., 8:100.

5. Philip J. King and Lawrence E. Stager, *Life in Biblical Israel*, Library of Ancient Israel (Louisville: Westminster John Knox, 2001), 265.

6. Xuang Huong Thi Pham, *Mourning in the Ancient Near East and the Hebrew Bible* (Sheffield, UK: Sheffield Academic, 1999), 24–25.

7. For a discussion, see Leland Ryken, James C. Wilhoit, and Tremper Longman III, eds., *Dictionary of Biblical Imagery* (Downers Grove, IL: InterVarsity, 1998), 320.

8. For a discussion, see James C. Martin, John A. Beck, and David G. Hansen, *A Visual Guide to Gospel Events* (Grand Rapids: Baker, 2010), 182–83.

9. John H. Walton, Victor H. Matthews, and Mark W. Chavalas, *The IVP Bible Background Commentary: Old Testament* (Downers Grove, IL: InterVarsity, 2000), 634.

10. For a discussion, see J. Scott Duvall and J. Daniel Hays, *Grasping God's Word: A Hands-On Approach to Reading, Interpreting, and Applying the Bible* (Grand Rapids: Zondervan, 2001), 192–93.

11. The prayer of Ezra may have this image-filled promise in view because he speaks about the remnant as a stake in God's sanctuary (Ezra 9:8).

12. For a more detailed discussion of the process, see Oded Borowski, *Agriculture in Iron Age Israel* (Boston: ASOR, 2002), 62–65.

13. For a discussion of this processing facility and associated biblical imagery, see John A. Beck, ed., *Zondervan Dictionary of Biblical Imagery* (Grand Rapids: Zondervan, 2011), 254–56.

14. For a helpful introduction to this topic, see Othmar Keel, *The Symbolism of the Biblical World: Ancient Near Eastern Iconography and the Book of Psalms* (Winona Lake, IN: Eisenbrauns, 1997), 89–94.

15. Willem A. VanGemeren, ed., *New International Dictionary of Old Testament Theology and Exegesis*, vol. 3 (Grand Rapids: Zondervan, 1997), 595.

16. Wolfram von Soden, *The Ancient Orient: An Introduction to the Study of the Ancient Near East* (Grand Rapids: Eerdmans, 1994), 89–90; Keel, *Symbolism of the Biblical World*, 91.

V

1. Denis Baly, *The Geography of the Bible: A Study in Historical Geography* (London: Lutterworth, 1957), 102.

2. For a more complete discussion, see Victor H. Matthews, "Treading the Winepress: Actual and Metaphorical Viticulture in the Ancient Near East," in *Food and Drink in the Biblical Worlds*, ed. Athalya Brenner, Semeia 86 (Atlanta: Society of Biblical Literature, 1999), 19–32.

3. Oded Borowski, *Agriculture in Iron Age Israel* (Boston: ASOR, 2002), 110.

4. For a description of this floor and the biblical imagery linked to it, see John A. Beck, ed., *Zondervan Dictionary of Biblical Imagery* (Grand Rapids: Zondervan, 2011), 274–76.

W

1. Willem A. VanGemeren, ed., *New International Dictionary of Old Testament Theology and Exegesis*, vol. 2 (Grand Rapids: Zondervan, 1997), 593.

2. Oded Borowski, *Daily Life in Biblical Times*, Archaeology and Biblical Studies (Atlanta: Society of Biblical Literature, 2003), 78.

3. W. Gunther Plaut and David E. Stein, eds., *The Torah: A Modern Commentary* (New York: URJ Press, 2005), 952.

4. Jack M. Sasson, ed., *Civilizations of the Ancient Near East*, vol. 1 (Peabody, MA: Hendrickson, 2000), 390–91.

5. For a detailed discussion of hydrology in the biblical world, see Arie S. Issar, *Water Shall Flow from the Rock: Hydrogeology and Climate in the Lands of the Bible* (Heidelberg, Germany: Springer-Verlag, 1990).

6. The use of aqueducts and tunnels to bring water into a central location within a city was mentioned in the Bible only during those times and in those circumstances when a strong central government made that possible (2 Kings 20:20; 2 Chron. 32:30).

7. Daniel Hillel, *Rivers of Eden* (New York: Oxford University Press, 1994), 66; Philip J. King and Lawrence E. Stager, *Life in Biblical Israel*, Library of Ancient Israel (Louisville: Westminster John Knox, 2001), 126–27.

8. Sasson, *Civilizations of the Ancient Near East*, 2:1571–74.

9. King and Stager, *Life in Biblical Israel*, 198.

10. For a further discussion of the balance scale and its imagery, see John A. Beck, ed., *Zondervan Dictionary of Biblical Imagery* (Grand Rapids: Zondervan, 2011), 223–25.

11. For a detailed overview of the ancient Near Eastern literature on this topic, see Hennie J. Marsman, *Women in Ugarit and Israel: Their Social and Religious Position in the Context of the Ancient Near East*, Oudtestamentiche Studiën 49 (Leiden, the Netherlands: Brill, 2003), 291–307.

12. Ibid., 319.

13. John H. Walton, ed., *Zondervan Illustrated Bible Backgrounds Commentary*, vol. 2 (Grand Rapids: Zondervan, 2009), 247.

14. For a more detailed look at the entire harvesting process, see Oded Borowski, *Agriculture in Iron Age Israel* (Boston: ASOR, 2002), 57–69.

15. Note that this is a west wind, not the hot khamsin wind that came off the desert (Jer. 4:11–12).

16. Mary Anne Murray, "Cereal Production and Processing," in *Ancient Egyptian Materials and Technology*, ed. Paul T. Nicholson and Ian Shaw (Cambridge: Cambridge University Press, 2000), 525.

Y

1. For a discussion of the yoke in agriculture, see Oded Borowski, *Agriculture in Iron Age Israel* (Boston: ASOR, 2002), 51–52. For a discussion of the yoke used with the Egyptian chariot, see M. A. Littauer and J. H. Crouwel, *Wheeled Vehicles and Ridden Animals of the Ancient Near East* (Leiden, the Netherlands: Brill, 1979), 85.

2. This image is not only used by the biblical authors but also appears in other ancient Near Eastern writings. See Moshe Anbar, "To Put One's Neck Under the Yoke," in *Essays on Ancient Israel in Its Near Eastern Context: A Tribute to Nadav Na'aman*, ed. Yaira Amit, Ehud Ben Zvi, Israel Finkelstein, and Oded Lipschits (Winona Lake, IN: Eisenbrauns, 2006), 17–19.

IMAGE CREDITS

Unless otherwise indicated, photos, illustrations, and maps are copyright © Baker Photo Archive.

The Baker Photo Archive acknowledges the permission of the following institutions and individuals.

Photo on page 110 © Baker Photo Archive. Courtesy of the Art Institute of Chicago.

Photos on pages 13, 14 (upper), 15, 16, 17 (upper), 26 (upper), 33 (upper), 36, 46 (lower), 48, 50 (upper), 55, 56, 61 (upper), 64 (upper), 73 (upper), 75, 76, 79 (lower), 82 (upper), 88 (lower), 94 (upper), 97 (upper), 98 (upper), 100, 104 (upper), 108, 122 (lower), 128 (upper), 138, 140, 144, 145, 146, 150, 152 (2x), 165, 169, 175, 176 (upper), 178 (2x), 182 (lower), 183, 194, 206 (upper), 212 (lower), 220 (upper), 225, 230 (upper right), 233 (upper), 237, 241, 242 (upper), 250 (upper), 255, 256, 281, 282 (upper), 282–83 (lower), 294, 295, 296 (upper), 302 © Baker Photo Archive. Courtesy of the British Museum, London, England.

Photos on pages 20, 49, 62, 66, 79 (upper), 84, 86, 137 (lower), 160 (upper), 226 (upper), 232 (lower), 247 (lower), 262, 272 © Baker Photo Archive. Courtesy of the Egyptian Ministry of Antiquities and the Cairo Museum.

Photo on page 32 (upper) © Baker Photo Archive. Courtesy of the Egyptian Ministry of Antiquities and the Elephantine Museum.

Photo on page 167 © Baker Photo Archive. Courtesy of the Egyptian Ministry of Antiquities and the Ismailia Museum.

Photos on pages 26 (lower), 292 © Baker Photo Archive. Courtesy of the Eretz Museum, Tel Aviv, Israel.

Photos on pages 232 (upper), 296 (lower) © Baker Photo Archive. Courtesy of the Field Museum.

Photo on page 229 (upper) © Baker Photo Archive. Courtesy of the Greek Ministry of Antiquities and the Archeological Museum of Thessaloniki, Greece.

Photos on pages 25, 215 © Baker Photo Archive. Courtesy of the Metropolitan Museum of Art.

Photos on pages 80 (lower), 114, 118–19 (upper), 120, 170 (upper), 177, 188, 193, 197 (upper), 226 (lower), 230 (lower left), 247 (upper), 268, 305 © Baker Photo Archive. Courtesy of the Musée du Louvre; Autorisation de photographer et de filmer. Louvre, Paris, France.

Photos on pages 23, 116 (upper), 201, 217 (lower), 231, 258 (upper), 270 (upper), 283 (upper) © Baker Photo Archive. Courtesy of the Oriental Institute Museum, University of Chicago.

Photos on pages 22 (upper), 72 © Baker Photo Archive. Courtesy of the Skirball Museum, Hebrew Union College—Jewish Institute of Religion, 13 King David Street, Jerusalem 94101.

Photos on pages 19, 51, 235 © Baker Photo Archive. Courtesy of the Turkish Ministry of Antiquities and the Antalya Museum, Turkey.

Photos on pages 158, 161, 187 (upper) © Baker Photo Archive. Courtesy of the Turkish Ministry of Antiquities and the Istanbul Archaeological Museum.

Photos on pages 28, 31, 38 (upper), 98 (lower), 299 © Baker Photo Archive. Courtesy of the Vatican Museum.

Photos on pages 222, 223 © Baker Photo Archive. Courtesy of the Wohl Archaeological Museum and Burnt House, Jerusalem.

Additional image credits

Photos on pages 81, 139 (upper), 197 (lower), 257, 269 © Dr. James C. Martin and the Israel Museum. Collection of the Israel Museum, Jerusalem, and courtesy of the Israel Antiquities Authority, exhibited at the Israel Museum, Jerusalem.

Photos on pages 9, 10, 12, 14 (lower), 17 (lower), 18, 22 (lower), 24, 27, 32 (lower), 33 (lower), 34, 35, 37, 38 (lower), 39, 40, 41 (lower), 42, 44, 45, 46 (upper), 47, 52 (lower), 53, 54, 57, 58, 59 (lower), 60, 61 (lower), 63, 64 (lower), 67, 69, 70 (lower), 71, 73 (lower), 74 (lower), 77 (upper), 78, 83, 85 (upper), 87, 88 (upper), 90, 91, 92, 93, 94 (lower), 95, 96, 99, 101 (lower), 102, 103, 104 (lower), 105, 107 (2x), 109, 111 (lower), 113, 115 (lower), 117, 118 (lower), 119 (lower), 121, 123, 124, 125, 126, 127, 128 (lower), 129, 130, 132, 133, 134 (lower), 135, 136 (lower), 139 (lower), 141, 142, 143 (upper), 146 (lower), 147, 148, 149, 151, 153, 154 (upper), 155, 156, 159, 160 (lower), 163, 166, 168, 170 (lower), 172, 173 (2x), 174, 176 (lower), 179, 180, 181, 184 (lower), 186, 187 (lower), 189, 191, 192, 195, 198, 199, 202 (2x), 203, 205, 207, 208, 209 (upper), 210, 211, 212 (upper), 213, 214, 216, 217 (upper), 219, 220 (lower), 221, 224, 227, 229 (lower), 233 (lower), 236, 238 (lower), 239, 240, 242 (lower), 243, 244, 245, 246, 248, 250 (lower), 251, 252, 253, 260, 261, 263, 264 (lower), 267, 270 (lower), 271, 274, 277, 278, 279, 280, 284, 285, 287, 288, 289, 290, 291 (2x), 293, 297, 300, 301, 304 © John A. Beck.

Photo on page 209 (lower) © John A. Beck. Courtesy of the Oriental Institute Museum, University of Chicago.

Photos on pages 80 (upper), 219 © R. Peter Beck.

SCRIPTURE INDEX

16:6 46, 174
16:9 43
16:16 113, 146
17:1 96, 98
17:3 200
17:7–8 191
17:21–22 216
17:23 262
17:25 210
17:27 217
18:1–4 203
18:1–6 310n15
18:5–6 203
18:20 283
18:22 281
19:2 310n15
19:9 95, 242
19:15 262
20:6 99
22:3 185, 299
22:4 210
22:19 46
23:25 85
23:27–28 86
24:5–7 101
24:6 191
25:8–10 77
25:10 43, 137, 153
25:27 89
25:33 46
26:18 197
27:6 100
27:8 304
27:9–10 80
27:11–14 304
27:20 99
28:14 304
29:1–14 101
29:5 189
29:7 101
29:8–9 80
29:28 189
31:4 74
31:9 110
31:10 301
31:13 74
31:37 164
32:9 295
32:22 169
33:11 43
34:8–11 250
36:4 229
36:11–26 230
36:23 273
36:24 273
36:32 229
38:9 40
40:9–10 141
41:5 232
47:5 174, 232
48:26 89
48:37 232
48:40 119
49:9 131
49:22 119
49:32 301

49:36 301
50:3 91
50:11 278, 279
50:12 91
50:14 15, 16
50:21 77
50:25–26 77
50:38 91
51:1–3 77
51:2 301
51:19 203
51:21 211
51:33 280
51:35–36 91
51:37–39 89
51:43 91
51:57 89
52:25 229

Lamentations
1:1 249, 299
1:1–2 297
1:2 175
1:4 175
1:8 179
2:15 55
2:19 138
2:20 95
3:5 242
3:52–53 146
3:53 263
4:2 201
4:9 103
4:18 146
4:19 119
4:20 283
4:21 89
5:2 148
5:3 185
5:13 137
5:15 74, 174
5:16 67

Ezekiel
1:1 101
3:11 101
4:1–13 242
4:9–13 23
5:1–17 233
5:10 301
5:16–17 104
6:8 301
6:11 56
6:13 172
11:15 101
12:13 146
12:14–15 301
12:18–19 100
12:19 102
12:24 80
13:6 80
13:7–9 80
13:23 80
15:2–3 276
16 206
16:7–8 179

16:8 192
16:12 66
16:22 179
16:30 204
16:32–33 206
16:35–39 179
17:20 146
18:6 94
18:10–11 94
18:11 172
18:15 94
19:8 283
20:5 140
20:6 169
20:12 216
20:13–16 217
20:15 140, 169
20:20 216
20:23 140, 301
20.42 140
21:14 56
21:17 56
21:18–21 79
21:26–27 67
21:29 79
22:7 185, 267, 299
22:13 56
22:17–22 259
22:20–22 165, 166
22:28 80
23:1–14 206
23:10 179
23:18 179
23:29 179
23:33 89
24:16–17 174
24:17 226
24:23 226
25:6 55
26:5 112
26:14 112
29:19 199
30:11–12 91
30:26 301
32:3 112
36:9 196
36:19 301
37:1–4 92
37:4–5 92
37:11 92
39:21 158
39:23 101
39:28 100
40–43 163
40:3 163
47:10 112

Daniel
1:3–5 100
1:6–7 182
2 85
2:1–2 84
2:27 79
4:4–37 85
4:7 79

4:28–31 18
4:28–37 19
5:7–12 79
5:27 296
7 85
7:1–8 19
7:13 273
7:14 19
8 85
8:18 252
9:3 106
9:25–26 11
10:3 9
10:5 24
11:30 237
11:40 237
11:44 77
12:2 253

Hosea
1:2 83
2:3 178, 179
2:9 179
2:11 217
2:19–20 194
2:23 191
3:1 83
4:13 172
6:5 209
6:11 143
8:7 143, 191
8:14 124
9:4 175
9:11 117
10:1–2 221
10:2 221
10:11 196, 304
10:12 191, 197
10:12–13 143
10:13 191
13:2 151
13:15 92, 200

Joel
1:8 194
1:9 175
1:10–12 92
1:14 106
1:17–20 92
2:12 106, 176
2:13 274
2:15 106
2:16 43
2:23–24 279
2:28 86
3:12 247
3:13 143
3:18 170

Amos
1:2 92
1:3 280
2:6 226
2:8 34
2:16 177
3:5 281

4:2 112, 113
4:7–8 103
4:13 202
5:16 175
5:27 100
6:12 196
8:5 163, 217
8:10 174, 232
8:11 104
9:9 245
9:13 142
9:15 191

Obadiah
1:4 118, 119
1:5 131

Jonah
1 238
1:4 237, 239
1:5–6 253
1:7 160
1:17 113
2:1 113

Micah
1:4 165, 166, 172
1:8 178, 226
1:16 174, 232
2:2 148
3:3 95
3:6–7 80
3:11 78
3:12 197
4:1 173
4:4 247, 285
4:12–13 280
4:13 77
5:1 242
5:13 221
6:7 110
6:10–11 163
6:11 296
6:15 142, 189
7:1 130
7:2 146

Nahum
1:5 166, 172
1:10 89
1:13 304
2:10 166
3:5 178
3:16 117
3:19 55

Habakkuk
1:6 124
1:8 119
1:10 124
1:12–17 100
1:14–15 113
1:15 112
2:15–16 89, 177
3:11 117

Zephaniah
1:13 189
1:17 31
2:13 91

Haggai
1:2–11 127
1:6 142, 189
2:6 90
2:22 211

Zechariah
1:21 301
2:1 162
2:1–2 163
3:9 98
3:10 247, 285
4:7 172
7:4–5 107
7:10 185, 267, 299
9:9 212
9:15 256
9:16 66
10:2 80, 86
10:4 277
12:1 128, 202
12:4 211
13:9 259

Malachi
1:8 30
2:16 81
3:2 288
3:5 185, 267, 299

1 Maccabees
7:33–34 133

Sirach
29:5 150

Matthew
1:5 205
1:11–12 101
1:17 101
1:18 193
1:18–19 193
1:18–25 28
1:20 85
1:20–24 252
1:21 182
2:4 230
2:11 38
2:12 85
2:13 85
2:19–22 85
3:7 223
3:12 302
3:17 20
4:1–2 106
4:1–4 40, 41
4:2 105

4:8–9 38
4:9 38
4:16 154
4:18 112
4:19 113
5:1 247
5:4 176
5:15 154
5:15–16 155
5:20 188, 230
5:31–32 82
5:46 270
5:47 134
6:16 107
6:31–33 94
7:2 164
7:24–27 126, 128
7:29 230
8:2–3 58
8:21–22 47, 306n21
8:24 252
9:9 271
9:10 270
9:10–12 271
9:11 94, 187
9:14–15 107
9:15 43
9:16 272
9:34 187
9:37–38 142
10:3 271
10:9 25
10:12 133
10:17 114
10:38 71
11:5 32
11:16–17 73
11:17 74, 174
11:19 88, 270
11:28 218
11:29–30 305
12:1–2 217
12:2–8 188
12:3–6 218
12:9–14 218
12:11 218
12:24 187
13:1–2 247
13:1–32 191
13:8 142
13:30 142, 143
13:39 143
13:47–48 112
13:47–50 113
14:3–5 73
14:6–11 73
14:13–21 40
14:19 247
15:1–8 188
15:14 31
15:29 247
15:30–31 31
15:32–38 40
15:35 247
16:4 223
16:5–12 224
16:16–17 11

16:24 71
17:24 269
17:27 112
18:17 270
18:23–24 35
18:35 35
19:3 82, 187
19:3–10 82
19:9 82
19:29 149
20:17–19 70
20:19 115
20:21–23 246
20:27 251
21:1–5 212
21:23 19, 187
21:31 205, 271
21:33–39 285
21:38 148
21:46 187
22:15 187
22:23 223, 224
22:29 223
22:29–33 224
22:44 246
23 31
23:1–3 186, 188
23:1–36 188
23:2 247
23:7 134
23:16–26 31
23:34 114
23:37 265
24:7 104
24:20 90
24:38–39 93
24:41 136
25:1 154
25:1–4 154
25:1–10 44
25:7 154
25:31–32 247
25:34 149
25:35–46 267
25:44–45 177
26:1–2 70
26:3–5 224
26:26 39, 94
26:48–49 151
26:49 133, 134
26:55 247
27:12–14 236
27:19 85
27:22–23 70
27:26 70, 115
27:27–29 67
27:31 70
27:32 71
27:35 70, 160
27:50–51 273
27:60 207
28:5 70
28:8 214
28:9 133
28:18–19 20

John A. Beck (PhD, Trinity International University) has taught courses in Hebrew and Old Testament at various colleges and universities for more than twenty years. He currently is an adjunct faculty member at Jerusalem University College in Israel. His articles have appeared in numerous academic journals and books. His books include *The Land of Milk and Honey: An Introduction to the Geography of Israel*; *God as Storyteller: Seeking Meaning in Biblical Narrative*; *A Visual Guide to Bible Events*; *A Visual Guide to Gospel Events*; *Zondervan Dictionary of Biblical Imagery*; and *Understand Your Bible*. Beck lives in Wisconsin.